Wrapped in White

Kevin Brooks has written twelve children's novels and has won several awards including the Canongate Prize for New Writing, Branford Boase Award, Kingston Youth Book Award, North East Book Award, Deutschen Jugendliteraturpreis Jury Prize, Buxtehude Bulle and the Golden Bookworm. His first adult novel, *A Dance of Ghosts*, was published by Arrow in 2011. He lives in North Yorkshire with his wife, Susan.

Also by Kevin Brooks

A Dance of Ghosts
Until the Darkness Comes

Kevin Brooks

Wrapped in White

arrow books

Published by Arrow Books 2013

4 6 8 10 9 7 5 3

First published in Great Britain in 2013 by
Arrow Books
Random House, 20 Vauxhall Bridge Road,
London SW1V 2SA

www.randomhouse.co.uk

Addresses for companies within The Random House Group Limited can be found
at: www.randomhouse.co.uk/offices.htm

The Random House Group Limited Reg. No. 954009

A CIP catalogue record for this book
is available from the British Library

Penguin Random House is committed to a sustainable future for
our business, our readers and our planet. This book is made from
Forest Stewardship Council® certified paper.

Printed and bound in Great Britain by Clays Ltd, St Ives plc

Typeset in Stempel Garamond by Palimpsest Book Production Limited
Falkirk, Stirlingshire

Wrapped in White

Fire devours. It consumes, destroys, obliterates. It lays the world to waste. Fire deforms. It craves disorder, its only purpose to burn and burn and light the skies until all that's left is dust. Fire has no limits. Everything burns: wood, plastic, stone, metal, flesh, bone, blood. And everything will burn in the end. Today, tomorrow, a thousand million years from now . . . at some point in time, fire will reduce everything to nothing.

But not tonight.

Tonight the fire is just another house fire.

The house stands in a secluded avenue at the edge of town. It's a pleasant area – broad pavements planted with lime trees, well-tended gardens, security lights, block-paved driveways – and the house is comfortable and spacious. Grey stone walls, rolling lawns, mullioned windows, a solid oak door set in an old stone porchway. Beyond the front door, a rolling cloud of thick black smoke is beginning to fill the hallway. At the far end of the hall, the kitchen is ablaze. The fire has spread quickly. Fuelled by the boiling cooking oil spilled across the floor, fierce flames have engulfed the kitchen in minutes. The old linoleum is melting, bubbling, smoking. Wooden cupboards are alight, the kitchen table is burning. Flames erupt from a plastic waste bin, a smouldering rug bursts into fire. The smoke thickens and billows, the heat feeding upon itself, and within a short while everything will be alight – sockets and plugs, ornaments, cookery books, the old oak beams, the smoke alarm fixed to the ceiling . . .

The smoke alarm is silent.

But even if it wasn't, even if the kitchen was filled with the shrieking siren of the alarm, the old man lying face-down on the floor wouldn't hear it. He's senseless, motionless, aware of nothing. He doesn't hear the roar of the fire, the crash of breaking glass as a crystal vase falls from the table. He doesn't see the heavy saucepan resting beside his head. He doesn't smell the acrid stink of his own scorched hair. And as his clothing burns, and the flames begin to blacken his skin, it can only be hoped that the old man feels no pain.

1

'What do you do if a bird shits on your windscreen?'

The man standing beside me at the bar was the kind of man who tells you a joke as if he's doing you a favour. The joke itself, to this kind of man, is neither here nor there. It's a joke. It's funny. It makes people laugh. And that's how this kind of man defines himself. He's a funny man. He tells jokes, he makes people laugh. He's a real character, this fellow. He's the kind of man who says, 'Cheer up, mate, it might never happen.'

And I fucking hate people like that.

But as I looked more closely at him, already weighing up how to brush him off, I realised that as well as being the kind of man who happily tells jokes to complete strangers, he was also the kind of man whose natural response to any perceived slight is to shove a broken glass in your face. He was, without doubt, a nasty piece of work. He wasn't particularly big – in fact, physically, he wasn't up to much at all – it was just that everything about him exuded violence. From the way he was standing at the bar – taking up far too much room, almost inviting someone to bump into him and spill his drink – to the lunatic gleam in his slightly off-kilter eyes, he was clearly a mean little bastard. He even had tough-looking teeth. So instead of just blanking him, or giving him a fuck-off look, I decided it was best to play safe and go along with him.

'Sorry?' I said, half-smiling at him, affecting a kind of harmlessly preoccupied look. 'I was miles away there . . .'

'What do you do,' he repeated, in exactly the same tone as before, 'if a bird shits on your windscreen?'

'I don't know,' I said. 'What *do* you do if a bird shits on your windscreen?'

He grinned. 'You don't ask her out again.'

I'd been preparing myself to force a smile whatever the punchline was, but the little snort of laughter I let out when it came was actually quite genuine.

'You like that one, eh?' the joker said.

'Yeah, not bad,' I admitted.

'I got plenty more.'

I bet you have, I thought.

Thankfully, I saw the barman approaching then, and by the time I'd caught his eye and ordered two pints of Stella, paid for them and got my change, the joker had found someone else to talk to – a big lunk of a man with a massive head, an equally massive neck, and arms like two legs of pork. From the way the joker was leaning in towards this man, the man bowing down to let him whisper in his ear, I guessed they weren't complete strangers. I should have left then. I should have just walked away. But I made the mistake of glancing at the joker and giving him a see-you-later nod, and just as I was doing that, he dismissed the lunk with a slap on the shoulder and turned his attention back to me.

4

'So,' he said, grinning his grin again, 'who do you fancy in the next one then?'

We were in a place called Juno's, an upmarket fitness and leisure complex on the south side of Riverside Business Park. It was a relatively new venture, having opened up just over a year ago, and it marketed itself as 'a high-class lifestyle experience' that catered for all the needs of an exclusive, membership-only clientele. As well as the usual state-of-the-art gymnasium and fitness facilities, it boasted an Olympic-size swimming pool, squash courts, saunas, spas, jacuzzis, a sports hall, a fancy restaurant, several bars, a high-tech conference hall, and a dozen or so private rooms available to members at daily or weekly rates.

I'd never been to Juno's before – I feel sick if I go anywhere near a gymnasium – but I'd seen it in passing quite often, and from the outside it looked fairly anonymous. A three-storey pale-brick building set in three barren acres of concrete, metal fencing, and prefabricated warehouses, it had always reminded me of the kind of place where you'd find the local tax office or a citizen's advice centre or something. But on the inside it couldn't have looked less like a tax office. The top two floors were cordoned off for the night, and the only areas of the ground floor open to the public were the lobby, the sports hall, the bar, and the toilets, so admittedly I hadn't seen all that much of the place, but what I had seen was all quite luxurious, albeit in a tacky kind of way. Thick red carpeting, marble pillars, brass railings, gilt-framed oil paintings on the walls. Several of the paintings were of the same female figure – a stern and

5

rather portly woman dressed in layers of white robing, with a garland of flowers in her hair – and there were more representations of female figures dotted around the lobby, this time in the form of sleek silver statues set on squat stone pillars. The statues depicted a series of artistically naked women, all of them impossibly lean and large-breasted, and they all seemed to be gazing upwards, with their hands raised and their backs arched, thrusting out their metallic hips as if their silver lives depended on it.

It was a strange mix of decor – part plush hotel, part gentlemen's club, part brothel – and in view of the entertainment on offer that night, it somehow seemed quite appropriate.

Tonight was Juno's inaugural 'Big Fight Night'.

According to the advertising, it was to be the first in a regular programme of 'action-packed evenings featuring some of the biggest names in professional boxing', and for one night only, non-members were 'invited to enjoy the exclusive facilities of Hey's most prestigious leisure complex'. Which wasn't strictly accurate, of course, as the only facilities available were the bar and the toilets, and the only really big-name fighter on the card that night was a so-so heavyweight whose only claim to fame was that he'd broken the jaw of a well-known sports presenter in a bad-tempered post-fight interview on live TV. That said, though, the fights had all been pretty good so far, and everything seemed about as well run and professional as boxing ever gets, and although Juno's was no Caesar's Palace, and the attendance was no more than a few hundred at best, there was definitely something about the place, and the kind of people who were there, that somehow felt just right.

The undercard was almost over now, and a lot of people had left their seats to go to the bar while the ring was being prepared for the final preliminary bout before the main event of the evening, the one featuring the so-so heavyweight. I wasn't bothered about the main event. It was the final preliminary fight that interested me. So when the joker asked me who I fancied in it, I was torn for a moment between finding out what he knew about it, if anything, or getting back to the ring to make sure I didn't miss the first round.

I glanced across at the sports hall. The ring was still empty, and there was no sign yet of the boxers making their entrance. I scanned the ringside seats and saw Cal – my nephew-in-law and colleague – sitting where I'd left him. He seemed happy enough, staring intently at the screen of one of his many mobile phones while his thumb skipped rapidly over the keys. I took a sip of beer, thought for a second, then turned back to the joker.

'What do *you* think?' I asked him.

His answer, in essence, was that the next bout was so one-sided that it wasn't even worth betting on.

'Everyone knows the black kid's got it,' he said. 'I mean, last I heard the odds were ridiculous, 10–1 on or something. Which is all right if you've got a couple hundred grand to spare, but otherwise it's just not worth the bother, is it? And there's no point putting anything on the gypsy kid because he's got no chance.' The joker shrugged. 'Might as well save your money for the big one.'

The 'black kid' was an up-and-coming young fighter

from Hey called Hassan Tan, and the 'gypsy kid', as far as I knew, was an Irish-born boxer from Liverpool who billed himself as Joe 'Boy' Rooney.

'Is Tan really that good then?' I asked the joker.

He nodded. 'He's the best young featherweight I've seen in years. Only turned pro about six months ago, and he's already making a name for himself. Two fights, two KOs, both in the second round. Six amateur fights, six wins inside the distance . . .' The joker shook his head. 'I tell you, the kid's going to be fighting for titles in a year or so. I mean, Rooney's no mug, he's been in with some good fighters and had a couple of decent results, but he's just not in the same league as Tan. I can't see him lasting three rounds, if that.'

'Sounds like you know your stuff,' I said.

The joker grinned. 'Well, you got to know what's what, don't you?'

I nodded, gazing casually around the bar. 'This is where Tan trains, isn't it? In Juno's, I mean. This is where he works out.'

'Yeah . . .'

'Looks like a good set-up.'

'It's the best.'

'And I hear he's got a good team behind him too – top trainers, ambitious management . . .' I looked at the joker. 'Do you know Curt Dempsey?'

The joker's smile suddenly went cold.

I said, 'He owns this place, doesn't he?'

The joker shrugged. 'So I've heard.'

'Right,' I said, nodding again. 'I was just wondering, that's all . . .'

'Wondering what?'

'Well, I've been thinking of joining, you know . . . applying for membership of Juno's.' I grinned, patting my stomach. 'I really need to get myself in shape.' I smiled at him. 'Are you a member? I mean, could you put in a good word for me or something?'

He stared emptily at me. 'Ask at reception. They'll give you a form.'

'Right . . . and you think it's worth it, do you? Becoming a member, I mean. Are the facilities really as good as I've heard?'

The joker looked away for a moment, gazing round the bar, then he turned back and stepped towards me, his eyes fixed coldly on mine. 'You know what really pisses me off?' he said quietly.

I almost said, 'Is this another joke?' but I quickly thought better of it. Instead, I just kept my mouth shut and stared back at him.

'What really pisses me off,' he went on, leaning in even closer, 'is people who ask too many questions. It makes me start wondering who they really are and what they really want. Do you know what I mean?'

'Hey, I'm sorry,' I said meekly, holding up my hands and backing away. 'I didn't mean anything. Honestly, I was just asking—'

'Well, fucking don't, OK?'

'Yeah, of course . . .'

He carried on staring at me for a moment or two, and I carried on looking as submissive and spineless as possible – which wasn't all that difficult – and then eventually, seemingly convinced that I wasn't worth wasting any more time on, he just gave me a final tough-guy look and said, 'Go on then, cunt, get the fuck out of my face.'

And I wandered away, smiling contentedly to myself.

After I'd gone outside for a quick smoke, I went back into the sports hall, sat down next to Cal, and passed him his beer.

'Thanks,' he said, taking the pint from me without looking up from his phone. 'You took your time.'

'I was talking to someone at the bar.'

'Yeah? Anyone interesting?'

'Not really.' I drank some beer and looked around. The hall was filling up again, people coming back from the bar carrying trays of drinks, finding their seats, sitting down. I turned back to Cal. 'He told me a joke,' I said.

'Who did?'

'The man at the bar.'

'Was it funny?'

I told Cal the joke. He laughed. I said, 'It's not a bad joke, is it?'

'Not bad at all.'

'Do you think it's OK to like it?'

He looked up from his phone. 'What do you mean?'

'You know . . .'

'No, I *don't* know.'

'Is it acceptable?'

'*Acceptable?*'

'Yeah. I mean, is it offensive or anything?'

Cal thought about it. 'No, I don't think so . . . it's just a play on words, isn't it? You assume that the bird in question is a seagull or something, a real bird, because that's the kind of bird that's known to shit on windscreens, but then you find out that in this case the word "bird" is being used in its slang sense, meaning a girl or young woman, and you're suddenly presented with the image of being out on a date with a girl or young woman who for some reason shits on your windscreen.'

'Which is funny.'

Cal grinned. 'Yeah.'

'But actually,' I said, looking at him, 'if you were out with a girl, and she did shit on your windscreen, she'd probably be suffering from some kind of mental illness, wouldn't she? I mean, a sane person wouldn't shit on your windscreen, would they?'

'They might if they were really angry with you about something.'

'No,' I said, shaking my head. 'They might shit *in* your car, but they're not going to bother climbing up onto the bonnet or the roof to shit on your windscreen, are they? Only a certified lunatic's going to go that far.'

Cal was laughing now.

'We should both be ashamed of ourselves,' I said, keeping a straight face. 'Laughing at people with mental problems . . . it's disgraceful.'

'You're right,' Cal agreed, still laughing. 'There's nothing remotely funny about it at all. I can see that now.' He looked at me, grinning madly. 'You're a wise man, Uncle John. I really don't know what I'd do without you.'

I smiled back at him. 'Have you heard the one about the tiny piano and the twelve-inch pianist?'

*

11

The Tan–Rooney fight was delayed. No reason was given for the hold-up, and no one seemed too bothered, we all just sat there waiting patiently until eventually things started to get moving again. The MC got back into the ring, the two ring-girls reappeared – both over-tanned, over made-up, and barely dressed in tight shorts, tight spangly vests, and ridiculously high heels – and eventually the boxers were introduced. There were no big fanfares, no special effects or dramatic entrances, the MC simply announced the fighters by name – Rooney first, then Hassan Tan – and once they were both in the ring, he read out their respective details: age, weight, fight record, home town. There was a smattering of boos and jeers for Rooney, and Tan's introduction was greeted with loud cheers and some half-hearted chanting from the back of the hall – *Has-san! Has-san!* Tan raised a gloved hand in appreciation, but he didn't make a big deal of it. He was too focused to get involved with the crowd – bobbing up and down, throwing punches, keeping himself nice and loose. I was watching him closely, and even at this stage it was obvious that he was a class act. He looked calm and confident, perfectly in control, totally unfazed by everything around him. Not once did I see him so much as glance at his opponent. He wore plain black shorts, no tassels, no fringes, nothing fancy. And although he was fairly slight, and a good two inches shorter than Rooney, he looked to be in really good shape – strong, powerful, well balanced. He had a light olive complexion, high cheekbones, and a very faint oriental look to his eyes.

The MC had left the ring now and the referee was giving

his last instructions to the two fighters. They nodded their heads, touched gloves, and went back to their respective corners.

As the trainers climbed out of the ring, and the expectant buzz of the crowd grew louder, Cal leaned over to me and said, 'You're really enjoying this, aren't you?'

'I'm working,' I reminded him. 'It's just part of the job.'

'Yeah, but you're still enjoying it.'

I smiled. 'It's the sport of kings, Cal. The noble art, the sweet science—'

'It's two guys beating the shit out of each other.'

The bell rang, and I turned my attention back to the ring.

As soon as the fight started it was obvious that the joker was right about Hassan Tan – he *was* in a different league. Rooney was the more aggressive fighter – constantly barrelling forward, his head down, shoulders hunched, fists pumping like pistons – but very few of his punches actually landed, and those that did were mostly on Tan's arms and shoulders. Tan, meanwhile, was just biding his time, effortlessly moving around the ring, happy to let Rooney tire himself out, while at the same time taking every opportunity to catch him hard with a straight left jab to the head. Unlike Rooney's punches, Tan's were telling and accurate, and by the end of the first round there was a cut over Rooney's right eye and a visible swelling under his left. He was struggling for breath too, and as he went back to his corner and sat down, he already looked like a beaten man. Tan, on the other hand, was unmarked and barely even sweating.

As one of the ring-girls climbed somewhat ungracefully

into the ring and began strutting her stuff – to the inevitable chorus of whistles, hoots, and crude comments – I gazed around the seats nearest the ring, trying to spot Curt Dempsey. From what I knew of him, he rarely missed a chance to show his face in public if he thought it would benefit him in any way, and as this was his club, and Hassan Tan was supposedly his protégé, the least I would have expected from Dempsey was a ringside appearance at this fight, if not at any of the others. But so far I hadn't seen him all night, and as I looked around now, there was still no sign of him.

In the second round, Tan began stepping things up. He started throwing more jabs, working on Rooney's cut eye, and as Rooney reacted to the barrage of left jabs by raising his guard more and more, Tan suddenly unleashed a devastating volley of body shots – four or five clubbing punches that caught Rooney just below the ribs. He staggered to one side, clearly hurt, and when Tan hit him again with a perfect right hook to the head, Rooney almost went down. I was expecting Tan to finish him off then, but Rooney was an experienced fighter, and he knew how to buy time – blocking, clinching, boxing dirty, using his head – and somehow he made it to the end of the round. I couldn't see him surviving another one though, and I began to wonder if the joker's prediction that Rooney wouldn't last three rounds was more than just an idle guess. Maybe he really did know what he was talking about. Maybe it wasn't so much Rooney's experience that had got him through the second round as the fact that Tan had been holding back, because maybe Tan knew – as the joker did – that all the clever money was on a Rooney KO in the third. This was boxing, after all. And boxing isn't exactly the straightest business in the world. So it wouldn't have surprised me in the least if Rooney had gone down in the third. But he didn't. In fact, if anything, as the round went on, it was Rooney who began to get the upper hand. Which really *was* surprising. Especially as he didn't seem to be doing anything different. He was still using the same basic tactic he'd used in the first round – barrelling forward with his head down, throwing as many punches as he could in the hope that one of them might do some damage – but Tan seemed to have forgotten how to deal with it. Instead of skipping out of Rooney's way and constantly stinging him with a sharp left jab, or switching his attack to his body, Tan was just defending himself now – backing off, blocking, clinching. And he seemed to have lost his air of self-belief too. He no longer looked in control.

'What's the matter with him?' I muttered.

'What?' Cal said, looking up from his mobile.

'He's not fighting any more.'

'Who isn't?'

'Tan . . . there's something wrong with him.'

Cal glanced up at the ring. 'Maybe he's hurt.'

I shook my head. 'He's not hurt.'

In fact, it struck me then that he looked more confused than hurt, as if he had something on his mind, something that troubled him. A couple of times I saw him glance over at his corner, and towards the end of the round, as Rooney had him backed up against the ropes, he quite clearly turned his head and looked out over the crowd towards the back of the hall. Rooney landed one then, a short right hook to Tan's chin. It wasn't a killer punch, but it was enough to remind Tan that he was in a fight, and for the next ten seconds or so he actually threw a few punches himself. But there was no real venom to them, and by the time the bell rang there was no doubt that Rooney had won the round.

I was watching Tan really closely now, and as he went back to his corner and sat down on his stool, it was clear that he was seriously bothered about something. As soon as his gum shield was out of his mouth he started arguing with his trainer, whispering furiously in his ear. His trainer snapped back at him, hissing through his teeth. Tan glared at him, cursing and shaking his head, and when his cutman tried to give him a drink he angrily swatted the bottle away. More words were exchanged, and then the trainer said something that seemed to stop Tan in his tracks. As the bell sounded, Tan gave his trainer a resigned-looking nod, the trainer shrugged sadly and patted him on the cheek, and Tan got to his feet, blew out his cheeks, and got ready to carry on fighting.

He didn't last very long.

The round started off promisingly enough, with Tan reverting to his skip-and-jab routine, and for a while I thought he'd sorted himself out, but after about thirty seconds he mistimed a jab and momentarily lost his balance, and as he stumbled to one side Rooney caught him with a left hook to his belly. It didn't look like much of a punch, but Tan gasped and doubled over, and Rooney was onto him in a flash. A vicious uppercut to the chin, a clubbing right cross to the side of his head, and Tan was down and out. The referee jumped in and started to count, but everyone knew it was already over. Tan was flat out on his back, his trainer was rushing across the ring, and Rooney was up on the ropes, his arms raised in triumph. The crowd, meanwhile, were jeering and booing.

'What's going on?' Cal said, looking round.

'He threw it,' I said, shaking my head.

'What?'

'Hassan Tan . . . he threw the fight.'

Cal looked at me, puzzled by my annoyance. 'Is that a problem?'

'It is for me,' I sighed.

'Why?'

'Because now Ada's going to kill me.'

2

My interest in Hassan Tan had begun four days earlier when his aunt had showed up at my office in Wyre Street. It was a cold January morning, the rooftops opposite my second-floor window still glittering with frost, and nothing much was happening. Things had been quiet since the lengthy Christmas and New Year break, and although it was the middle of January now, there was still no sign of any work coming in. Times were hard, and the private investigation business, just like everything else, was struggling to survive.

That morning, as usual, I was sitting with Ada on the battered old settee beneath the window in my private office, drinking coffee and smoking cigarettes, chatting idly about this and that, just passing the time, waiting for something to happen. Ada is my only full-time employee. An over-weight and perpetually grumpy old woman, with very poor social skills and the dress sense of a bag lady, she does almost everything for me. She's my secretary, my recep-tionist, the office administrator. She looks after all the paperwork, the contracts, the finance, and – in her own special way – she looks after me. And despite all her faults, and maybe even because of some of them, I'm inordinately fond of her.

For the last couple of days we'd been trying to work out if there was anything we could do to get the business going, but so far we hadn't come up with much.

'No one's got any money,' Ada said simply, 'that's all there is to it. The economy's fucked, the banks aren't lending, businesses are cutting back, and everyone's maxed out their credit cards to pay for Christmas.' She took a long drag on her cigarette. 'It's not just us, John. I was talking to someone at Mercer's the other day, and they said their business is down at least 50% on last year.'

I nodded. Mercer Associates is a large corporate investigation company based in Hey, owned and run by two old friends of mine, Leon Mercer and his daughter Imogen. When times were better, Mercer would often subcontract some of their smaller cases to me, but that hadn't been happening for a while.

'The whole country's fucked,' Ada went on. 'The only people making any money at the moment are pawnshops and loan companies.'

'That's what I like about you, Ada,' I said. 'You're always so full of optimism.'

She shrugged. 'I'm just being realistic, that's all. There's no point in pretending everything's OK when it's not.'

'Yeah, well . . . maybe if things get really bad there'll be some more riots, only this time the entire social order will start to break down and we'll descend into a state of anarchy. *Then* I might get some work.'

Ada shook her head. 'If we descend into a state of anarchy, no one's going to bother hiring a private investigator, are they? In a lawless world, if you thought your

19

wife was having an affair, all you'd have to do was follow her yourself, catch her with her lover, and then kill them both. Problem solved.' Ada looked at me, a glint of amusement in her eyes. 'No one would need you any more. You'd be redundant.'

'Yeah, but I'm your employer, don't forget. So you'd be redundant too.'

She smiled. 'I'd get by. I'm resourceful.'

'What, and I'm not?'

'You wouldn't last ten minutes.'

'Why not?'

'Because—'

It was at that point that the door to the main office swung open and a sad-eyed black woman wearing a thick woollen coat and a bright red headscarf came in.

'Can I help you?' I asked her, getting to my feet.

'I'm looking for Mr Craine.'

'I'm John Craine,' I told her. 'What can I do for you?'

'My name's Ayanna Osman,' she said. 'And I'm hoping you can put my mind at rest.'

After asking her if she'd like some coffee, which Ayanna politely declined, Ada left us alone in my office and I showed Ayanna to the chair in front of my desk. She had the kind of face that doesn't give much away, but I guessed she was probably in her early forties, and I got the impression that she'd been through a lot in her life. She had the world-weary look of someone who's learned the hard way that showing your true feelings can sometimes be dangerous.

As she settled herself down in the chair, and I sat down

opposite her and took out a pad of writing paper, I found myself wondering where she came from. Her English was excellent, but it clearly wasn't her first language, and my best guess was that she was originally from somewhere in Africa but that she'd been in the UK for quite some time. Even as the phrase 'somewhere in Africa' entered my head, I realised what a ridiculously inept and narrow-minded description it was, and that if I'd said it out loud my ignorance could quite possibly be taken as an insult. And for a second or two I actually felt quite uncomfortable with myself. But then I thought – *well, firstly, you* didn't *say it out loud, did you? And secondly, all it really means is that you're reasonably sure she comes from an African country, but that your knowledge of African countries is insufficient to allow you to be more specific.*

'Before we start,' Ayanna said, refocusing my attention, 'can I ask if there's a fee for this?'

'For hiring me?'

'No, I mean for the consultation. Do you charge for the consultation?'

I shook my head. 'You only have to pay if you hire me. We usually ask for a part-payment in advance, and then we'll bill you for the remainder of the payment when the job's finished.'

'Right . . .' she said, a touch hesitantly. 'And whatever I tell you now, is that in confidence?'

'If you do decide to hire me,' I explained, 'we'll draw up a contract that guarantees your confidentiality, but until then I can't promise anything.' I smiled. 'There's no one else here though, it's just the two of us, and unless you confess to some heinous crime, I'm quite happy to respect your privacy.'

She nodded. 'I hope you don't mind me asking.'

'Not at all,' I said.

'It's just . . . well, it's always best to know where you stand, isn't it?'

'Of course it is.' I looked at her. 'So, Ms Osman—'

'Ayanna, please.'

'Right,' I said. 'And I'm John, OK?'

She nodded again.

'So, Ayanna,' I went on, 'how can I put your mind at rest?'

She started off by telling me about her nephew Jamaal, but then all of a sudden she went off on a tangent and began talking about her sister, Sudi, and how it wasn't really Sudi's fault that she'd abandoned her children soon after leaving Somalia . . . and within a minute or two I was totally lost.

'Hold on a second,' I said, holding up my hands. 'I'm getting a bit confused here.'

'I'm sorry,' she said. 'It's just that it's a long and quite complicated story, and I'm not really sure how much you need to know and how much I should leave out.'

'All right,' I said, picking up a pen. 'Well, the first thing I need to know is what it's actually about.'

'Right . . .'

I looked at her, waiting for her to go on, but she still seemed unsure what to say. 'Is it about your sister?' I asked.

'Not really . . .'

'Your nephew then?'

'Yes . . . yes, it's about Jamaal.'

'OK,' I said. 'So let's start with him. He's your sister's son, is that right?'

'Yes.'

'Full name?'

'Jamaal Tan.'

I wrote it down. 'And his mother's full name?'

'Sudi Tan.'

'How old is Jamaal?'

'Seventeen . . . or rather, he *was* seventeen. He died last year.'

'How did he die?'

'He was killed, murdered.'

I stared at her. 'Murdered?'

She nodded.

I said, 'And where did this happen?'

'Here . . . in Hey.'

'When?'

'27 August last year,' she said. 'It was a Saturday.'

I paused for a moment, thinking back to last year, but I couldn't remember hearing anything about the murder of a teenage boy, and I found that hard to believe. Hey has its fair share of violence and death, but it's no worse than any other medium-sized British town, and any murder is still rare enough to be a big deal, let alone the murder of a teenage boy, so I should have heard something about it, especially as it's part of my job to know what's going on in this town.

'What happened to him?' I asked Ayanna.

'Jamaal's body was found in one of the underpasses down

by the river,' she said quietly. 'He'd been badly beaten, sexually assaulted, and stabbed to death. A man walking his dog called the police early on Sunday morning.'

I frowned. 'And this was definitely in August last year?'

'I know when my nephew was killed, Mr Craine.'

'I'm sorry,' I said, 'it's just that I don't understand why I haven't heard about this before.' I looked at her. 'I mean, as far as I know, there hasn't been anything about Jamaal's murder in any of the papers, local or national, and there was nothing on the news, TV or radio . . .'

'There was one newspaper reporter,' she said. 'A young man, he came round to my flat with a photographer a few days after Jamaal was killed. He said he was from the *Hey Gazette* and was writing a story about my son's murder.'

'He thought Jamaal was your son?'

She nodded. 'I didn't want to speak to him. I told him to go away. He carried on asking me questions, but when the photographer took a picture of me, I just slammed the door in their faces.'

'Did the reporter try getting in touch with you again?'

'No.'

'What was his name?'

She closed her eyes, trying to remember. 'I think it was Morton, or Morgan . . . something like that.'

I wrote down the names. 'And nothing about Jamaal was ever published in the *Gazette*?'

She shook her head. 'I haven't seen anything in any of the papers.'

I thought about that for a while, wondering if it really was as unusual as it seemed, and it did cross my mind for a moment that maybe I was wrong, maybe some murders just don't make the news, for whatever reason. Maybe it happens all the time? If something doesn't make the news, you're not going to know, are you?

I shook my head. A seventeen-year-old boy, beaten, raped, stabbed to death . . . and that doesn't make the news? It was definitely unusual.

I looked at Ayanna. She was sitting very still, just staring down at her lap, a picture of long-suffering patience.

'What about the police?' I asked her.

She looked up. 'They aren't being very cooperative with me.'

'Why not?'

'That's what I was hoping you could find out.'

I paused, staring at her, momentarily reminded of a woman called Helen Gerrish who'd come into my office just over two years ago. I could see Helen now, sitting in the same chair as Ayanna, telling me of her dissatisfaction with the police, asking me to see what I could find out . . .

I'd found out a lot for her.

And even more for myself.

I'd awoken ghosts, some of which were still haunting me now, and I wondered for a moment if it was happening all over again.

'All right,' I said to Ayanna, shaking the memories from my mind, 'tell me everything you know about Jamaal's death.'

She knew he'd been stabbed twenty-two times, and that at least four of the knife wounds would have been fatal. She knew he'd been punched and kicked repeatedly, and brutally beaten around the head and body with some kind of blunt object, most likely a baseball bat. He'd suffered a fractured skull, three broken ribs, and a ruptured spleen. He'd been found with his trousers pulled down, and there were indications that he'd been raped. Twenty-eight wraps of heroin and thirteen rocks of crack cocaine were found in his pockets. Ayanna also knew that as yet no one had been arrested or charged in connection with Jamaal's murder.

I wrote all this down, and then I asked her to take me through her dealings with the police. She told me that the officer in charge of the investigation, Detective Inspector Gavin Lilley, had spoken to her and Jamaal's older brother, Hassan, at some length on the day Jamaal's body was found, and that at first Lilley had seemed reasonably understanding and sympathetic.

'He apologised for having to ask us so many questions so soon after Jamaal's death, but he said it was vital to gather as much information as soon as possible in order to find out what had happened.'

I nodded, noting down Lilley's name. I didn't know him personally, but I'd heard of him.

'I did my best to answer all his questions,' Ayanna went on, 'but it was . . . well, it was difficult. I have to be very careful.'

'What do you mean?'

'Well, as I said, it's a long and complicated story . . .'

I smiled. 'I've got the time if you have.'

She sighed. 'My sister and I were brought to this country in 1999 to work as domestic staff for a wealthy Russian businessman. When we arrived in London, the man who'd arranged everything for us took away our passports and told us they wouldn't be returned until we'd paid off the fee we owed him for bringing us over and arranging our accommodation and employment.' Ayanna shook her head. 'The fee was so large that even if we'd earned any money it would have taken us years to pay off, but the Russian never paid us a penny.'

'You worked for nothing?'

She nodded. 'We weren't the only ones. Most of the others were either African or East European, and we were all in the same position. We'd all had our passports taken away, so we had nothing to prove we had a right to be in the country, and it was made perfectly clear to us that if we went to the authorities without any documents, the best we could hope for was a long spell in prison, and for those with children, like Sudi, they'd never see them again. But there were stronger threats too, stories about those who *had* tried to contact the authorities, or those who'd decided to leave the house and try their luck on their own, and how these people had simply disappeared without trace.' Ayanna sighed again. 'So we all just did what we were told. We cleaned, cooked, served drinks at parties. We kept our mouths shut. We worked all day and slept at night in an annexe building at the back of the house . . .' She lowered her eyes. 'Two or three times a week, some of the younger women would be collected from the annexe in the early evening and we wouldn't see them again until late the following day. Sudi was almost always one of those taken. None of us talked about it, but everyone knew what was happening.'

'Forced prostitution?' I said.

Ayanna nodded. 'It was all too much for Sudi. She'd already been through an incredibly abusive marriage in Somalia, and part of the reason she was so desperate to leave in the first place was to get away from her husband, and now here she was being violated and abused all over again . . . it was just too much for her. She stopped caring altogether – about herself, her children, me . . . she just gave up on everything. She started spending more and more time away from the house, sometimes with the Russian, but more often with friends of his, or business colleagues . . . she was passed around like a favoured toy. They played with her, dressed her up, did what they wanted to do, then had her taken away when they were done. On the rare occasions when I did see her back at the house, she was almost always drugged-up on something. I didn't know at the time it was heroin, all I knew was that whatever she was taking, or being given, it was slowly sucking all the life out of her. I was looking after the two boys by then, and sometimes they went weeks without seeing their mother, and even when they did see her . . . well, Sudi was in no state to be anything to them.' Ayanna took a deep breath and let it out slowly. 'Even when we finally managed to get away from the Russian, things didn't get much better, especially for Sudi. She was too far gone by then.'

'How did you get away from him?' I asked.

'He just abandoned the house one night, cleared everything out in a hurry, then drove off and left us behind.' She shrugged. 'We assumed he'd been tipped off that some kind of raid was imminent – the police, the Inland Revenue, rival gangsters – but we didn't hang around to find out. The four of us left with a Nigerian woman who said she knew someone in Southend who might be able to help us, maybe even find us all somewhere to stay for a while . . .' Ayanna smiled. 'We didn't even know where Southend was at the time, let alone how we were going to get there, but we made it in the end.' Her smile faded. 'But, as I said, it was already too late for Sudi. She was heavily addicted to heroin by then, and the only way she knew how to get it was by selling her body. I did everything I could to help her, but it was hopeless really. She was never going to make it. She died from an overdose five years ago.'

I nodded, saddened but not surprised.

'I did my best for Hassan and Jamaal,' Ayanna went on, sniffing back a tear. 'I worked as hard as I could, I made sure we had somewhere to live, I even managed to get the boys into school now and then . . . but it's hard to live a normal life when you have no right to be in the country. You can't get a decent job, everything has to be cash in hand, and if you don't pay the rent on time or your land-lord just wants you out, there's nothing you can do about it.' She sighed. 'We must have lived in a dozen different places over the last few years – Southend, Chelmsford, Harwich, Jaywick . . .'

'Couldn't you have gone to the relevant authorities?' I asked her. 'I mean, if you'd told them how you came to be here, explained the whole situation . . .?'

She smiled wryly. 'And what do you think the authorities would have done with us?'

'I don't know,' I said.

'Do you know anything about Somalia, Mr Craine?'

'Not really,' I admitted. 'I read the newspapers and watch the news, so I've got some idea of what it's like, but I wouldn't say that I really *know* anything about it.'

'Sometimes it's best not to know,' she said sadly. 'There's so much cruelty and violence in the world, so many atrocities taking place every day, every hour, so many unspeakable things . . . if we knew about all of them, if we were made aware of every single act of human monstrosity, we simply couldn't cope.'

I didn't know what to say, so I just sat there, quietly moved, and waited for her to go on.

'Somalia is my home, Mr Craine,' she went on. 'It's my country, my birthplace. But I have no love for it, and despite everything I've been through here, I don't want to go back there. And it's certainly no place for a young man like Hassan.'

'Right,' I said, 'so you had to be careful what you told DI Lilley because you were worried about getting deported.'

She nodded. 'I told him as much as I could, but when he began asking me detailed questions about our history, I kept my answers as vague as possible. I couldn't really see why it was relevant anyway. But Mr Lilley seemed to think it was important, and it was obvious he was getting annoyed with me. And then, when he started asking me about Jamaal's day-to-day life, and I told him that neither of the boys lived with me any more, so I didn't really know what Jamaal got up to every day . . . well, that's when he turned his attention to Hassan, and that didn't go very well at all.' Ayanna looked at me. 'Hassan doesn't like the police.

He doesn't like *any*one in authority, full stop. He doesn't trust them, doesn't respect them, doesn't want anything to do with them. And although, on this occasion, the police officer in question was supposedly trying to help him, Hassan's instinctive response was to tell him as little as possible. He was happy enough answering the straight-forward questions – where did your brother live? where did he work? – but when Mr Lilley moved on to Jamaal's lifestyle – who were his friends? what did he get up to? did he have any enemies? – Hassan became very surly and defensive. When Mr Lilley brought up the subject of the drugs that had been found in Jamaal's pocket, and he asked Hassan if he knew that his brother used drugs, Hassan just shrugged off the question at first, saying he had no idea what his brother got up to. But when Mr Lilley asked him outright if Jamaal had been a dealer, and if he'd had any connections with the local gangs, Hassan completely lost it.' Ayanna shook her head at the memory. 'He just started yelling at Mr Lilley, telling him that it was obvious the drugs had been planted after Jamaal had been killed, it was just *so* obvious, why couldn't he *see* that? Why would anyone beat him up and stab him to death but *not* steal the drugs from his pockets, especially if it was a gang-related killing?'

'I was wondering about that myself,' I said.

'Hassan eventually calmed down a bit, but I could tell he was still seething inside. He told Mr Lilley, in no uncertain terms, that yes, his brother had used drugs – who doesn't? – but he'd never been a dealer, he'd never had anything to do with gangs, and that whoever had killed him had also planted the drugs on him. When Mr Lilley stared at Hassan and asked him why he thought the killer would do that, Hassan just stared back at him and said, "You tell me."'

I smiled to myself. I was beginning to like the sound of Hassan.

'After that,' Ayanna said, 'Mr Lilley suggested that we call it a day for now and give ourselves a chance to cool off.'

I jotted down some notes, a few initial thoughts, then I turned back to Ayanna. She looked tired, physically and emotionally drained.

'Are you all right carrying on?' I asked her. 'We can stop now if you want, finish off another time. Or just take a quick break if you'd prefer.'

'No, I'm fine, thank you.'

'Do you want a cup of tea, coffee? A drink of water?'

She shook her head. 'No, thank you.'

'OK,' I said. 'So what happened next?'

She didn't see very much of DI Lilley after that first interview. As far as Ayanna knew, he was still in overall charge of the investigation, but most of her subsequent dealings, such as they were, were with two younger officers: Detective Sergeant Alan Proven and Detective Constable Jessica Scales. DC Scales was supposed to be the Family Liaison Officer.

'She came round to see me a couple of times,' Ayanna said, 'but I wouldn't say she *liaised* with me all that much. All she ever had to say about the investigation was that they were "following up leads", or they were "looking into things". She was very reluctant to go into any real detail about anything.'

'What about DS Proven?' I asked. 'Was he any help?'

'Not especially. Every time I rang him up to find out how things were going, there was always some kind of hold-up – they were waiting on forensics, they were trying to trace a possible witness – and he kept assuring me that someone would be in touch as soon as there was any definite news. So I'd leave it for a while, a week or so, waiting for someone to get in touch, but no one ever did. So then I'd call back, and it'd be the same old story all over again – we're still waiting on this, chasing up that . . . we'll get back to you as soon as we know anything – and then another few weeks would go by without hearing anything . . .'

'When they told you they were "looking into things", did they ever elaborate at all? Did they tell you what kinds of things they were looking into?'

Ayanna frowned. 'Not really . . . they talked about the drug gangs quite a lot—'

'Which gangs?'

'Well, they seem to think there's some kind of turf war going on between the local Somalis and a Chinese gang, and that Jamaal might have been killed because he was somehow involved in one of these gangs.'

'You don't sound very convinced.'

She smiled sadly. 'I'm a realist, Mr Craine. Both the boys have had a very hard life, and they've both been in trouble with the police now and then, and Jamaal in particular had lots of personal problems. So I know he was no angel, and I can't see any reason why he *wouldn't* get involved with a gang, but – as Hassan said – it all just seems a little too obvious. Sudi's husband was Chinese-American, so Jamaal

33

and Hassan are both Somali and part Chinese, and the gangs the police are talking about just happen to be Somali and Chinese. And again, as Hassan pointed out, if Jamaal was killed by a member of a drug gang, and the drugs in his pockets *were* his, why didn't the killer take them? And why would a rival gang member plant drugs on him? It doesn't make any sense, does it?'

'Not at the moment, no,' I admitted.

'And I'm not even sure that this so-called Somali drug gang actually exists anyway. I know there's a small community of Somalis in Hey, and I know that a lot of them live on the Redhills estate, and sometimes there's a bit of trouble down there – young men taking drugs, getting into fights, that kind of thing – but taking drugs and getting into fights doesn't necessarily mean you're part of an organised drug gang, does it?'

'Not necessarily, no.'

She looked at me, half-smiling. 'You don't sound very convinced.'

'I like to keep my options open,' I said, smiling back at her.

She nodded.

'So, anyway,' I said, getting back to the subject, 'what you're basically telling me is that you don't think the police are doing their job, they're not keeping you informed, and the only line of enquiry they seem to be following is this idea that Jamaal was mixed up with a drug gang. Is that about right?'

'I wouldn't even call it a line of enquiry really,' she said. 'It's just something that keeps coming up. They all keep mentioning it – Proven, Scales, DI Lilley. It's almost as if they're hoping that if they talk about it enough, I'll get so used to the idea that eventually I'll just accept it, and then maybe I'll stop bothering them.'

'Is that really the impression you're getting from them, that you're *bothering* them?'

'It's not just an impression. It's what I've been told.'

'By the police?'

She nodded. 'I think it must have been sometime in November. It had been weeks since I'd heard anything, so I rang up again to find out what was going on, and when DS Proven started giving me the same old excuses, I lost my temper with him. I told him what I really thought, that I was fed up with being fobbed off all the time, and I told him I wanted to speak to someone in charge. Not DI Lilley, but whoever was really in charge.'

'And what did Proven do?'

'He put me through to DI Lilley, who proceeded to tell me, quite calmly, that if I carried on bothering his officers, ringing up every few days and swearing at them – which I'd *never* done – he'd pass on all my details to the Border Agency and let them deal with me.'

'He *said* that?'

She nodded. 'I swear to God.'

'He actually threatened you?'

She nodded again.

'What did you do?' I asked.

She shrugged. 'What could I do?'

'Did you stop calling them?'

'I didn't have much choice.'

'Have they been in touch with you at all since then?'

'DC Scales came round to see me just before Christmas. She said it was a courtesy call, just to let me know that there was still no news, but they were making some progress.'

'Making some progress . . .?'

'That's what she said.'

'And that's it? You've heard nothing since then?'

'No.'

I stared down at my notepad for a while, not actually reading anything on the page, just thinking things through, trying to make some kind of sense out of what Ayanna was telling me, but I didn't get very far.

'So, Ayanna,' I said, looking up, 'what is it you want me to do?'

She gazed at me, a flicker of hope in her eyes. 'Do you think you can help me?'

'Well, that depends.'

'On what?'

'On what you want from me. If you're asking me to find out who killed Jamaal, I'm not sure I can—'

'No,' she said quietly. 'That's not what I'm looking for. I'd *like* to know who did it, of course. I'd like to see justice done. But justice . . .' She shrugged. 'Well, I lost faith in justice a long time ago. It's never done me any good, and I'm not even sure I know what it means any more.'

'So what *do* you want me to do?'

She hesitated. 'I just . . . I think I just need to know.'

'Know what?'

'Whatever it is I don't know.' She smiled, slightly

embarrassed. 'Sorry, that doesn't make much sense, does it? It's just . . . how can I put it?' She paused for a moment to think, then tried again. 'I just want to know why the police are keeping things from me, why they're so reluctant to tell me the truth. If Jamaal was involved with drugs and gangs, and that's what led to his death, if that really is what happened . . . well, all right. It's not going to make me feel any better, but at least I'll know. Whatever the truth is, I can accept it. I can deal with it. But the way I've been treated, the way I'm still being treated, as if Jamaal's death somehow doesn't have anything to do with me, and it doesn't matter what I want or how I feel, or how they deal with me, because I'm nothing . . . nothing at all, just another illegal immigrant.' She sighed. 'Well, I can accept that too, if I have to. But if there's any chance that I don't have to . . .'

'It'd put your mind at rest?'

She smiled. 'Perhaps.'

'OK,' I said. 'Well, I can certainly look into things for you—'

'Really?'

I nodded. 'I can't promise anything—'

'Of course not.'

'But I'll do what I can.'

'Thank you, Mr Craine. Thank you *so* much. I really appreciate it.'

'No problem,' I said, smiling at her. 'Have you talked to Hassan about this? I mean, does he know you were coming to see me?'

She shook her head. 'There was no point in telling him. He'd only have told me to forget it. The way he sees it now, his brother's dead, and there's nothing anyone can do to bring him back. So why bother doing anything? It's like he's just given up. Doesn't want to think about it, doesn't want to talk about it. He doesn't even get angry with the police any more.'

'Will he talk to me?'

'Probably not.'

I asked her for his address and phone number anyway, and as I was writing them down she said, 'He spends most of his time at the gym these days, either training or working, so if you can't get him at home . . .'

'The gym?'

She smiled. 'He started getting into boxing about eighteen months ago. I only found out when he came round to see me about a year ago and I noticed how well he was looking – fit and healthy, strong, more confident – and he told me that he'd been going to a gym for the last six months and had started doing a bit of boxing. It turned out that he'd already had a couple of fights by then, and he'd not only won them both, but won them in some style.' Ayanna looked at me. 'I didn't like the idea of him boxing, but if it gave him a sense of purpose and kept him out of trouble, which it definitely seemed to be doing, I was happy enough to let him get on with it. And I was even happier when he told me that he'd managed to get some part-time work for both himself and Jamaal at the gym where he trained.'

'What kind of work?'

'He didn't say.'

'What's the gym called?'

'Juno's.'

'Juno's?'

'Do you know it?'

I nodded, noting down the name. I didn't actually know very much about Juno's then, but I knew where it was.

'He's fighting there on Tuesday night,' Ayanna said.

'Sorry?'

'Hassan . . . there's a big boxing thing at Juno's on Tuesday night. I don't know what you call it – a boxing show, boxing night? Anyway, whatever it's called, Hassan's going to be there. It's a really big night for him. A big fight, apparently. Good money too.'

'Is he going to win?'

'He'd better.'

'Why?' I said, smiling. 'Have you got money on him?'

It was meant as a joke, just a light-hearted comment, but Ayanna didn't seem to find it funny. If anything, it seemed to make her feel uncomfortable, and I wondered for a moment if I'd somehow offended her, touched a nerve or something. Maybe for someone like Ayanna, who'd probably never had enough money to bet on anything, it just wasn't funny. Or maybe, I thought, gambling was against her religion.

'I'm sorry,' I started to say to her. 'I didn't mean—'

'No, please,' she said, waving away my apology. 'It's just . . . well, the thing about the money . . .' She lowered her eyes for a moment, almost as if she were ashamed, then she looked up at me again. 'You said you usually ask for a retainer for your services . . .'

I nodded.

'Well, you see . . .' she went on hesitantly, 'I have *some* money I can give you now, but I'm not sure . . . I mean, how much would you normally ask for?'

'It's probably best if you talk to Ada, my secretary,' I suggested. 'She'll explain the rates and draw up the contract—'

'I've got about £35 on me,' she said, pulling a big old purse from her pocket and digging out some notes and a handful of coins. 'Well, almost £35 . . . I could probably get another ten or fifteen for you by the end of the day.' She stopped counting her money and looked at me. 'But if you could possibly wait until next week, after Hassan's fight . . . you see, he's on a £5,000 win bonus, and he told me a few weeks ago that he's going to give me half of it, so by next week I'll easily have enough to pay you.'

'Right . . .' I said doubtfully. 'But that's only if he wins?'

'Well, yes, but there's no question of him losing. He's very good, apparently.'

I looked at her, not knowing what to do or what to say. The only thing I knew for sure was that if I accepted Ayanna's terms, which basically came down to no payment up front – I couldn't take her last £35, could I? – and quite possibly no payment at all if Hassan lost his fight . . . if I agreed to work for Ayanna on that basis, Ada would go ballistic.

I thought about that for a moment, imagining her reaction – the initial look of stunned disbelief on her face, a brief attempt to reason with me, and then, inevitably, the eruption, a foul-mouthed spewing out of contempt, derision, disdain – *Jesus fucking Christ, John, you're so fucking gullible* . . .

I leaned back in my chair, stretching the stiffness from my back, and then, smiling quietly to myself, I got to my feet.

'If you'd just like to wait there a minute,' I said to Ayanna. 'I'll go and have a quick word with my secretary and see what we can sort out, OK?'

3

My prediction of how Ada would react to Ayanna's 'promise' of payment – the disbelief, the reasoning, the rage – was just about spot on. She managed to hold herself back long enough to suggest, reasonably calmly, that rather than drawing up a contract right now, we should tell Ayanna that we'd work out the terms over the weekend and get back to her with the details on Monday. But once I'd explained this to Ayanna, and she'd left the office, Ada really let rip at me. *What do you think you're doing? What the fuck's the matter with you? How can you be so fucking naïve? Jesus Christ, John, you're such a fucking pushover . . .*

I didn't try to stop her, I just let her rant on and on, until gradually she began to run out of steam. And when her fury was finally spent, and the veins in her neck were no longer popping, I gave her a cigarette, made us some coffee, and we sat down together on the settee in my office and smoked ourselves back to normality.

'God, John,' she sighed, 'why do you always have to do this?'

'Do what?'

'You *know* what.' She looked at me, blowing out a stream of smoke. 'You're always doing something to get me going, aren't you? And it's not good for me. Not at my age.'

'Not at your weight either.'

'Fuck off.'

I smiled at her.

She scowled, shaking her head. 'I mean, this woman—'

'Ayanna.'

'OK, so this Ayanna, she's had a really tough life, she's been through a lot, she's been victimised, abused, blah, blah, blah—'

'You're all heart, Ada.'

'Yeah, I know. But what I'm saying is, it's not your job to solve the problems of every poor bastard in the world. Not for nothing, anyway. We're not a fucking charity, John. We're a business. And the way businesses generally work is that they charge money for their services. If you want them to do something for you, you have to pay them.'

'Ayanna *is* going to pay us.'

'Yeah, right . . . she's going to pay us *if* her nephew wins some poxy boxing match.' Ada looked at me. 'For all you know, he might be the world's worst boxer, he might get knocked out in the first round . . . he might not even *be* a boxer. Ayanna might be lying through her teeth—'

'But you could say that about every client,' I argued. 'We never really know if they're going to pay or not until we send them the bill, do we?'

'No,' she said, speaking very slowly, like a spiteful teacher talking to a very dumb kid, 'and that's why we ask for a retainer, John. So if the client doesn't pay their bill, we're not completely out of pocket.'

'Yeah, all right,' I said. 'You've made your point. But this is different.'

'How is it different?'

'How?'

She grinned at me. 'Yes, what exactly is it about this case that makes it different?'

'Well . . .'

'You feel sorry for her?'

'No. Well, yes, but—'

'You *like* her?'

'Yeah, actually, I *do* like her. I think she's a good woman.'

'*A good woman?*' Ada laughed. 'Who do you think you are, the hero in a Wilkie Collins novel or something?'

'No,' I said, shaking my head. 'I'd like to think I'm a bit more modern than that, you know . . . more Philip Marlowe than Wilkie Collins.'

She laughed again, coughing on a lungful of smoke. 'Oh, right, I see . . . *that's* who you model yourself on, is it? Philip Marlowe.' Cough, cough. 'Yeah, of course, I can see the resemblance now . . . the heavy drinking, the loneliness—'

'Marlowe wasn't lonely. He was lonesome.'

'What's the difference?'

I smiled. 'Lonesome is heroic. Lonely is just sad.'

Ada shook her head. 'It's not a valid comparison anyway.'

'What isn't?'

'Marlowe's a fictional character.'

'So what?'

'So you can't compare a fictional character with an author, can you?'

'I didn't.'

'Yes, you did. You said you were more Philip Marlowe than Wilkie Collins.'

'So?'

'So it's not a valid comparison, is it? It's like saying you're more Hans Solo than Federico Fellini . . . it doesn't make sense.'

'*Han* Solo,' I corrected her.

'What?'

'You said *Hans* Solo. It's not *Hans*, it's *Han*.'

'*Han* isn't a real name.'

'And Chewbacca is, I suppose?'

We carried on in this vein for another hour or so, just rambling away about nothing, smoking cigarettes and drinking coffee, and by the time it got to around two o'clock, I told Ada she might as well call it a day and go home.

She smiled knowingly at me. 'You think you're smart, don't you?'

'What do you mean?'

'Either that, or you think I'm really stupid.'

I sighed. 'I honestly don't know what you're talking about.'

'Of course you don't. I mean, you wouldn't sneakily change the subject on purpose, would you? And it'd never even *occur* to you that if you jabbered on about something else for an hour, and then oh-so-kindly sent me home early, I'd forget all about Ayanna Osman and leave you in peace for the rest of the day.' She grinned at me. 'You wouldn't do anything like that, would you, John?'

'Not me,' I said, shaking my head. 'My conscience wouldn't let me.'

We both just sat there smiling at each other for a while, quite comfortable sharing the silence, and then Ada took a final puff on her cigarette, stubbed it out in the ashtray, and turned back to me. The smile had gone from her face now, and as her eyes fixed on mine, I knew she meant business.

'Just be careful you're not putting your heart over your head on this one, John, that's all. I know you can't help being swayed by your feelings, but sometimes you have to take a step back. Otherwise . . . well, you know what can happen.'

'Yeah, I know,' I said quietly, putting my hand on her knee. 'But all I'm going to do is look into things for her, see if I can find out what's going on. I'll give it a couple of days at most, wait to see what happens at the fight, and then just take it from there. It's not going to cost us anything, is it? And it's not as if I'm being paid to do anything else at the moment, so I might as well spend my time doing something I might get paid for rather than sitting around here all day doing nothing.'

'Well, I suppose . . .' Ada said, far from convinced.

'And I promise that if something else turns up in the meantime, a nice, boring, proper job, I'll take it. How's that?'

Ada shrugged. 'You're the boss.'

'Yeah?' I said, smiling at her. 'Since when?'

After Ada had gone home, I spent a couple of hours on my own in the office, mostly just nosing around on the Internet. The list of reporters on the *Hey Gazette* website didn't include anyone called Morgan or Morton, but when I checked through the archives I came across a couple of articles written by someone called Jason Morgan. I called the *Gazette* and asked to speak to him, but after being put on hold for a few minutes, then passed around from department to department, I was finally informed that Jason Morgan was no longer employed by the *Gazette*.

'Do you know where he works now?' I asked.

'No, I'm sorry.'

'When did he leave?'

'September last year.'

'Do you know why he left?'

'You'd have to take that up with Mr Morgan.'

I made a note to that effect, then started looking into some of the other details Ayanna had given me – names, dates, places – anything that might throw some light on her story. I didn't find very much. There was nothing about her or Sudi, nothing about Jamaal's murder, and nothing particularly useful about DI Lilley, DS Proven, or DC Scales. For a while I got distracted by some articles about Somalia, and I also spent a bit of time reading about human trafficking, the 21st-century slave trade – how it all works, who controls it, how much money they make – but then I reminded myself that however intriguing it might be, none of it was really relevant. So I went back to checking out some of the names and places that Ayanna had mentioned, and when I Googled 'Juno's', and started looking into the club's background and history, the first thing I discovered was that the club was owned and run by a man called Curt Dempsey.

It wasn't hard to discover a few basic facts about Dempsey – aged fifty-five, a self-made multi-millionaire, he'd begun his business life at the age of fifteen selling fruit and vegetables from a market stall in the East End of London. There was little or no explanation as to how he'd progressed from working on a market stall to owning a string of businesses and a number of luxury properties in Essex, London, and Spain – in fact, there was virtually no information at all about his pre-millionaire existence – but there was plenty of information about the public face of Curt Dempsey. As well as Juno's, he also owned the local ice rink, a couple of restaurants, a property development company, a haulage business, a number of taxi firms . . . and I got the feeling that this was just the tip of his corporate iceberg, and that below the surface he probably owned dozens more companies. He was the kind of businessman who fancies himself as a bit of a philanthropist too, and there were lots of photographs of him with local dignitaries and D-list celebrities at various charity events and gala dinners. In at least half of these pictures he was shown smiling into the camera as he handed over a giant-sized cheque to yet another lucky unfortunate – some poor kid in a wheelchair, a wounded soldier, a mad old woman from a hedgehog sanctuary. But while there was always a smile on Dempsey's face in these photos – a big wide grin, showing perfect white teeth – there was no trace of a smile in his steely grey eyes. They were the eyes of a man who always gets what he wants, and doesn't care how he gets it. And this air of ruthlessness was reflected in his overall appearance too – his broad shoulders, his stocky figure, his battle-scarred face and close-cropped white hair . . . he couldn't have looked more like a crook if he'd tried. Even the clothes he wore – conspicuously expensive but totally without style – were the clothes of a man who's seen too many Guy Ritchie films. In fact, it was all so obvious it was almost laughable . . . but all you had to do to stop yourself smiling was look into those cold grey eyes. There was nothing funny about them. Nothing funny at all. And I'd be willing to bet that if you were stupid enough, or suicidal enough, to make so much as a light-hearted comment to Dempsey about his appearance, you'd regret it for the rest of your life . . . however short a time that might be.

I realised, of course, that all this was pure speculation. I was, after all, judging a man's character wholly on the evidence of a handful of photographs and some stuff I'd read on the Internet, which was hardly the most constructive way to go about it. So I was well aware that my gut feelings about Dempsey could be way off the mark, and although I have a certain amount of faith in my instincts, I'm never really surprised, or disappointed, if they're wrong.

It so happened that in this case my instincts would prove to be right.

But I wasn't to know that then.

All I knew then, as I sat alone in my office on that cold afternoon, was a visceral sense of unease about the man staring out at me from my computer screen.

I couldn't find anything at all about Curt Dempsey's personal life – where he lived, who he lived with, whether he had a family or not – and the only other snippets of possibly useful information I came across were a brief mention of him in the archives of the *Hey Gazette*, and some anonymous comments on YouTube. The piece in the *Gazette* was from 25 October 2009. A single paragraph sneaked in at the bottom of page seven, all it said was that 52-year-old Curt Dempsey had been charged with assault after an affray at The Grape and Vine restaurant in East Harbour Street, Hey, on Saturday 3 October. There were no further details. I scanned the rest of the archives, but that was it – no follow-up, no court case, nothing.

The anonymous comments on YouTube related to a short video showing Dempsey at yet another charity function, this time at the town hall. The video itself was nothing much, just a ten-second shot of Dempsey shaking hands with a local MP called Meredith Chase, and the quality of the comments posted about the video were par for the course for YouTube. The first one read – *cunt depsy + another dirty cunt!* This was followed by – *yah but u woldnt call him cunt to his face wud u?* Then – *whyd they call him cunt anyway?* Answer – *cos hes a cunt u fuking cunt.*

That was enough for me.

I closed YouTube, logged off the Internet, and lit a cigarette.

I'm old enough to remember the pre-Internet world, and I wouldn't want to go back to it. The Internet, the World Wide Web, email, Google, whatever . . . it's all incredibly useful, and I still find it amazing that most of us take it for granted now – instant communication, a world of information at our fingertips, an almost infinite reservoir of facts and figures, sounds and images, thoughts, opinions, attitudes. It's all just *there*, and I don't know what I'd do without it. But there's always a downside to everything, and sometimes, when I'm immersed in places like YouTube, I can't help feeling that the whole world is just a vast and nightmarish playground, a planet-sized school yard filled with billions of nasty children, all of them running around like lunatics, screaming and shouting, shoving each other around, picking on each other, calling each other names . . .

And I could do without that.

It was four-thirty by then. The daylight was fading.

I finished my cigarette, fetched my coat, and went home.

4

And so it was that four days later I was sitting in the sports hall at Juno's watching the still-dazed Hassan Tan being helped out of the ring by his trainer. I'd called Ayanna Osman earlier that day and told her that I didn't think there was any point in signing a contract just yet, but that I'd make some preliminary investigations and get back to her as soon as possible, and she'd seemed happy enough with that. I wasn't really expecting to find out very much at Juno's, and apart from the fact that my chances of getting paid were virtually non-existent now that Hassan had lost the fight – which was bound to mean even more grief from Ada – I couldn't see how it had any real relevance to anything. I was intrigued as to why he'd thrown the fight, and I couldn't help wondering what, or who, had made him do it, but I doubted very much if it had anything to do with his brother's death. It probably didn't mean anything at all. But the only reason I'd come here was to do a bit of nosing around, and so far I hadn't found anything else worth sticking my nose into . . .

'I'm going to see if I can talk to Hassan,' I told Cal, getting to my feet and gazing out over the crowd towards the backstage area at the rear of the hall. 'I won't be long.'

He nodded. I hadn't told him everything about the case,

partly because I still wasn't sure if it actually *was* a case, and partly because – at this stage – he didn't need to know everything about it, but I'd told him enough to put him in the picture.

As I made my way over to the back of the hall, I had no idea what I was going to say to Hassan Tan if I saw him, but I didn't give it too much thought. Right now, I was more concerned with how I was going to get to see him in the first place. The backstage area was closed off behind a pair of double doors, which were guarded by two burly security guards, one on either side. They were both standing with their legs apart and their arms crossed over their chests, bouncer-style, and they were both wearing T-shirts with the Juno's logo printed on the front. It was the same logo I'd seen on a neon sign above the main entrance, and on the vests of the round-card girls – the word *Juno's*, spelled out in fancy gold lettering, with the *J* formed into the figure of an outstretched female body . . . just like the statues in the lobby.

I turned on my friendly smile and went up to the bruiser on the left.

'Hi,' I said breezily, holding out my hand, 'Ray Thornton, boxing correspondent with the *Mirror*. I was told I could have a quick word with Hassan.'

The bruiser didn't return my smile or shake my hand. He just stared down at me and grunted, 'Pass?'

'Sorry?'

'Press pass.'

'Didn't you get the message?'

'What message?'

I sighed, the sigh of a man who's used to this kind of frustration. 'Curt said he'd leave a message with you . . . Curt Dempsey? I saw him earlier. I told him I'd left my pass at the hotel and he said not to worry, he'd sort it out. He said he'd leave a message with you.'

'With me?'

'Not you personally, no. With security. You *are* security, aren't you?'

'We didn't get any message.'

'Are you sure?'

He turned his head towards his colleague – the first time he'd actually moved since I'd started talking to him. 'You got any messages, Dan?' he said. Dan shook his head. The bruiser turned back to me. 'We didn't get any message.'

I sighed again, scratching my head. 'Can't you just—?'

'No pass, no access.'

'All I want is five minutes—'

'Bye bye,' he said, staring hard at me.

I wouldn't have thought it was possible to say 'bye bye' with any real menace, but somehow the bruiser managed it, and when I glanced over at his colleague and saw the way he was looking at me too, I thought it was probably a good idea to cut my losses and make a tactical retreat. There was no point in getting beaten up just yet, and I could always try to see him again later. And maybe, after another few beers at the bar, I might come up with an idea that actually had a chance of working.

But just as I was about to turn away, the double doors swung open and the so-so heavyweight came out with his entourage. As they hustled past – in a blur of flesh, sweat, and satin – and the two bruisers stepped back and held the doors open to let them through, my curiosity got the better of me, and before I really knew what I was doing, I'd dodged to one side and was heading through the doorway.

'Hey!' the bruiser yelled, coming after me. '*HEY!*'

The doorway led into a brightly lit corridor with white-washed stone walls and a bare concrete floor. At the far end of the corridor, three men were standing together outside a closed door, and as they all turned their heads at the sound of the bruiser's raised voice, I immediately recognised two of them. One was Curt Dempsey – dressed for the night in a garish white dinner jacket over a tight black T-shirt – and the other was a man I hadn't seen for over two years, and that wasn't nearly long enough. His name was Bishop, Detective Chief Inspector Mick Bishop. The third man looked like another security guard – big, well muscled, dressed in a grey Juno's T-shirt and tracksuit bottoms – but I barely even glanced at him. My eyes were inexorably drawn to Mick Bishop. The sight of him standing there next to Curt Dempsey sent a cold ugly shiver through my heart.

The first bruiser caught up with me then, and as he hooked his arm round my throat and began dragging me back through the doorway, I saw the flash of recognition in Bishop's eyes, and then almost immediately I saw him say something to Dempsey. Dempsey glared at me for a moment, and then – just as the second bruiser grabbed hold of my arm, and I felt myself being lifted off my feet – I saw Dempsey point at me and say something to the security guard standing next to him. The guard called out to the two bruisers – 'Hold him!' – and began walking up the corridor towards us. The two bruisers did as they were told, keeping hold of me while the other one made his way up to the doorway, but although the first one still had his arm round my throat, squeezing so hard I thought my head was going to explode, and the second one was gripping me so tightly with his giant-sized fingers that my hand had already gone numb, they had at least lowered me back to the floor now, so I didn't feel quite so bad. Helpless, yes. And kind of pathetic too. But I'm fairly well versed in the art of feeling helpless and pathetic, so it didn't really bother me that much. What *was* bothering me though was the feeling in my guts as I watched the other guard approaching. It was that unnervingly primitive feeling you get when your body senses danger, that visceral fear that empties your belly and drains the blood from your veins. I couldn't quite understand it at first, as there didn't seem to be any reason to feel so afraid. The man coming towards me didn't look any scarier than the other two, and although the other two were undeniably big and strong, and perfectly capable of beating the shit out of me, they weren't actually all that scary anyway.

Being scary is a state of mind. It doesn't have anything to do with how big or tough you are. The man, or woman, you need to be afraid of is the one who'll put a gun to your head and pull the trigger without thinking about it. And as the third security guard stopped in front of me, and I got my first really good look at him, I knew that my body had been right all along. This *was* a man worth fearing. I still didn't quite understand it, because even up close there was nothing obviously menacing about him. He was fairly big – around the six-foot mark, maybe sixteen stone – but not as massive as the other two, and while his arms and his neck were quite muscular, he was nowhere near as unnaturally pumped up as his colleagues. He was a little older than them too. They were both in their mid- to late twenties, he was around thirty-five, thirty-six. But it was his face that puzzled me the most. It was just so . . . I don't know. So *un*threatening, I suppose. It was a nothing kind of face – neither soft nor hard, mean nor kind, smart nor dumb . . . it somehow seemed to have no characteristics at all, either physical or personal. Even his eyes said nothing about him. They were brown, and that was it. They were just eyes. The only vaguely notable thing about him was the way he wore his dirty-blond hair. He had the kind of haircut a thirty-five-year-old man might have worn in 1973: longish – but not *too* long – only just covering the ears, with a reasonably neat and well-maintained side parting. But even that didn't really come across as anything out of the ordinary. Slightly incongruous, perhaps. But it wouldn't make you look twice at him.

Nothing would.

He didn't look like anything.

But he was. My body knew it, and so did I. There was just something about him, some indefinable yet over-whelming sense of otherness. This was a man who was just plain *wrong*.

'Let him go,' he said calmly to the other two, staring at me.

They let me go, and I stretched my neck and rubbed at

my throat, waggling the fingers of my other hand to get the blood running again.

'What are you doing here?' he said, still staring at me. His voice had no accent, no expression.

'I'm not doing anything,' I told him. 'I was just—'

'Come here,' he said, taking me by the arm and leading me firmly, but not aggressively, away from the doors and over to the wall. He positioned me with my back to the wall, let go of my arm, and stood right in front of me, his face no more than six inches from mine. 'Now,' he went on, his voice still perfectly calm, 'I'm only going to ask you once more, OK? What are you doing here?'

I briefly considered giving him the same story I'd given the other two, but I was fairly sure that Bishop would have said who I was, to Dempsey if not directly to him, so I quickly gave up on that idea, and for want of any better options, I just said the first thing that came into my mind.

'Look, I'm sorry, OK?' I said, holding up my hands to show him how sorry I was. 'I didn't mean to cause any trouble, I was just trying to see Hassan Tan, that's all.'

'Why?'

I sighed. 'I lost a lot of money on him, a *lot* of money, and I was just, you know . . . I was just a bit pissed off with him for losing the fight.'

'What price did you get?'

'What?'

'On Hassan. What odds did you get?'

I frowned. 'I can't remember exactly . . . I mean, they were fucking low, I know that. That's why I put so much on him.'

He didn't say anything, he just looked at me.

'I wasn't going to *do* anything,' I said. 'I just got a bit carried away, you know . . . lost my head in the heat of the moment.' I smiled a self-mocking smile. 'I feel kind of stupid now, to be honest.'

He still didn't say anything, he just stepped even closer to me, getting right up into my face, and then paused, staring impassively into my eyes. I had no idea what he was going to do then. If it had been one of the others, I'd have guessed that I was about to get hit – a vicious jab to the belly, maybe, or even something worse – but with this man, I really didn't know what to expect. So as he stood there, breathing his surprisingly sweet breath into my face, I was preparing myself for anything . . . at least, I thought I was. But when I felt him place his hand between my legs and gently cup my genitals . . . well, I wasn't prepared for that.

'What the fuck—?' I started to say, squirming away from him, but then he suddenly tightened his grip and squeezed hard, paralysing me with a sickening bolt of pain. It hurt so much that I couldn't do anything – couldn't move, couldn't speak, couldn't even breathe.

'All right,' he said quietly. 'Now listen. Mr Dempsey would like you to leave the premises.' He paused, staring at me. 'Did you hear me?'

I nodded, gritting my teeth.

'Good. You leave now, and you don't come back. Do you understand?'

I nodded again.

'And if I ever see you in here again, or if I hear that you've been here, I'll break your spine. Is that understood?'

'Yes . . . yeah . . .'

He paused for a few moments again, looking at me as if I was of no more interest to him than a stain on the wall, and then – without another word – he just let go of me, turned around, and walked off.

I watched him go, then sank down to my haunches, put my head between my knees, and moaned like a baby.

The first thing Cal said to me when I got back to him was, 'Why are you walking like that?'

'I'll tell you later. Come on, we're going.'

'What, now?'

'Yes, now.'

He gave me a questioning look. 'Has something just happened?'

'You could say that.'

He was about to ask me something else, but then he saw how I was looking at him and he changed his mind. He passed me my coat, picked up his, and we headed for the exit.

5

I've never quite understood why certain agonies are taken more seriously than others, and I've always been particularly puzzled by the all-round hilarity associated with any kind of kick in the balls. I get the fact that it's to do with a man's testicles, which are difficult to take seriously at the best of times, but the thing is, if you get kicked or punched in the balls, or someone grabs hold of them and squeezes as hard as possible, it really fucking hurts. It doesn't just hurt a bit, it's absolutely fucking agonising. And what's so funny about that?

So when I was telling Cal what had happened as he drove me back home, and I got to the bit where the scary guy grabbed my balls, I was quietly glad that Cal didn't make light of it.

'Are you all right now?' he asked, giving me a worried glance. 'I mean, he didn't do any serious damage, did he?'

I shook my head. 'I don't think so . . . it still fucking hurts though, you know? Right down in my guts.'

Cal frowned. 'It's kind of a weird thing to do to someone, isn't it?'

'He was kind of a weird guy.' I opened the window a couple of inches and lit a cigarette. 'Although, actually, if you think about it, it's not really such a weird thing to do.

I mean, if you want to hurt someone, it kind of makes sense to grab them where it hurts the most, doesn't it?'

'Well, yeah, I suppose . . .'

'The only reason it seems odd is that it's not the kind of thing you expect from your average day-to-day tough guy.' I flicked ash out of the window. 'But I don't think this guy was an average day-to-day *anything* . . .'

We drove on in silence for a while, and I just sat there smoking, looking out through the window as the world passed by. It was warm and quiet in the car, and for once I was grateful for Cal's love of luxury. Until quite recently, he'd owned a series of customised Mondeos. Each one was totally anonymous from the outside – no different from any other bog-standard Mondeo – but on the inside, and under the bonnet, they were all as well equipped, if not better, than cars worth twenty times as much. In the last twelve months or so though, he'd sold all his Mondeos and was now driving the kind of cars that *did* cost twenty times as much – top-of-the-range Audis, BMWs, Jaguars, Range Rovers. Tonight he was driving a Lexus. I don't know what kind of Lexus it was, as I have no knowledge and no interest whatsoever in cars, and I only knew it was a Lexus because Cal had told me. But I had to admit that it was kind of nice being in a car that didn't rattle and cough all the time, as my crappy old Renault usually did, and as we cruised along the bypass on the outskirts of town, it was all too easy to sink down into the warmth and comfort and gaze out mindlessly at the cold night outside. A fine rain had begun to fall, and as we passed the familiar red-brick sprawl of Rollerworld, McDonald's, and Beautiful Homes, I was quite content just sitting there watching the urban lights dazzling in the misted darkness – traffic lights, headlights, shop lights, streetlights . . . like neon sweets glowing in a black glass jar. I was happy enough not thinking or talking about anything. But Cal wasn't.

'What do you think Bishop was doing there?' he said.

'Sorry?'

'Mick Bishop,' he repeated. 'What do you think he was doing at Juno's tonight?'

'I'd like to think it was just a coincidence, you know . . . he just happened to be there. He's bound to know someone like Dempsey, isn't he? So there's no reason to suppose that he wasn't just there as a guest . . .'

Cal glanced at me. 'But you don't think he was?'

'I don't know,' I sighed. 'Maybe I'm just being paranoid. Even if he wasn't just there as a guest, there could be any number of other reasons he was there. Just because I'm interested in Hassan and Jamaal Tan, it doesn't necessarily mean that Bishop's got anything to do with them.'

'Right,' said Cal. 'But Bishop's bound to know who Jamaal is, isn't he? Even if he's not personally involved in the murder case, he'll know all about it.'

'Yeah.'

'And if he knows all about it, and it *is* being covered up for some reason . . .'

Cal didn't have to finish the sentence. We both knew there was nothing Mick Bishop didn't know about the workings of Hey CID – and very little he didn't know about Essex Police as a whole – and if there was something going on, especially something shady, Bishop would at the very least know about it, and he'd more than likely be part of it, or even directly responsible for it.

'Shit,' I said wearily, flicking my cigarette end out of the window. 'Maybe Ada was right about this one. Maybe I should give it a miss. I mean, it doesn't look as if I'm going to get paid now, and if Bishop *is* mixed up in whatever's going on . . . well, I'm not sure I can deal with that. Not after the last time.'

The last time . . .

How could I forget?

The last time I was involved in a case with Mick Bishop, a lot of very bad stuff happened. People died, people I cared about got hurt. Cal was beaten half to death. I witnessed things too ugly to think about . . .

'Do you want me to look into Bishop and Dempsey for you?' Cal said, lighting a cigarette. 'I mean, if they are connected, it might be a good idea to know how.'

'I don't know, Cal. If I'm not going to work this case, you'd just be wasting your time.'

'What about Ayanna?'

I looked at him.

He shrugged. 'I'm just saying . . .'

'What?'

'You promised her you'd look into it, didn't you?'

'I have looked into it. And I don't like what I've seen.'

'So you're just going to turn your back on her?'

'Maybe . . . have you got a problem with that?'

'Nope,' he said, shaking his head. 'But I think you probably have.'

'Yeah?'

He grinned at me. 'Yeah.'

I glared at him for a moment, trying to be annoyed, but I couldn't keep it up for long.

'Smart arse,' I muttered, turning away to hide my smile.

'Sorry?' he said, cupping a hand to his ear. 'What was that?'

It was around eleven when Cal swung the Lexus into Paxman Street and started heading down towards my house. The narrow old street looked the same as it always did – a row of terraced houses on one side, dozens of cars parked beneath the high brick wall on the other. A bank of mist was rising from the cooling pond on the other side of the wall, and through the mist I could just make out the familiar shapes of tall factory buildings and chimney tops blocked against the moonlit sky. It's a sight that's always fascinated me, and as Cal pulled up across the road from my house, and I gazed out at the industrial gloom, I wondered – as I've wondered many times before – what actually goes on in those buildings.

I've lived in this street for fifteen years, and while I know that all the houses around here were originally built as factory houses, constructed over a century ago by the owners of the neighbouring engineering plant to accommodate the company's workers, I still don't know what the plant actually does. I've always assumed that it manufactures some kind of heavy machinery, but since I don't know what heavy machinery is, and I don't have anything to support my assumption anyway, it's a pretty pointless bit of reasoning all round.

I keep promising myself I'll look it up, Google it, find out what really goes on in there . . . but I never do. And I suppose if I really did want to know, I'd make the effort. So maybe I don't want to know after all. Maybe, deep down, I'm happier not knowing. Or maybe I just can't be bothered.

'All right then?' Cal said, breaking into my thoughts.

'Yep.' I looked at him. 'Do you want to come in for a coffee or something?'

He shook his head. 'Things to do, you know . . . people to see . . .' He lit a cigarette. 'I'll get back to you if I find out anything about Bishop and Dempsey, OK?'

I nodded, but I still had serious reservations about this case, and I couldn't keep the uncertainty from my face.

'Hey,' Cal said gently, putting his hand on my shoulder. 'Don't fret about it, John, all right? Just think about it for a while, see how you feel, and then if you want to do it, that's fine, but it's perfectly OK if you don't.' He smiled. 'It's your life, John. You've got to live it by your rules.'

I looked at him. 'Since when did you get all grown up and wise?'

He laughed. 'I've always been wise. I just make out I'm dumb to fit in with the cool kids.'

'Yeah, well,' I said, unfastening my seat belt. 'You do it very convincingly, I'll give you that.'

He patted my shoulder. 'All thanks to you, Nunc.'

'Yeah, very good.'

I opened the car door and got out. The rain had stopped, the air was cold and icy. Tendrils of mist were creeping over the factory wall, and I could hear a low rumble of machinery coming from one of the factory buildings.

'I'll call you tomorrow,' I said to Cal, leaning back into the car.

He nodded. 'OK.'

'And Cal?'

'Yeah?'

'Thanks.'

He grinned. 'No problem. Say hello to Bridget for me, OK?'

'Yeah, see you later.'

I stepped back, closed the car door, and watched him drive off into the night. The red tail lights of his Lexus hazed in a swathe of mist, and as they disappeared round the corner at the bottom of the street, I took out my keys, paused for a moment, then crossed over the road.

My house is split into two separate flats – one upstairs, one downstairs – and when I inherited it from my mother fifteen years ago, Bridget Moran was renting the flat upstairs.

My mother had also left me the family home in her will, and as I'd already decided to sell that and use the money to set up my own private investigation business, it had seemed sensible and convenient to move into the downstairs flat at Paxman Street which had been empty for quite some time. The flat itself is nothing special – a large front room, spacious and high, with solid old walls, a broad bay window, and heavy double doors that lead through to the bedroom, and then on into a cramped little kitchen area at the back – and the house isn't anything to shout about either, it's just an old terraced place with a small front yard and a brick-walled garden at the rear. But it's mine, and I like it. It makes me feel safe and comfortable.

Although I'd always liked Bridget, and we'd always been reasonably good friends as well as being landlord and tenant, we didn't actually get together until just over two years ago. We'd had a few problems at first. I hadn't been in any kind of relationship since the death of my wife Stacy, so I probably wasn't the easiest person to be with, and soon after we'd begun seeing each other, Bridget had been badly hurt after getting mixed up in the Gerrish case, and for a while it had looked as if our relationship was over before it had a chance to begin. But we'd worked things out, and over the last two years we'd grown really close to each other and were gradually putting most of our problems behind us. I wasn't drinking so much any more, and apart from the odd line of coke at Cal's now and then, and maybe the occasional joint, I was hardly taking any drugs at all. The intermittent bouts of depression that had plagued me for years weren't quite so frequent or debilitating any more either, and although my dead wife was still never far from my mind, I was no longer hearing her voice in my heart every day. In fact, I couldn't actually remember the last time we'd talked to each other. I still missed her, of course. I missed everything about her. But I knew she was happy for me. And she knew I still loved her.

Bridget, too, was happier than she'd been for a long time. The young dog we now shared our lives with – a lurcher/rottweiler cross called Finn – had helped her get over the traumatic loss of her beloved old greyhound, Walter, and while it would be wrong to say that everything was always perfect between the three of us, it was about as close to perfect as it gets. We still kept our own flats – Bridget's upstairs, mine downstairs – so if either of us ever wanted to be alone, it was never a problem. But at the same time we happily shared each other's flats as well. Some nights we slept upstairs, other nights we slept in my room. I'd cook for Bridget sometimes, other times she'd cook for me. She could spend all day in my flat if she wanted to, and I could spend all day in hers. Finn, meanwhile, had the run of the whole house, so he could go wherever he liked.

I suppose it was a little unconventional, but it worked for us.

It made us happy.

And that's all that counts.

That night, as I opened the front door and went into the hallway, Finn was waiting for me as usual, and as I dropped my keys on the hall table, he gave me his customary greeting – jumping up at me, putting his front legs on my shoulders, and barking madly into my face.

'Hey, Finn,' I said, gently pushing him off and wiping dog spit from my face. 'How's it going?'

He barked again – 'Fine, thanks,' – and wagged his tail, thumping it against the wall.

'Where's Bridget?' I asked him, glancing up the stairs.

He answered me by turning round, lolloping down the hallway, and barging in through my door. I followed him. The door to my flat leads directly into the bedroom, to the left of which are the double doors that lead into the sitting room. The bed was empty when I went in, but as I followed Finn through the doors, I saw Bridget sitting on my old settee in front of the glowing gas fire. She was dressed up warmly in pyjamas, an old woolly dressing gown, furry slippers, and a big furry hat with the earflaps down, and she was sitting upright, with her knees pulled up to her chest, reading a paperback book.

She looked beautiful.

'Hey, you,' she said, turning to me and smiling.

I went over, leaned down, and kissed her.

'Oooh,' she said, 'cold lips.'

I smiled. As Finn jumped up and sat down beside her, I took off my coat, went over to a corner table by the window, and poured myself a small whisky.

'Why are you walking like that?' Bridget asked.

'Like what?'

'Like you've got a broom handle stuck up your bum.'

I grinned at her, but it didn't work. She just glared at me, waiting for an answer. I briefly considered telling her that I didn't want to talk about it, but I could tell from the look in her eyes that the only option I had was to tell her what she wanted to know.

So I told her.

We slept in my bed that night. Bridget made a big fuss about my injury, insisting – quite seriously – on a thorough examination to make sure that nothing was damaged, and when she'd satisfied herself that I was probably going to be OK, she asked me if there was anything else I needed – paracetamol, a glass of water, an extra pillow? I told her I was fine, and that she didn't have to do anything for me, but she wouldn't hear of it.

'I like doing things for you,' she said with a smile.

And I wasn't going to argue with that.

I did put up an argument when she suggested that a strategically placed bag of ice might be a good idea, and I'm glad to say that in this case she listened to me.

We both read for a while in bed – Joseph O'Connor for her, John D. MacDonald for me – but by one o'clock we'd turned off the lights and were falling asleep in each other's arms while Finn snored contentedly at the foot of the bed.

I was dreaming about something when the phone rang, but it wasn't anything memorable, and by the time I'd opened my eyes and squinted at the alarm clock, the dream had already gone. It was 4.31 a.m. The phone was still ringing. Bridget was half-awake now, rubbing her eyes and muttering sleepily – 'Wha's 'at? Wha's going on?' – and Finn's ears had pricked up and he was whining quietly at the noise. I groaned, coughed, cleared my throat, and picked up the phone.

'Hello?'

'John?' a woman's voice sobbed. 'Oh, Christ, John . . . is that you?'

'Imogen?' I said, sitting up quickly.

'It's Mum and Dad . . . I can't . . . oh, *Jesus* . . .'

She was crying so hard, her voice so broken and breathless, that I could barely understand what she was saying.

'Please, John,' she sobbed. '*Please*. . . I don't know what to do—'

'Just try to slow down a second, OK?' I said as calmly as possible.

'But I don't—'

'What's happened, Imogen? Just tell me what's happened.'

'They're dead . . . they died . . . they didn't—'

71

'Who's dead?'

'Mum and Dad . . . they were in the house, they didn't get out . . . I don't *understand*—'

'Where are you?'

'I'm here, the police called me—'

'Where?'

'At the house . . . it's gone, John, it's all burned down . . . everything's gone—'

'Is somebody there with you?'

'Yes, but I don't *want*—'

'Just stay where you are, OK?' I told her. 'I'll be there in fifteen minutes.'

'Yes . . . yes, please . . . I'm sorry—'

'I'm putting the phone down now, Imogen. Just wait there, all right? I'm on my way.'

I wasn't aware of how shocked I was until I'd thrown on some clothes, quickly explained things to Bridget, and hurried outside to my car. It was only when I'd started the engine and was about to get going that the nausea suddenly struck me, and I realised then that my head was spinning, my legs were shaking, and my hands were trembling so much I could barely hold onto the steering wheel.

I sat there for a few seconds, just breathing steadily and trying to calm myself down, but the longer I waited, the more I started to think, and all that did was make things worse. So in the end I just lit a cigarette, slammed the Renault into gear, and sped off into the morning darkness.

6

Leon Mercer was my father's closest, and possibly only, friend. They'd first got to know each other in the late 1970s when they were both Detective Constables with Hey CID, and as their career paths had progressed over the years, and they'd risen through the ranks together – from Detective Constable to Detective Sergeant, and eventually to Detective Inspector – they'd always remained good friends. They didn't socialise a lot, but Leon was often at our house when I was growing up, so although I didn't really know very much about him – he was just another grown-up to me – he'd always been a presence in my life. I got to know him a little better when, at the age of seventeen, I started going out with his daughter Imogen, but all he was to me then was my girlfriend's father, which basically meant that I was scared of him. He didn't actually do anything to frighten me – in fact, as girlfriends' fathers go, he was remarkably restrained and approachable – but I was a seventeen-year-old boy lusting after his seventeen-year-old daughter . . . there would have to have been something wrong with me if I hadn't been scared of him.

It was after my father's suicide in 1992 that Leon and I became close friends. It was a very difficult time for me, for all kinds of different reasons, and Leon was the only one of my father's police colleagues who kept in touch with my mother and me. He did what he could to look after my mother, and he became something of a surrogate father to me, and then, a year later, when my wife was murdered, and I started falling apart – drinking myself into oblivion, taking every drug I could find . . . losing my job, my dignity, my will to live – it was Leon who pulled me back from the brink. Even when everyone else had – quite rightly – given up on me, Leon still kept in contact, ringing me up, coming round to see me, making sure I was OK. He didn't try to change me or anything, he was always just there, looking out for me, caring for me. And despite the fact that I was pretty much a non-functional 24-hour drunk, and I didn't know the first thing about investigation work, he even offered to take me on at Mercer Associates, the private investigation company he'd set up after retiring from the force. And although it took a while, it was that kindness, that unconditional show of faith, that dragged me out of my wallowing self-pity and gave me back at least some sense of purpose. I must have turned down his offer about half a dozen times before I finally agreed to give it a go, and that was the start of everything really. Leon took me under his wing, taught me everything he knew about the business, and it wasn't long before I realised that not only did I enjoy the work, but I was reasonably good at it too. So much so that when my mother died in 1997, I decided to use the money from the sale of her house to set up my own investigation agency. And even then Leon was really good to me – giving me his support and advice, helping me with the practicalities, the legal stuff . . . and he didn't really mind too much when I poached Ada from his company either.

Since then I'd stayed good friends with both Leon and his wife, Claudia – who'd always been incredibly kind to me too – and Leon had carried on helping me out, subcontracting cases to me, offering advice if I asked for it – and I'd stayed in touch with Imogen as well. Our teenage romance hadn't lasted very long, and while I'd gone on to marry Stacy, Imogen met and married a wealthy financier named Martin Rand. They were divorced a few years ago, at about the same time that Leon was diagnosed with pancreatic cancer, and since then Imogen has taken over the day-to-day running of Mercer Associates. Leon never officially retired, but as his health slowly deteriorated, he began spending more and more time at home, and the last time I'd seen him, about two months ago, I'd got the feeling that he wasn't going to live much longer.

And now . . .

Now, it seemed, he and Claudia were both dead.

I found it hard to digest, and as I drove along the empty roads that morning, heading out of town towards the Mercers' house, I tried not to think about the reality of what I was going to find. I'd deal with it when I got there. Whatever it was, whatever it meant, whatever I had to do . . . I'd deal with it when I got there.

It was raining again, a cold sleety rain that shone like silver needles in the dark. The roads were deserted, no traffic, no people, and everything had a strangely timeless feel to it. The lime trees along the pavements, the lightless houses, the pelican crossings waiting for someone to cross . . . it was all just there, without human witness, like a scene from the end of the world.

It was around quarter to five now, and the sun wouldn't be up for at least another two hours or so, but as I left the Eastway roundabout behind and headed into the area known as Lexden Vale where Leon and Claudia lived, I could see a faint glow of light spreading across the morning sky about half a mile up ahead, a shimmering haze of electric blue, pulsing and flashing in the darkness . . . the lights of multiple emergency vehicles – police, fire brigade, ambulance. I didn't see the smoke at first, but as I approached the turning that leads down into Lexden Vale, the flash of lights momentarily lit up a thick greyish cloud hanging in the sky to my left.

I made the turning, and as I accelerated down a steepish slope, the lights disappeared for a few seconds, hidden behind a wall of towering Leylandii trees, but when I slowed the Renault and turned left into a tree-lined avenue, the lights came back again. And now I could see everything – the dazzling glare of strobing emergency lights from the dozen or so vehicles parked at the end of the street, the uniformed police officers, the firemen, the ladders, the hoses . . . the smouldering shell of an all-too-familiar house.

'Shit,' I muttered, slowing the car to a crawl.

There were people out in the street – concerned neighbours in coats and pyjamas, people carrying torches, people filming the scene on their mobiles – and others were watching from the safety of their homes – parents, children, curious faces peering out through upstairs windows. It was too crowded to drive – I was barely topping 5 mph – so I pulled in at the first available space at the kerb, got out of the car, and started to run. An ambulance passed by, going away from the house. Its siren blipped a couple of times, warning people to get off the road, but its lights weren't flashing, and it clearly wasn't in a rush to get anywhere. As I approached the scene, slowing to a jog, I couldn't take my eyes off the Mercers' ruined house. It had always been an impressive home – a grey-walled four-storey building with a gated driveway and well-tended gardens – and when I'd first started coming here, as a nervous teenager, I'd felt quite intimidated by its size and comparative luxury. It wasn't until some years later, when I'd got to know Leon and Claudia, and I'd got to know a little bit more about the world, that I realised it wasn't the marble-halled mansion I'd thought it was when I was a kid, it was just a reasonably large detached house in a secluded avenue in a nice part of town. It was where Leon and Claudia lived, that was all. It was their home.

There wasn't much left of it now.

It hadn't looked too badly damaged from a distance, but as I approached the driveway and stopped at the gates, the full extent of the devastation became clear. Most of the roof was missing, just a few charred rafters remaining, and all the windows were gone, the glass blown out. The grey stone walls around the broken windows were blackened with fire, like great smudges of tear-stained mascara. Smoke was still drifting from the ruined roof, and firemen were still pumping water into the building. Steam was rising in the heat. Empty ladders leaned against the walls. The gardens and the driveway were flooded.

It wasn't a home any more, it wasn't anything.

I looked around, trying to spot Imogen, but all I could see were uniformed men in fluorescent yellow jackets – police officers, firemen – all of them bustling around, shouting out orders, talking on radios. A tall PC and a fireman were coming down the driveway together, the fire officer wiping soot and sweat from his face.

I went up to the PC and said, 'Excuse me, I'm looking for—'

'Sorry, sir,' he said, cutting me off, 'you can't come in here.'

'I'm a friend of the family. I'm trying to find—'

'John!'

I turned at the sound of the voice and saw Imogen hurrying along the pavement at the foot of the drive. She looked in a bad way – white with shock, her face streaked with tears, her eyes all puffy and red – and as I went over to her, and she threw her arms around me and held me tight, I could feel her whole body shaking.

'Oh, *God*, John,' she sobbed into my shoulder. 'They're gone . . . they're just . . . I can't . . . oh, God . . .'

Five minutes later, after she'd calmed down a little, I suggested we find somewhere quiet so we could sit down and talk for a while. She led me along the pavement to a parked BMW, opened the back door, and we got in. She took a tissue from her pocket, wiped her eyes and blew her nose, and then – after a quick glance over her shoulder at the still-smouldering house – she started telling me what had happened.

The police had called her at just gone three o'clock, she

78

said. All they could tell her then was that there'd been a fire at her parents' home, and they didn't know if Leon and Claudia were in the house or not. Imogen immediately drove over from her flat on the other side of town, getting to Lexden Vale at around three-twenty. By this time, three fire engines were at the scene, and the worst of the fire was under control.

'That's when they found them,' Imogen said, sniffing back tears again. 'Once they could get inside, you know . . . when the fire was out. They went inside to see if Mum and Dad were there . . . and they found two bodies . . .'

The bodies were so badly burned that the police wouldn't let Imogen see them. And because they were burned beyond recognition, they couldn't be officially identified until forensic tests had been carried out. But from the identifying evidence that Imogen had been shown – articles of jewellery found on the bodies, wedding rings, a necklace, a wristwatch – and from the police doctor's estimation of the age, height, and build of the bodies, there was little doubt they were Leon and Claudia.

'I keep trying to kid myself that it's not them,' Imogen said quietly. 'You know, as long as there's a chance, however small, however unlikely . . .' She shrugged. 'But I know it's ridiculous.'

'Have you tried their mobiles?'

'First thing I did.' She shook her head. 'They both go straight to voicemail.' She looked at me. 'I know it's Mum and Dad, John. I mean, who else could it be? I just . . . I don't know. I just can't believe it, I suppose.'

'Do the police know how the fire started?'

'No one seems to know anything yet.'

I wound down the window and lit a cigarette.

Imogen said, 'I'm sorry I woke you up—'

'Don't be silly.'

'I didn't know who else to call.'

'I'm glad you called me,' I said. 'I just wish there was something I could do.'

'You're doing it,' she said, looking at me. 'You know, just being here . . .'

I nodded, wondering why I felt so calm, so accepting, so unemotional. I wasn't shaking any more, I didn't feel sick. What was the matter with me? Why wasn't I crying for Leon and Claudia? Why wasn't I mourning them? Was it some kind of denial? Or had I become so inured to death that it no longer had any effect on me?

'Have the police told you how long it'll take to confirm the ID?' I asked Imogen, dropping the half-smoked cigarette out of the window.

She shook her head. 'They're trying to get hold of Mum and Dad's dental records but they're having problems contacting their dentist.' She glanced at her watch. 'I'm going to the police station now to see if there's any more news.'

'Do you want me to come with you?'

'Thanks, John, but the police are probably going to want to talk to me for a while, ask me a few questions about Mum and Dad. And Bob Smith is meeting me there, he's Dad's solicitor, and he'll want to talk to me too. You'd just be hanging around waiting for me.'

'I don't mind.'

'No, really,' she said, putting her hand on my knee. 'I'll be fine.'

'Are you sure?'

She nodded.

I said, 'Will you let me know as soon as anything's confirmed?'

'Of course.' She looked at me, tears welling up in her eyes.

'Come here,' I said quietly.

We just held each other for a while then, both of us knowing that words weren't necessary any more. Sometimes there just isn't anything worth saying, and this was one of those times. There were a lot of questions running through my mind – when did the fire start? how did it start? why couldn't Leon and Claudia get out? – but I knew there'd be plenty of time for questions in the days to come, and that in the end the answers wouldn't make any difference anyway.

Leon and Claudia were dead.

What else was there to know?

As far as I know, I wasn't consciously aware of where I was going when I drove away from Lexden Vale that morning, I was just driving – away from town, out into the suburbs, towards the bordering countryside. I didn't intend stopping off at the big Sainsbury's in Stangate Rise, I didn't even know it'd be open this early in the morning, but it was, and before I really knew what I was doing, I'd parked in the car park, gone inside and bought a half-bottle of Teacher's and a large Americano to take away. Back in the Renault, I poured half the coffee away, topped it up with whisky, and took a long warming drink from the cup. It made me retch a little, but once I'd lit a cigarette and taken another long drink, the sickness soon passed.

I sat in the car park for a while, just smoking and sipping, not really thinking about anything, then I fixed the cup in the cup holder, put out my cigarette, and drove away.

Before the mid-eighties, when the commuter suburb known as Stangate Rise was built, Stangate was just another village on the outskirts of Hey – a few dozen houses, a couple of shops, a post office, a church, playing fields. There was no Sainsbury's back then, no DIY super-stores, no Burger Kings, and there was nothing on the hilly expanse to the east of the village except woods and fields and the remains of a disused quarry. So, of course, when it first became known that the woods and the fields were all going to be dug up to make way for a vast new housing estate consisting of thousands of affordable homes marketed almost exclusively at the growing number of people who worked in London but couldn't afford to live in London, the local residents inevitably rose up in protest. Despite a long and bitter campaign, the housing development still went ahead, but even now there's still a lot of bad feeling between some of the villagers and those who live on the estate. My father though – who was born and brought up in Stangate, and whose family had lived there for generations – he never seemed bothered about it at all.

'Things change,' I remember him saying once. 'That's

just the way it is. There's no point in getting all worked up about it.'

I'd always kind of admired him for that.

Although he moved away from Stangate when he was seventeen – and as far as I know he never showed any interest in going back – my father left instructions in his will that his body was to be laid to rest in the grounds of the village church, St Leonard's, where both his parents and his grandparents were buried. Five years after my father's death, my mother joined him in the graveyard at St Leonard's. And that morning, as I parked outside the small stone church and headed round the back to the cemetery gardens, I realised that this was the first time I'd been here in almost fifteen years. It wasn't something I regretted or felt guilty about – I've always preferred memories to gravestones – but it did beg the question as to what I was doing here now.

I didn't have an answer.

And I didn't really give it much thought.

I was here, that was all. I was opening the gate to the gardens, threading my way along the gravel paths between the gravestones, heading slowly down to the far side of the graveyard where my mother and father were buried. A light rain was falling, the air was damp and earthy. The skies were still dark, but the first faint flickers of the morning sun were beginning to show on the horizon, and as I sat down on a wooden bench and gazed out over the low stone wall that borders the cemetery, I could just make out the soft grey outlines of the hills and fields beyond.

I lit a cigarette, sipped from my whiskied coffee, and

looked at the two gravestones in front of me. They were matching granite stones, standing side by side, each as plain as the other. The one closest to me read simply: *James John Craine, 1945–1992*. The inscription on the other was equally straightforward: *Alice Craine, 1946–1997*.

'Hey, Dad,' I muttered, raising my cup to them. 'Mum . . .'

Their graves were surprisingly well tended – no weeds, no overgrown grass, everything nice and neat – and I wondered who was responsible. I looked around at the other graves. They weren't all neat and tidy, which I guessed they would be if someone from the church looked after the whole cemetery, so I assumed that someone else must have been tending to my parents' graves. The only close family they had left was my mother's elderly sister, but she lived somewhere in Hampshire, so it obviously wasn't her. It could be someone I didn't know, of course – an old friend of Mum's or Dad's perhaps – but knowing how close Leon had been to my father, and how kind a man he'd always been, I was pretty sure that this was his doing. I could just see him coming up here once a month, cleaning things up a bit, clearing away the weeds, refreshing the flowers in the vases. There was a grey granite vase at the base of each gravestone, and the flowers in both of them looked fresh: white irises in my mother's, yellow roses in my father's.

Yellow roses . . .

A distant memory floated into my mind, a hazy remembrance of a brief conversation I'd had with Leon a few days before my father's funeral. I couldn't recall too much about it – my father died almost twenty years ago – but as I gazed down at the vase of roses now I could clearly remember Leon asking me about flowers. He'd wanted to know what kind of flowers I thought Dad would like. And I'd told him, quite honestly, that I had no idea. I didn't even know if he liked flowers or not.

'You'd be better off asking Mum,' I'd said to Leon, slightly surprised that he'd asked me in the first place.

'What about roses?' he'd suggested. 'Yellow roses . . . do you think they'd be suitable?'

'I suppose so,' I'd shrugged. 'But, like I said, Mum'll know better than me.'

I don't know if he did ask my mother or not, and I can't remember what kind of flowers he chose in the end, but I definitely remember him asking me about roses.

Yellow roses . . .

'Thanks, Leon,' I said now, raising my cup again. 'You were a good man.'

I didn't say anything else for the next hour or so, I just sat there, smoking and drinking, watching the sun come up. I wondered if the reason I'd come here was to let my father know that Leon was dead, and on a couple of occasions I almost said something out loud, but the words didn't seem to want to come out. And I didn't see any point in forcing them. They were there – in my mind, my heart – and that was enough.

It was just gone eight o'clock when I decided I'd better get going. A pale January sun hung low in the sky, and flat grey clouds were spreading out across the horizon. Away to my right, on the other side of a misted vale, I could see the dark dereliction of Morden Hall glowering down from its hilltop plateau. The old brick ruins looked exactly the same as they had for years. A partially roof-less structure, with the walls still mostly intact, the crumbling old mansion house stood in a wire-fenced courtyard surrounded by piles of bricks and rubble. I gazed at it for a while, wondering idly how long it would take for all traces of the building to meld back into the ground on which it was built. Ten years? A hundred? A thousand?

It was all too long for me.

As I got to my feet and started heading back to my car, I suddenly realised that I'd drunk a lot more than I'd thought. I wasn't quite sure how it had happened, but the half-bottle of Teacher's in my pocket was almost empty, and I didn't feel too steady on my feet. I stopped at the church gate and lit another cigarette, and I was just beginning to consider the ramifications of leaving my car here and getting a taxi back, when my mobile rang.

It was Bridget.

After I'd apologised for not calling her, and then told her all about the fire, she asked me where I was and when I was coming home.

'I'm just on my way back now,' I said. 'I should be home in about half an hour. Are you working today?'

Bridget and her friend Sarah co-own a small pet shop in town. They take turns running the shop – one week Bridget works Monday, Wednesday, and Friday, the following week she does Tuesday, Thursday, and Saturday

– and I can never remember which days are Bridget's and which are Sarah's.

'I'm supposed to be working,' Bridget said, 'but I can call Sarah if you want and get her to swap—'

'No, it's all right,' I said. 'I'm a bit tired anyway, so I'm probably just going to sleep for a while when I get back, and then I might go into the office later.'

'Are you sure? I don't mind staying here—'

'There's no need, Bridge. Really, I'm fine.'

'Honestly?'

'Yeah.'

'It's just that you sound a bit—'

'I'm really tired, that's all. And it's all been a bit of a shock, you know . . . I'll be all right when I've had some sleep.'

'Well . . . OK,' she said hesitantly. 'I'll probably be gone by the time you get back, but if you need me for anything, or if you change your mind, just call me, all right?'

'Yeah, of course. Are you taking Finn with you?'

'I was going to, yeah. But I can leave him if you want some company.'

'No, that's OK.'

'Sure?'

'Yeah.'

'All right . . . well, I'd better start getting ready now if I'm going to get the shop open on time.'

'Right.'

'See you later, OK?'

'Yeah.'

*

The house was empty when I got back, and my heart was empty too. I didn't like myself at all just then. I shouldn't have drunk so much, I shouldn't have driven home in the state I was in, and I should have been more honest with Bridget. I should have just told her that I'd gone to the church and drunk myself stupid, and that I didn't know why I'd done it.

I went into the front room, poured myself a drink, and sat down in the armchair beneath the high window. I lit a cigarette and sat there in the dusty light, wondering what to do. But there isn't much you can do when you don't like yourself, is there? You can't ignore yourself. You can't run away. You can't pretend that it doesn't matter, that it's just the way it is sometimes, and there's nothing you can do about it. You can't do anything that means anything. All you can do is sit in your chair in the dull morning light and drink yourself to sleep.

7

At nine-thirty on Friday morning I was sitting in an office on the third floor of Hey police station, waiting for DI Lilley to show up. My appointment with him was at nine, but according to the Detective Constable who'd brought me a cup of cold coffee, the DI had been 'unavoidably delayed due to pressing operational matters'. The DC told me that he didn't know how long Lilley was going to be, and that it was up to me if I wanted to carry on waiting for him or rearrange the appointment for another day.

I was quite happy waiting.

I don't have that many skills, but I'm excellent at waiting.

I'd already had a good look round the office, and it hadn't taken long to see everything there was to see. It was virtually bare – a grey metal desk, two grey metal chairs, an empty grey filing cabinet, a fire extinguisher mounted on the wall. I'd gone over to the window and spent another five minutes watching the last of the rush-hour traffic as it coiled back and forth along Eastway, and then I'd sat down on one of the grey metal chairs, placed my cold coffee on the grey metal desk, and for the last twenty minutes or so I'd been lost in my head, just staring blindly at the wall, thinking without really thinking.

Yesterday, six in the evening, Imogen's tearful voice on

the phone . . . *it's been confirmed, John, it's Mum and Dad . . . I can't talk now . . . ring me tomorrow, OK? I need to see you.*

OK, tomorrow, today . . .

OK.

Bridget, this morning . . . *are you sure you're all right, John? You just seem a bit . . . I don't know, a bit distant.*

It's nothing, really. I'm just a bit . . . it's nothing. I'll see you later.

And then that look in her eyes as you leave, that confused mixture of uncertainty, annoyance, anger, fear. *Why won't you just talk to me?*

Why don't you just talk to her?

About what?

Tell her how you feel.

I don't fucking know how I feel, do I? I don't know what's the matter with me. I don't even know what I'm doing here. What the fuck am I doing in this shithole of an office, waiting for someone who I'm probably not going to like?

It's your job. It's what you do.

Yeah, well—

The door opened then, and a pudgy-faced man in his late thirties came in. He was wearing the kind of plain white shirt that comes in a pack of three, costs virtually nothing, and is made so cheaply you can see through it. And like most men who favour cheap see-through shirts, he was wearing a vest underneath. Stylish.

'Morning, Mr Craine,' he said, coming over to shake my hand. 'I'm DI Lilley. Sorry to keep you waiting.'

I nodded, shook his hand, and watched him as he sat down opposite me at the desk. He wasn't much to look at. Thinning brown hair, dull grey eyes, a mouth too small for his face. He was on the short side, but not noticeably so, and fattish without being obese. Like a chubby child in the body of a man.

'So, Mr Craine,' he said, placing his hands on the desk and lacing his fingers together, 'what can I do for you?'

'Well,' I said, smiling pleasantly, 'as my secretary explained when she spoke to you on the phone yesterday—'

'I know what your secretary said, Mr Craine. All I'm interested in is what *you* have to say.'

I looked at him, staring into his eyes, and for a moment or two I really had to force myself to remain in the chair. What I wanted to do was get up, grab the fire extinguisher off the wall, and hammer it into his fat head. But I didn't. Instead, I just smiled to myself for a few seconds, imagining the headlines – *LOCAL PI SLAYS LOCAL DI* – and then, as straight-faced as possible, I got on with it.

'OK,' I said. 'Well, it's quite simple really. I'm a private investigator, as you know, and I'm acting on behalf of a client regarding the progress of your investigation into the murder of Jamaal Tan.'

'Who's your client?'

'Ayanna Osman.'

Lilley raised his eyebrows. I wasn't sure if it was an authentic expression of surprise at the fact that I hadn't refused to name my client, or if it was supposed to convey something else. Not that it made any difference. I'd called Ayanna the night before and told her I was meeting with

Lilley, and that I didn't think there was any point in trying to keep her name out of it, as he was bound to know who I was working for anyway. And although she hadn't liked it, she'd seen sense in the end and agreed to waive her right to confidentiality.

'I take it you're aware that I'm not obliged to tell you anything?' Lilley said.

I nodded.

'In fact,' he went on, 'we're not obliged to liaise with Miss Osman at all, either directly or through an agent. She has no legal standing in the matter.'

'So you're not going to talk to me?'

'That's not what I said—'

'I don't mind,' I told him. 'If you're not going to talk to me, that's fine. Just tell me. But I don't have time to sit around playing games with you, OK?' I shrugged. 'So what's it to be? Do you want me to go?'

He shook his head. 'All I'm saying is we're not legally bound to share any information with either you or Miss Osman.'

'I'm perfectly aware of that. And all I'm saying is, are you going to talk to me about it or not?'

'What are you going to do if I don't?'

'Oh, come *on*, for Christ's sake,' I said, rapidly losing patience. 'You either talk to me or you don't, OK? It's up to you. I really don't give a shit.'

He didn't say anything for a few seconds, he just sat there frowning at me, as if he really couldn't understand my impatience. And I just gave up then. That was it, I'd had enough.

'All right,' I sighed, getting to my feet, 'thanks for your time—'

'Hold on a second,' he said.

I looked at him.

He smiled. 'Just sit down, OK?'

'Why? What's the point?'

'Please? Just sit down.'

I sighed again, and reluctantly sat down.

Lilley examined his fingernails for a moment, sniffed, rubbed his nose, then looked up at me and said, 'What exactly is it you want to know?'

The first thing I asked him was how the investigation was going.

'It's going very well,' he said.

'Can you expand on that a little?'

He shook his head. 'I can't reveal any details of the investigation, Mr Craine. You know that.'

'Have you charged anyone?'

'Not yet.'

'Arrested anyone?'

'No.'

'Has anyone been questioned?'

'We've questioned a number of people, yes.'

'Do you expect to be charging anyone soon?'

'I can't tell you that.'

I sighed. 'What *can* you tell me?'

He thought about this one for a while, his eyes fixed on the desk in front of him, and then eventually he looked up and said, 'Jamaal Tan was stabbed to death between 1 a.m. and

2 a.m. on 27 August last year. The post-mortem examination revealed extensive injuries to the head and body consistent with a severe and prolonged physical attack, and the pathologist also found evidence of anal rape.' Lilley paused, looking at me. 'Our investigation into Mr Tan's death has uncovered incontrovertible evidence that he was heavily involved in both the use and supply of Class A drugs, and that he had close connections with several criminal gangs in the area who we know are responsible for at least 90% of the drug-related violence in Hey.'

As Lilley sat there looking at me, waiting for my response, I wondered how long it had taken him to learn that little speech. Had he practised it? Had he written it himself? Was he proud of it? From the faint look of satisfaction in his eyes, I got the feeling that he was, at the very least, quite pleased with himself.

'So you think that's why he was killed?' I said. 'He was mixed up with the local drug gangs, and he did something that one of them didn't like?'

'We don't *think* that's why he was killed, Mr Craine. We *know* it.'

'His brother claims he wasn't using drugs any more.'

Lilley smiled knowingly. 'His brother's wrong.'

'Do you know which gangs he was involved with?'

'Yes.'

'The Somalis?'

Lilley said nothing.

I tried again. 'The Chinese?'

He shrugged. 'As I said before, I'm not in a position to reveal any details of our investigation.'

'Why did you threaten Ayanna Osman?'

He frowned. 'What?'

'You told her that if she didn't stop bothering you, you'd report her to the Border Agency.'

'Who told you that?'

'She did.'

He laughed. 'I'm afraid you've been misled, Mr Craine. I can assure you that I've never so much as mentioned the Border Agency to Miss Osman, and neither have any of my team.'

'Are you saying she lied to me?'

He shrugged again. 'All I can tell you is what I know. Perhaps she misheard me, or misunderstood something I said. It's sometimes a problem if English isn't your first language—'

'She speaks perfect English.'

Lilley stared at me. 'What do you want me to say? Yes, she lied to you? She made up a story to make you pity her – the poor little woman being threatened by the big bad policeman?' He shook his head. 'I'm sorry, Mr Craine, but it's not my job to pass judgement on your clients. I've got more important things to do.'

'You know she's here illegally though, don't you?'

'Her immigration status bears no relevance to my investigation.'

'Would you say she's been bothering you?'

He hesitated for just a moment. 'There have been occasions when the sheer frequency of Miss Osman's enquiries has led to some difficulties. It can be very frustrating if you're trying to do your job and you have to keep stopping to explain to someone what you're doing. But my investigation team are all experienced officers. They understand the difficulties, and they know how to deal with them.' He gave me his knowing smile again. 'If Miss Osman is unhappy with any aspect of our investigation, there are numerous ways of making an official complaint.'

'Are you happy with the way you've dealt with her?'

'Perfectly.'

'So you wouldn't agree that you've been uncooperative with her at all?'

'In what way?'

'Well, by refusing to tell her anything, for a start.'

'We tell her as much as we can. That's how it has to be in a murder investigation.'

'When was the last time you spoke to her?'

'Look,' he said, leaning forward, 'we've treated Miss Osman as fairly and courteously as possible, OK? But she's not Jamaal's mother, she's not his legal guardian, she's just his aunt, that's all. We don't *have* to tell her anything—'

'Why wasn't the murder reported in the press?'

Lilley glared at me, and I could tell he was beginning to lose his composure now. 'All right, listen,' he said sternly, pointing his finger at me. 'I know you think you've got a right to come in here and question me, but I don't give a fuck about your rights, OK? All I care about is getting the job done. And I *know* how to do it. You just think you do. The truth is, you don't have a fucking clue.' He paused for a second or two, calming himself down a bit, then went on. 'I've been working on this case for five months now, and I'm not going to allow you or anyone else to mess it up. Do you understand that?'

I didn't respond.

He said, 'Well, you'd better understand it, and I'll tell you why.' He sniffed, wiping his nose with the back of his hand, and for a fleeting moment I caught a glimpse of uncertainty in his eyes. 'Sometimes things aren't as straightforward as they seem. Sometimes, for example, when we're investigating a murder, we know for a *fact* who the killer is. We know their name, we know who they are, where they are, we have evidence against them . . . there's absolutely no doubt of their guilt. But sometimes that's not enough to get a conviction. There are rules to follow, legal complexities . . . all kinds of hoops to jump through before the CPS will even consider prosecuting a case. So sometimes we have to make compromises. And occasionally we find ourselves in a position where the suspect we can't prosecute for crime A is already in custody for committing crime B, and we know that he's going down for crime B, and that the sentence he'll get will be just as severe as the sentence he'd get for crime A, but if we try to convict him of crime A as well as crime B, there's a chance he'll be acquitted of both. So we just have to forget about A, no matter how much it hurts, and get the fucker for B.' Lilley looked hard at me. 'Do you understand what I'm saying, Mr Craine?'

I nodded.

'And do you understand that if crime A were to be made public, all the lurid details revealed in the press and on TV, then the successful prosecution of crime B might be jeopardised?'

'Yeah, I understand.'

'Good.'

I scratched my head. 'So let me get this straight. You know who killed Jamaal, but the CPS don't think you've got enough to convict him. But he's been arrested and charged for another murder which the CPS are confident he'll go down for. And there are aspects of Jamaal's murder that could prejudice the trial for this other murder.' I looked at Lilley. 'Is that what you're saying?'

Lilley held my gaze. 'I'm not saying any more than I've just said.'

'Right . . .'

'But I would remind you that it's a criminal offence to interfere with the administration of justice.'

'OK,' I said, nodding thoughtfully.

'Now, if that's all—'

'Just one more thing.'

He glanced impatiently at his watch. 'I have to be somewhere in two minutes.'

'It won't take two minutes,' I assured him.

'Go on then,' he sighed. 'What is it?'

'The drugs found in Jamaal's pockets.'

'What about them?'

'Were they his?'

'They were in his pockets.'

'Kind of odd the killer didn't take them, don't you think?'

He shrugged. 'People do odd things all the time. Maybe the killer was disturbed by something, ran off before he had time to search the kid's pockets. I mean, who knows?'

'Right. But they were definitely Jamaal's drugs?'

'I just told you—'

'Did you find his prints on them?'

'That's it,' Lilley said sharply, getting to his feet. 'No more questions.' He stared down at me, waiting for me to get up.

'Is DCI Bishop pulling the strings on this one?' I said.

Lilley went blank for a moment, he just stood there looking at me with his mouth half-open. Then he blinked twice, sniffed hard, and said, 'This interview is over. If you don't leave right now, I'll have you physically removed.'

'I only—'

'Right,' he snapped, pulling a mobile from his pocket.

'OK, OK . . .' I said, getting up. 'I'm going, all right?'

He glared at me, keeping hold of his mobile, and I could feel his eyes burning into the back of my head as I crossed the room, opened the door, and left.

8

Apart from being one of my very few genuine friends, and the only living connection I have left with my wife, Cal Franks has worked on and off for me since he was little more than a spotty little teenager. He's nearly thirty now, and over the years he's helped me out in all kinds of different ways, but while I'm always happy to have an extra pair of eyes, or just someone to drive me around if I need it, Cal himself would be the first to admit that it's his technological wizardry that helps me the most. All he needs is a computer and a phone and he can do virtually anything. He can hack into just about anywhere, he can track and trace phones, crack security codes . . . he can write software and design programs that no one else has ever even thought about. He's a techno-genius, basically. And, what's more, he knows how to make the most of it. You wouldn't know it from the look of him – he looks and dresses like some kind of death-metal scare-crow, and he gives the impression of a man who doesn't have any money and doesn't care about it either – but the reality is somewhat different. Cal's always made money, and lots of it. Not always legally, especially when he was younger, but then a lot of the things he does for me aren't strictly legal either. But as he keeps telling me, the thing about cyber laws, the thing that makes them so difficult to police, is that what's illegal in one country can be totally lawful in another country, and since cyber criminals have the ability to commit crimes a thousand miles away from where they're actually located, who's to say if they're breaking the law or not?

That's my excuse anyway.

I don't know about Cal. I don't ask him how he makes his money, and he doesn't talk about it. And that suits us both. My guess is that he answers to his own set of values, his own moral code, and he just does what he does, legal or not, without the slightest trace of remorse. But, like I said, it's not something we generally talk about. I get the odd little hint of what he's up to now and then, usually when I'm at his place and he's working away on something, but because I very rarely understand the first thing about what he does, it's never any more than just a hint. In the past year or so, for example, I've been at Cal's on a number of occasions when I've seen or heard a couple of things that have given me the impression he's beginning to branch out into more legitimate lines of work. I'm not sure exactly what they might be, but I think he's probably being paid a lot of money by big corporations, both private and state, to tighten up their cyber security. A sort of poacher turned gamekeeper scenario, if you like. Set a thief to catch a thief, that sort of thing. Unless, of course, Cal's just playing them at their own game. The poacher who just pretends to turn gamekeeper. The thief set to catch a thief who's actually the thief himself . . .

I wouldn't put it past him.

He still lives in the same big old four-storey house that he'd first moved into when he was seventeen years old. It was a squat back then, populated by an everchanging mish-mash of hippies, punks, dealers, poets . . . anyone who didn't fit in anywhere else, basically. Somewhere along the line, Cal had quietly become the legal owner of the house – buying it outright with cash, so rumour has it – and while it now looks from the outside just as rundown as it always did, and most of the rooms are still inhabited by all kinds of weird and wonderful people, it's undoubtedly not a squat any more. The other residents pay rent, for a start, and the rooms have all been refurbished and modernised. The whole house is protected by high-tech surveillance equipment, CCTV, the very latest security systems, and there's so much electronic gadgetry and cyber stuff installed in the attic and under the floorboards, all of it constantly humming away, that the house doesn't actually need any central heating. Cal's flat is in the basement. It was originally two separate flats, but Cal converted it into a single large living space, with a small bedroom and bathroom at the far end, and a poky little kitchen area off to one side. It's a low-ceilinged room, painted white all over, and almost all of it is taken up with the tools of Cal's trade: computers, laptops, routers, printers, scanners, work desks, phones, cameras, TVs, recording equipment. There's a small recreation area in one corner, with a black leather settee and a huge widescreen TV, and that's where we were sitting that morning, drinking our coffee and talking about my meeting with DI Lilley.

'Do you think he was lying?' Cal asked me.

'Of course he was lying,' I said. 'He's a cop, he works for Bishop. What else is he going to do? My problem is trying to work out which bits he was lying about, which bits were true, and why he was lying about the bits that weren't true.'

'Maybe he was right about Ayanna,' Cal suggested. 'I mean, maybe he didn't threaten her. Maybe she *was* just making it up. It's possible, isn't it?'

'Yeah,' I agreed. 'But that doesn't mean he's not hiding something.'

'But what about his explanation . . . you know, that the guy who killed Jamaal is in custody for a different murder and they don't want to jeopardise that case? Do you think that's likely?'

'I suppose it could be. I mean, it's certainly not impossible. It might even be the truth. But I can't help feeling there's something about it that doesn't add up.'

'In what way?'

I shook my head. 'I honestly don't know.'

'You know what you need, don't you?'

I looked at him.

'Facts,' he said.

I smiled.

'No, seriously,' he went on, 'that's what you're lacking here, John. Hard facts. I mean, think about it. All you've got to go on at the moment is what you've been told – what Ayanna's told you, what Lilley's told you – and there's no way of knowing if either of them is telling the truth, is there? You're just guessing all the time. But you don't have to guess with facts. Facts are neutral, facts are unbiased, facts don't have any ulterior motives.'

'Is that a fact?'

'Fucking right it is.'

'All right,' I said, 'so get me some facts.'

*

We spent some time talking about which areas of the case we needed to focus on, and eventually we decided to concentrate on two separate angles: the local gangs, and the story about the killer who was already in custody. I didn't ask Cal how he was going to go about it, and he didn't offer to tell me.

He just said, 'Leave it to me, and I'll get back to you as soon as I can.'

In the meantime, he told me, he'd already uncovered a few things about Curt Dempsey that I might find interesting. I started to tell him that maybe he could show me another time, but he wasn't listening. He'd already got up, gone over to a worktop and picked up one of his laptops, and as he brought it back to the settee, sat down again, and began scrolling through dozens of images and scores of pages crammed full of cuttings and notes, my eyes were inexorably drawn to the screen.

A lot of the stuff he'd found out about Dempsey wasn't particularly useful – his address, phone number, what kind of cars he drove, a list of the companies he owned – and a lot of the stuff that might prove useful was for the most part unverifiable – rumours, hints, hearsay, stories. Cal had come up with *some* indisputable and possibly useful information about him – his criminal record, for example – but even as I sat there watching Cal scroll through Dempsey's criminal history, I knew there was a good chance we were wasting our time. If Dempsey did have anything to do with Jamaal's murder, it might be helpful to know that in 1987 he was sentenced to two years in prison for living off immoral earnings, or that in 1996 he was arrested and later released without charge in connection with the infamous Rettendon murders, but there was nothing to suggest that Dempsey *did* have anything to do with Jamaal's murder. Just because Jamaal had worked at Juno's, and Dempsey owned Juno's, and Dempsey was obviously a villain, or at least an ex-villain . . . well, so what? That didn't mean anything, did it?

'Listen, Cal,' I said, 'this is all really good stuff, and it's not that I don't appreciate it, but I just think that at the moment—'

'Look at this,' Cal said, ignoring me.

I looked at the screen. He'd brought up a report from the *Gazette*, dated 10 March 2011. The headline read: *DRUG SUSPECT IN FATAL ROAD ACCIDENT.* I moved closer to the screen and scanned through the article. The salient facts were that Anthony Gameiro, a 24-year-old unemployed fitness instructor, had died from his injuries following a hit-and-run incident outside his home on the East Whipton estate in Hey. Gameiro had recently been charged with possession and intent to supply Class A drugs and was due to stand trial the following week.

'I don't get it,' I said to Cal. 'What's this got to do with anything?'

'That's Gameiro, OK?' Cal said, pointing to the photograph that accompanied the article.

'Yeah . . .'

Cal touched the mouse pad and brought up another photo. This one showed a dozen or so fit-looking men and women – the men dressed in T-shirts and vests, the women in high-cut leotards – all of them smiling and flexing their muscles. 'This is an early promotional picture for Juno's,'

Cal said. 'And that . . .' He moved the cursor over one of the muscled men. 'That's Anthony Gameiro.'

I moved closer to the screen, staring at the smiling face. Cal was right, it was definitely Gameiro.

'So?' I said. 'He worked at Juno's . . . so what?'

'He was a dealer.'

'He was *accused* of dealing.'

'He was run over and killed a week before his trial.'

I looked at Cal. 'It happens . . .'

'Yeah, it happens when someone doesn't want the accused to stand trial.'

'Someone like who?'

Cal leaned back from the laptop and lit a cigarette. 'I know it's a bit far fetched—'

'A *bit*?'

He grinned. 'There's a connection though, isn't there? The Rettendon murders were all about drugs, and it looks like Dempsey was mixed up in that. Gameiro worked at Juno's, and he was a dealer. If Gameiro was dealing at Juno's, either for Dempsey or with his permission, and Dempsey got word that Gameiro had cut a deal, and that he was going to spill the beans about Juno's and Dempsey at his trial . . . well, maybe Dempsey sent someone out in a car to take care of him.' Cal looked at me, puffing on his cigarette. 'What do you think?'

'*Spill the beans?*' I said, smiling.

'What?' he said, blushing slightly. 'What's wrong with that? It's a perfectly acceptable phrase.'

'Yeah, in an episode of *Murder She Wrote* maybe.'

'Fuck off.'

I laughed.

He shook his head in disbelief, like I was an idiot child.

I said to him, 'Has anyone been arrested for the hit-and-run?'

'No.'

'Any witnesses?'

Cal leaned forward to the laptop again and brought up a page of notes. 'One of Gameiro's neighbours thought the car was a black Range Rover. Another one said it was a dark red Citroën.'

'Is that it?'

'That's it.' He looked at me. 'What do you think, John? Seriously.'

'I think the first thing we should do is have a chat with Hassan Tan. See what he's got to say, and then take it from there. How does that sound?'

'Yeah, OK. Do you want me to come with you?'

'If you're free.'

'No problem. Are we going right now?'

'Might as well.'

'All right, let me just close all this stuff down.'

As he clicked away on his laptop, shutting everything down, I happened to glance at the screen just as he was saving some articles from the *Gazette*, and in the instant before the page disappeared, a word in one of the articles suddenly jumped out at me. Two words actually.

'Let me see that again,' I said to Cal.

'What?'

'The page you just closed. Bring it up again.'

'What, this one?' he said, tapping the mouse pad.

'Yeah, that's it. Scroll down a bit . . . there.'
I leaned forward and read the article on the screen.

Around 130 jobs are to be created when a new £5 million operations centre opens near Hey next year. The new development, currently under tender, will house Ministry of Defence surveillance and information technology at Morden Hall in Stangate on the outskirts of Hey.

Detailed planning consent has already been obtained for the 110,000 sq ft site which has been unused since the collapse of the Xylonex plastics research laboratory in 1979. Built on a 5.25 acre plot, the centre will employ 130 people in a range of operation, administration and support services.

Curt Dempsey, director of Town Developments Ltd, said the contract to develop the site should be given to a local company to provide more jobs for local people.

He added: 'This would represent a major step forward for Town Developments. Our ability to offer a high level of service combined with our local work-force and knowledge would enable us to invest in this centre with complete confidence.'

'I was looking at it yesterday,' I muttered, remembering the sight of the old brick ruins across the misted vale.
'Looking at what?'
'Morden Hall. I saw it when I went out to Stangate.'
'What were you doing at Stangate?'
I'd told Cal about the fire at Leon's house, but I hadn't

mentioned my visit to the cemetery. 'I went there after the fire,' I told him now. 'My parents are buried at St Leonard's, and I just thought . . .' I shrugged. 'I don't know what I thought really. I just went to see them.' I looked at Cal. 'You can see the ruins of Morden Hall from the churchyard.'

'Sorry, John,' he said, his brow furrowed, 'but I'm not sure what you're saying. What's Morden Hall got to do with anything?'

'Nothing, as far as I know.'

'Right . . .' he said, still looking confused.

'I just saw it, that's all. On the screen . . . the reference to Morden Hall. And, you know, I was out there yesterday, so it just kind of grabbed my attention . . .' I shrugged again. 'It doesn't mean anything.'

'OK.'

I smiled at him. 'A lot of stuff doesn't mean anything. It's just stuff.'

'Is that your profound quote for the day?'

'It's as profound as you're going to get from me.'

The street where Hassan Tan lived was only about a mile or so from the Redhills estate, and as we headed south in Cal's Lexus, across the river and then right into Redhills Lane, I remembered Ayanna telling me about the Somali community in this part of town. 'Can you pull in over there a minute?' I said to Cal.

'Where?'

'Over there, by the shops.'

He slowed the Lexus, indicated right, and cut across Redhills Lane into a little square of streets. It was the kind of square you often come across near housing estates on the outskirts of towns – a three-sided greyish block of convenience stores, launderettes, and estate agents. Some of these edge-of-town squares have a kids' playground in the middle, or at least the remains of what was originally a kids' playground, and others have a patch of grass lined with long-dead saplings in cracked and weather-faded plastic tubes. This one had a bit of both – a rutted square of grass, dotted with dog shit, and the rusted frames of two swingless swings. The grass was surrounded by a low brick wall topped with concrete slabs, and even now – at just after one o'clock on a Friday afternoon – half a dozen teenage kids were perched on the wall, smoking and drinking, staring at their mobiles, waiting for something to happen. They were probably estate kids. The estate itself was just across from the square – a cluttering of granite-grey council houses and low-rise blocks of flats – and I guessed the local kids came over here to buy stuff or just hang around the shops.

'We're not leaving the car here, are we?' Cal said, eyeing the teenagers.

'Scared they'll nick it?' I asked, smiling at him.

He shook his head. 'This car's safer than Fort Knox. I just don't want them keying it or anything though.'

'You're getting to be more of an old fart every day, Cal. You'll be writing letters to *The Times* next, moaning on about the teenagers of today, how they don't have any respect—'

'Do you know how much this car cost?' he said indignantly. 'I'm not like you, you know. I don't refuse to spend more than £500 on a vehicle—'

'Excuse me, but I paid nearly £900 for that Renault.'

'Yeah, well that's about how much it'd cost me to get a scratch fixed on the Lexus, so I'm not leaving it here.'

'If you drove a cheaper car you wouldn't have to worry about it getting scratched. That's the whole point—'

'I'm not getting into all that again,' he said, shaking his head. 'Just tell me what you want me to do. Are we stopping here, or do you want me to drive on?'

'Pull in over there,' I said, nodding towards a parking spot across the square. 'And don't worry, we're not leaving the car.'

'What exactly *are* we doing?' he asked, driving on.

'I just want to see something.'

'What?'

'See that little café over there?'

He glanced to his right. 'Next to the fried chicken place?'

I nodded. 'And you see the two young kids on bikes outside the café?'

'Yeah,' he said, pulling into the parking spot.

'They're Somali, aren't they?'

Cal parked the Lexus and gazed over at the café again. It was about forty yards away on the other side of the street. 'I'm not sure,' he said, looking at the kids. 'I don't really know what a Somali looks like, to be honest.'

The two boys were about eleven or twelve years old. They were both quite lean, with high foreheads and close-cropped hair. Their skin was a lot darker than Hassan Tan's, but then Hassan was only half Somali – his father was Chinese-American – so comparing his skin colour with that of the two boys was pretty pointless anyway.

111

'Is it Somali or Somalian?' Cal said.

'What?'

'The descriptive term, you know . . . do they call themselves Somalis or Somalians?'

'I don't know . . . Somalis, I think.'

'Christ,' Cal said, shaking his head. 'I just realised how fucking ignorant I sound. I don't know what a Somali looks like, I don't know what to call them . . . shit, maybe you're right, John, maybe I am getting to be more of an old fart every day. Maybe I'm turning into one of those good old Essex boys, you know . . . *call me old-fashioned, and I ain't got nuffin against the coloureds, but . . .*'

'There's nothing wrong with not knowing stuff,' I said, still watching the café. The front window was too heavily plastered with menus and tatty old posters to get a clear view of the interior, but I got the impression that it was a dark and dingy little place. 'Just because you don't know what the people of a certain country look like,' I went on, 'or what they call themselves, that doesn't make you a racist, for God's sake.'

'Yeah, I suppose. I just feel as if . . . I don't know. Like I shouldn't even be talking about it.'

'Talking about what?'

'The whole thing, you know . . . what does a Somali look like, what does a Nigerian look like, what does an Iranian look like—'

'We don't all look the same, do we?'

'Well, no—'

'Someone from Germany doesn't look the same as someone from Mexico.'

'No.'

'Which is an entirely different thing from saying that all Germans look the same or all Mexicans look the same. That *would* be pretty ignorant.'

'Right.'

'But, as far as I can see, there's nothing wrong with me looking at those two kids over there and making an educated guess about their country of origin based on their overall physical appearance – skin colour, body shape, eyes, face . . . whatever. It seems a perfectly reasonable and acceptable thing to do.'

'Fair enough.'

I leaned closer to the window, peering over at the boys. 'The only trouble is . . .'

'What?'

'I don't know what a Somali looks like either.'

As Cal laughed, and I wound down the car window and lit a cigarette, the door of the café opened and a group of older kids came out. They were all black, all wearing the usual street gear – hoods, tracksuits, trainers, beanies – and most of them were about seventeen or eighteen. The one who was clearly in charge though, a tall imposing figure with a fearsomely gaunt face, was in his early to mid-twenties. I saw him pass something to a kid with a gold tooth – without looking at him – then the gold-toothed kid passed whatever it was to one of the boys on bikes. The bike boy slipped it into his pocket, said something to Gold Tooth, and I saw Gold Tooth glance over at me and Cal.

'I think we'd better go,' I said.

As Cal put the Lexus in gear, I saw Gold Tooth say

something to the tall guy. The tall guy turned slowly and stared at us – his raw-boned face carved out of stone, his eyes burning into my soul. They were the eyes of a man who's seen and done the unspeakable.

'Shit,' I muttered, breathing out hard as we pulled out of the parking spot and drove away. 'Did you *see* that guy?'

'Yeah,' Cal said, 'and I wish I hadn't.'

Hassan Tan's flat was in a mid-terrace Victorian house at the far end of Cowley Lane. Like most of the houses in the street, it was a run-down four-storey property that had been bought up cheaply a long time ago and converted into low-rent bedsits and flats. It was by no means the worst area in town, but most of the people who lived round here were the kind of people who couldn't afford to live anywhere else.

Sleet was falling as Cal followed me up the steep concrete steps to the front door of Hassan's house. Rusty old railings bounded the steps on either side, and there was a battered old intercom system on the wall by the door. I pulled up my collar and studied the list of handwritten name tags. The one at the bottom read *H Tan, Flat 8*. I pressed the buzzer and waited.

Nothing happened.

'Maybe he's out,' Cal said.

I pressed the buzzer again.

This time, after a couple of seconds, a tinny voice crackled out from the intercom. 'Yeah?'

'Hassan Tan?' I said, leaning in to the speaker.

'What do you want?'

'My name's John Craine,' I said. 'I'm a private investigator. Your aunt, Ayanna, has asked me to look into—'

'Fuck off.'

The intercom went dead.

I looked at Cal. He shrugged. I pressed the buzzer again. Nothing happened.

'What now?' Cal said.

I reached up to the intercom again and started pressing all the buzzers. There was no reply to the first two, but I struck lucky with the third.

'Hello?' a female voice said.

'DHL,' I announced. 'Delivery for a Mr Tan.'

'Flat 8, third floor,' she said brusquely, and an instant later the door buzzed open.

It was much as I expected inside – a dim hallway, junk mail piled on a ratty old table, a padlocked bike leaning against the wall – and as we climbed the stairs to the third floor we passed through a pot-pourri of typical bedsit smells: takeaway food, damp washing, cigarette smoke, marijuana . . .

'Brings back memories,' Cal said.

A TV was playing loudly somewhere – the sound of people getting excited about cheap antiques – and from somewhere else I could hear the muffled thump of booming drum and bass beats, but despite all the noise – or maybe *within* all the noise – the house felt strangely hushed. It was an odd feeling, and it didn't seem to make any sense at all. But I didn't have time to think about it. We'd reached the third floor now, and Cal was nudging my arm and nodding me in the direction of a door marked Flat 8.

'Do you think he'll talk to us?' he whispered.

'There's only one way to find out,' I said, going up to the door.

There was no bell, so I just reached up and knocked.

Again, nothing happened immediately. I waited a few seconds, then knocked again, a bit louder this time. Still nothing.

'Hassan!' I called out. 'It's John Craine. Could you open the door please? I just want to talk—'

The door opened suddenly and a flash of silver snaked out at me. I stepped back, leaning away from the knife in Hassan Tan's outstretched hand.

'I told you to fuck off,' he said, keeping the door half-closed.

'It's OK,' I said, trying to sound reassuring, 'there's no need—'

'So fuck off.'

'I'm only trying to—'

'Last time,' he said, moving the knife towards my face. 'You can fuck off right now or lose an eye. It's up to you.'

I only stared back at him for a moment or two, but that was all it took to recognise the look in his eyes. It wasn't anger or belligerence, it wasn't even aggression – it was pure fear. Hassan was scared to death of something. And I knew then that he wasn't bluffing, he'd use the knife if he had to.

'Come on, John,' Cal said quietly, taking hold of my arm. 'Let's go, OK?'

9

My mobile rang as we were getting back into Cal's Lexus, and the caller display told me it was Imogen.

'Hey, Immy,' I said, closing the car door and lighting a cigarette. 'How are you doing?'

'Not so good, John. You know . . .'

'Yeah.'

Cal got in the car and closed the driver's door.

'Where are you?' Imogen asked.

'Cowley Lane.'

'Are you working?'

'Sort of . . .'

'When do you think you'll be finished?'

'I can stop any time.'

'Are you sure? I don't want to—'

'Do you want me to come over now?'

'Could you?'

'Yeah, no problem. Are you at home?'

'No, I'm at the house.'

I hesitated for a moment, not sure what she meant.

'Mum and Dad's house,' she explained. 'The fire investigator was out here this morning and I've been talking to him about what happened . . .'

'What did he have to say?'

'Well, that's kind of what I want to see you about.'

'OK,' I said, quickly thinking things through. 'I'm with Cal at the moment, and my car's back at his place. So I'll have to go back to Cal's first to pick it up—'

'Bring him with you,' Imogen said.

'You sure?'

'He might be able to help.'

'All right,' I said, glancing at Cal and mouthing 'Are you free?' at him. He nodded. 'We'll be there in about twenty minutes,' I told Imogen.

Cal and Imogen didn't know each other that well, but they'd met in passing a couple of times, and I'd told Imogen enough about Cal's expertise for her to know the kinds of things he could do, so I was curious as to how she thought he might be able to help with anything to do with the fire. And so was he. But it was pointless trying to guess, so we didn't really bother. I just told Cal what Imogen had told me, he asked me where the house was, and we drove off across town towards Lexden Vale.

Imogen's BMW was parked in the driveway when we got there, and as Cal pulled in at the side of the road, Imogen got out of the car and waved at us. She looked very different to the last time I'd seen her. On the night of the fire she'd been distraught and dishevelled, and she'd obviously just thrown on whatever clothes she could find – jogging pants and an old sweatshirt and hood – but today she was back to her elegant and stylish self. Her jet-black hair was neatly tied back, her face was perfectly made up, and the clothes she was wearing were as classically simple as they were expensive. She looked how she usually looked: confident, capable, and graceful.

But looks are often deceiving, and as I got out of the Lexus and went over to meet her, it was clear to me that underneath it all she was still struggling to come to terms with everything.

'Thanks for coming, John,' she said as we hugged each other. 'I really appreciate it.'

I nodded, glancing over at the fire-ravaged remains of the house. It looked different in the daylight – more real, more humdrum. It somehow seemed less dramatic. It was still hard to believe though.

'Hey, Cal,' Imogen said, letting go of me as Cal came up and joined us.

'I'm so sorry for your loss,' he said to her. 'I know that doesn't really mean very much, but—'

'Thanks,' she said, giving him a quick embrace.

He seemed a little embarrassed for a moment, not quite sure what to do, and I found that rather endearing. I gave him a smile, then turned back to Imogen. She was gazing over at the house, and I could tell she was feeling more than just sadness. 'What is it?' I asked her.

She looked at me, then glanced up as the sleet began falling again. 'Let's go and sit in the car.'

The fire investigation officer, a man called Derek Lisbie, had told her that a full report into the causes of the fire would be sent to the coroner in due course, but he'd warned her that it was a long and exhaustive process, and it could be weeks or even months before the report was filed.

'It sounds like a very thorough investigation,' Imogen said. 'They locate and interview any witnesses, examine the scene, collect and evaluate evidence . . . I mean, it *sounds* like they know what they're doing.'

'But . . .?' I said.

She looked across at me. I was sitting in the passenger seat, she was in the driver's seat, and Cal was in the back. 'Well, first of all,' she said, 'as soon as Lisbie had finished telling me all this stuff about how long the full report was going to take, and why it was such a laborious process, he then started saying that he already knew pretty much everything that was going to be in the report anyway. How the fire had started, where it had started, why it had spread so quickly . . . he'd even pieced together Mum and Dad's last movements. All from just looking around the house for an hour or so.'

'They do know their stuff,' Cal said. 'I saw a thing on TV about fire investigators once, and it's amazing how quickly they can tell what happened just by poking around in all the ashes and stuff.'

'Yeah, but the thing is,' Imogen said, 'a lot of what Lisbie was saying . . . well, it just didn't make sense.'

'Like what?' I asked.

She went through it all then, giving us Lisbie's account of the fire. It had started in the kitchen, he'd told her. A chip pan had been left on the cooker, the oil had overheated. It had either ignited of its own accord or someone had knocked it over. As Leon's body had been found in the kitchen – and preliminary examinations suggested that he'd suffered a heavy fall and cracked his head on the floor – it was likely that it was Leon himself who'd upset the boiling chip pan. And while he was lying unconscious on the floor, the oil-fuelled fire had raged through the kitchen before spreading to the rest of the house.

'Do they know what time it started?' I asked her.

'Around quarter to two, Lisbie thinks. The kitchen clock was stopped at 1.54, and a neighbour called the emergency services at 2.11. The first fire engine didn't arrive until gone 2.30 though.'

'Why not?'

'There was a big fire earlier that night at a paper mill about ten miles away, and all the fire engines from Hey had already been called out.'

I nodded, going over the timings in my head. 'What about your mum?' I asked Imogen. 'Where does Lisbie think she was when the fire broke out?'

'They found her . . .' She paused, looking down for a moment, and I realised how hard this had to be for her.

'If you don't want to talk about it—' I started to say.

'Mum was in bed,' she said quietly. 'That's where they found her body. Lisbie thinks it's possible that she didn't wake up because she might have taken some sleeping pills . . . he found the remains of a packet of temazepam in the bathroom.' Imogen looked at me. 'Mum didn't take sleeping pills, John.'

'Are you sure?'

'She hated taking *any* kind of pills. She wouldn't even use aspirin.'

'But if Lisbie said he found the packet—'

'No,' Imogen said firmly. 'I don't care what he said. There's no way that Mum would have taken sleeping pills.'

'Maybe they weren't hers,' I suggested. 'Your dad was on a lot of medication, wasn't he?'

'Well, yes . . . but not sleeping pills. That was about the only thing he didn't need. He was tired enough as it was, and with all the painkillers and other drugs he was taking he could barely stay awake at times. And that's another thing about Lisbie's account that doesn't make sense. Dad was always in bed by nine or ten o'clock, eleven at the very latest. His routine never varied. He'd spend most of the evening alone in his study, working away on those old cases of his that he's never been able to let go of, and then he'd go downstairs and join Mum in the sitting room for an hour or so. They'd watch TV or listen to the radio together for a while, and then Dad would get off to bed.' Imogen shook her head. 'He wouldn't be in the kitchen at nearly two in the morning frying chips, for Christ's sake. I mean, who cooks chips at two o'clock in the morning? And Dad *never* cooked anyway. He wouldn't know how to make chips. He didn't even like the fucking things.'

'What about your mum?' I asked. 'Did she ever cook chips for herself?'

'Very occasionally,' Imogen admitted. 'But she'd never use that old chip pan they found in the kitchen . . . she had a really nice Russell Hobbs fryer, all digitally controlled and everything. The only reason she still had her old chip pan was that she couldn't bring herself to throw it away.'

'Did you mention any of this to Lisbie?' I asked.

'No.'

'Why not?'

'Because . . .' She shrugged. 'I don't really know, to be honest. Well, maybe . . .' She looked at me. 'Lisbie knew about Dad's illness. I can't remember if I told him, or if he found out from someone else, or perhaps he just came across some of Dad's medication . . . I don't know. But he definitely knew that Dad had cancer and that it was at a fairly advanced stage. I suppose I just thought that if I told Lisbie that Dad always went to bed early, and that he never cooked, and he didn't like chips . . .'

'Lisbie would blame it on his illness, or all the medication he was taking.'

Imogen nodded. 'I didn't want him telling me that Dad didn't know what he was doing any more, that he'd lost his mind . . . I wasn't having that.' There was a quiet ferocity in Imogen's voice now, a sad determination in her eyes. 'And besides,' she went on, 'I was already beginning to doubt Lisbie by then, and I thought it was best to keep my thoughts to myself.'

'Why would he lie to you?'

'I don't know . . .'

'Are you thinking the fire might not have been an accident?'

'I don't *know*, John . . . I don't know what I think. It just . . .' She sighed. 'It just doesn't add up, that's all. I mean, Lisbie *seemed* all right – courteous, professional, efficient – and I'm sure he knows what he's doing, but a lot of what he was telling me just didn't ring true.'

'Yeah, OK, but that doesn't mean he was lying to you. Maybe he just got a couple of things wrong.'

'It was more than just a couple of things.'

'Really?'

She nodded. 'He told me that the batteries were dead in all the smoke alarms . . . *all* of them. But Dad was always checking the alarms, making sure they still worked, checking the batteries. And there was the thing about the decorating too . . .'

'Decorating?'

'When I was in the house with Lisbie, he pointed out a load of burned-out decorating stuff in the hallway – paint cans and bottles of white spirit and paint stripper – and he said that was probably why the fire had spread so quickly.' Imogen looked at me. 'Mum never said anything to me about decorating, John. And I was round here for dinner only last week. She would have told me if they were thinking about redecorating. You know what she's like – she would have been going on about it for months, asking me what I thought of this colour, did I like that colour . . . there's no way she wouldn't have mentioned it.'

I nodded slowly, thinking things through, trying to work out if there was any substance to Imogen's suspicions or not. She was usually a very rational person, with a calm and reasoning mind, and it wasn't like her to make wild accusations based on very little evidence . . . but she was grieving, she wasn't herself. And I know better than most that a reasoning mind is no match for the demands of a grieving heart.

'Come on,' she said, opening the car door, 'I want to show you something.'

*

The heavy skies were dark with a blanket of slate-grey cloud as the three of us left the car and headed up the driveway towards the house, and just as we reached the stone porchway the sleet began turning to snow. The front door was jammed open, hanging skewed on a single hinge, and the hallway beyond was just a blackened tunnel strewn with debris.

'Are you sure it's all right to go in?' I asked Imogen.

She nodded, staring ahead, her eyes oddly distant. 'Lisbie said it's not safe to go upstairs, but everywhere else is OK.'

'Are we allowed in?' Cal asked.

'It's my house,' Imogen said simply, stepping through into the hallway.

Cal looked at me.

I shrugged.

We followed Imogen into the house.

The floors were still sodden everywhere, pooled with puddles of filthy black water, and the air was still thick with the smell of stale smoke – a pungent mixture of burned cloth, melted plastic, and God-knows what else.

'There's the decorating stuff I told you about,' Imogen said, indicating a pile of scorched paint cans at the end of the hallway.

'Your mum wouldn't have done the painting herself, would she?' I asked, gazing down at the pile.

Imogen shook her head. 'And Dad couldn't have done it.'

'So if they were decorating, they would have got someone in to do it.'

'They weren't decorating, John,' Imogen said, looking at me. 'I know you think I'm making this up—'

125

'I don't—'

'I can read you like a book, John,' she said, smiling. 'I always could.'

I shook my head. 'I'm just trying to be practical, that's all. All I'm saying is that if they did hire a decorating firm, we should be able to find out.' I turned to Cal. 'You could do that, couldn't you?'

He thought about it for a moment. 'I can check their phone records, landline and mobile, see if they called any decorators. That's no problem at all. But if they didn't use the phone to hire someone, if they just called in somewhere . . . well, that might be a bit more tricky.'

'But not impossible?'

'No . . .'

I turned back to Imogen. 'It's not that I don't believe you, Im. It's just—'

'Follow me,' she said, heading towards the burned-out staircase.

'Hold on,' I called out after her. 'I thought you said it wasn't safe to go upstairs?'

She didn't reply, she just started clambering up the remains of the staircase, keeping in close to the wall where the stairs were still mostly intact.

I looked at Cal.

He shrugged.

We followed Imogen up the stairs.

The upper floors of the house were almost as badly damaged as the ground floor, but most of the basic frame-work seemed solid enough – the floors, the walls – and although we had to be very careful on the way up, taking our time, watching where we stepped, it was nowhere near as treacherous as I'd expected. Leon's study was at the far end of the landing on the third floor. It was a ridiculously cramped little place, with far too much furniture, too many bookshelves, countless piles of clutter all over the place – files, papers, magazines, newspapers – but it was a room I'd always felt very comfortable in, and it held lots of memories for me. I'd spent many a long evening up here with Leon, the two of us just sitting around talking about things – the past, the future . . . my father, their friendship – and I'd got to know the room so well that everything about it was seared into my memory. Leon's big old mahogany desk, his writing table against the wall, the worn-out leather armchair in the corner where I'd always sit . . . I could picture it all. The cupboards and filing cabinets, the framed photographs and certificates on the wall, the small TV on the black glass table, the stacks of DVDs piled up next to it, the open fireplace with a wooden mantelpiece above the grate, the small circular window high up in the far wall . . .

I remembered it all.

But now, as I stood in the doorway of the study, all I could see were the blackened remains of my memories. Burned papers, ashes, broken glass, charred skeletons of chairs. The desk had collapsed, the writing table was little more than a heat-scorched board on the floor, and the window was just a gaping hole rimmed with broken glass. Snowflakes were fluttering in through the window now, turning black as they fell.

'Shit,' I muttered, suddenly overwhelmed with a weight of sadness.

'Yeah, I know,' Imogen said quietly, putting her hand on my arm. 'This was Dad's place . . . this was *him*.'

I looked at her.

'I came up here after Lisbie had gone,' she told me. 'I just had to see it, you know . . . just to say goodbye to him. I needed to say goodbye . . .'

I squeezed her hand.

She sniffed and wiped a tear from her eye. 'Anyway, I was just looking around while I was up here, you know, not really *looking* for anything, but then . . .'

'What?'

'Well, I'm not sure . . . maybe it's nothing.' She turned to Cal. 'Could you take a look at Dad's PC terminal and tell me what you think?'

'His PC terminal?'

'It's over there,' she said, pointing across the room.

We both looked over at the remains of a PC terminal lying in a puddle against the far wall. The plastic casing was burned away, and all that was left was a fire-blackened carcass of scorched metal and melted cables, but it was still recognisable as a PC terminal.

'What exactly do you want me to do with it?' Cal asked Imogen.

'Just have a look, that's all. See what you think.'

He frowned at her for a moment or two, still not sure what she meant, but eventually he realised that she wasn't going to tell him anything else and he nodded OK and headed across the room. I watched, intrigued, as he stopped by the terminal, crouched down beside it, and had a good long look – leaning to one side, angling his head, making sure he saw everything. After thirty seconds or so he glanced over at Imogen and said, 'Is it all right if I touch it?'

She nodded.

He turned back to the terminal, picked it up, placed it carefully on the floor with the back facing towards him, and then he just crouched there for a while, staring curiously into the scorched and melted interior. He moved his head a couple of times, peering intently inside, then he stood up and began gazing slowly around the floor. He carried on looking for a good few minutes or so, gradually increasing the area he was searching until he'd covered just about everywhere, and then finally he turned back to Imogen and said, 'The hard drive's missing.'

Imogen nodded. 'I wouldn't have noticed anything if the terminal had been by the desk,' she explained. 'But when I saw it lying right over there by the wall . . . well, it just seemed a bit odd, you know? It was always under Dad's desk. What the hell was it doing over there?' She shrugged. 'So I went over and had a look, and something just didn't seem right.' She half-smiled at me. 'I don't know much about computers, and the only reason I've got a vague idea of what should be inside a PC terminal is because mine crashed recently, and when the IT guy came round to fix it he insisted on showing me what he was doing, and I remember being really surprised at how little there actually was in there. So that's why, when I was looking at Dad's, I just had a feeling that something was missing. I mean, I didn't know what it was . . .' She turned to Cal. 'You're sure it's the hard drive that's gone?'

He nodded. 'And I'm also pretty sure it was removed before the fire.'

'How can you tell?' I asked.

'The screw holes where it's connected are blackened. If it'd been taken out after the fire, there'd be unblackened rings round the holes.'

'So you think someone removed the hard drive from Leon's PC before the fire?'

'It looks that way, yeah.'

'It couldn't have been destroyed in the fire?'

'Not completely, no. There'd be *some*thing left of it. I mean, the remains of everything else is in there – motherboard, processors, heat sink, graphics card. There's just no hard drive.' He turned to Imogen. 'Did your dad use any other computers?'

'He had a laptop,' she said, looking round the room. 'He usually kept it on his desk . . . hold on, there it is.'

It was half-hidden under a pile of charred books – an inverted V of seared black plastic and charred metal. As Cal went over to it, pulling a small penknife from his pocket and opening a screwdriver attachment, I lit a cigarette and turned to Imogen. She was watching Cal with a quiet intensity, her jaw set tight, her eyes burning with a curious mixture of emotions. She looked both relieved and frightened, angry and satisfied, hyped up and exhausted.

'I thought I was being paranoid,' she said shakily, still watching Cal. 'I really thought I was making it all up, you know . . . trying too hard to find some answers, desperately trying to convince myself that someone was to blame.' She looked at me. 'And now that it looks like I might be right, that maybe there is someone to blame after all . . . I don't know how that makes me feel, John. I don't know if it makes me feel better or worse . . .' She shook her head. 'It's all so confusing.'

I wanted to say something comforting to her then, something to ease her pain, but I couldn't seem to find the right words, or maybe there just weren't any. So rather than saying something simply for the sake of it, I didn't say anything. I put my arm round Imogen's shoulder and we stood there together watching Cal as he unscrewed the back of the laptop. It was quite badly damaged, with a lot of the casing melted out of shape, so it took him a while to get the screws out and lever the back off, but he managed it in the end. And then, after just a quick look inside, he turned to us and said, 'Yeah, this one's the same. The hard drive's gone.'

'Shit,' Imogen said quietly.

'Can you tell if anything else is missing?' I asked her.

'Not really,' she said, looking around and shaking her head. 'Even when I was living at home I didn't come in here all that much. Neither did Mum. It was Dad's private place, his little sanctuary.' She looked at me. 'You probably spent more time in here than I ever did.'

'Have you got any idea if he was working on anything in particular recently?'

She shrugged. 'Again, you probably know more than me. He never really talked about what he was working on, not to me anyway. The couple of times I did ask him about it he just said he was looking into some old cases.'

'Yeah, that's what he told me.'

I gazed around the study, taking everything in, trying to remember if Leon had ever said anything else to me about what he was working on . . . and something almost came to me then. As I scanned the fire-damaged walls, noting the empty spaces where Leon's framed pictures and photographs had hung – and wondering idly at the inherent sadness that such a space always seems to have – something began to stir in my mind, something that seemed to mean something, some half-forgotten flicker of something . . . but I couldn't get hold of it.

I turned to Cal. 'Is there any way of retrieving anything from the PC or the laptop?'

'Not without the hard drives.'

'Nothing at all?'

He shook his head.

'What about email?' I suggested.

'Yeah, that's no problem. I don't need his computer to check his email, just his address and password.'

'I know his address,' I said, looking at Imogen. 'Do you know his password?'

'No, sorry.'

'What's the address?' Cal asked me.

I spelled it out for him, and as he took out his iPhone and copied it down, his phone beeped quietly and he quickly checked the screen. 'Sorry,' he said, 'but I've really got to take this. I won't be a minute, OK?' He put the phone to his ear, started talking rapidly about stuff I didn't understand, and cautiously stepped out of the room.

'He's grown up a lot since I last saw him,' Imogen said. 'He's not quite so hyper any more.'

'That's probably his uncle's influence,' I said, smiling at her.

She tried to smile back, but couldn't quite manage it.

'How are you feeling?' I asked her.

She sighed. 'I don't know. Confused, tired . . . totally fucked-up, basically. I just don't know what's going on here, John. I mean, was this really deliberate? Did someone *do* all this?' She shook her head. 'I don't get it. Why would anyone want to kill Mum and Dad? They were just . . . they were just Mum and Dad, for God's sake. It's not right. And Dad was dying anyway . . . it's not fucking *right*.'

'I know.'

'Mum should have got old. She would have been sad when Dad died, but she should have been allowed to grow old and be sad. No one had the right to take that away from her.'

My head was empty again now, empty of any reassuring words, and all I could do was stand there in that ruined room, feeling distant and incapable, just staring vacantly at the snowflakes floating in through the broken window, their fluttered whiteness greying now against the dying daylight outside . . . and it was then, quite suddenly, that the half-forgotten flicker began coming back to me. It was still very vague, and I had no idea of its relevance, but it was something to do with Leon . . . something he'd once said to me . . . something about my father . . .

'John?'

I looked round and saw Cal standing in the doorway. 'Everything all right?' I asked him.

'Yeah, just a bit of business, you know.' He glanced at his watch. 'Look, I'm really sorry but I'm going to have to go now. There's a couple of things I need to sort out. It shouldn't take too long though, and if you want me to try getting into Leon's emails, I could probably get started on it later tonight.'

'What about his password?' Imogen said.

'That shouldn't be a problem.' He glanced at me, then looked back at Imogen. 'I'll only do it if you want me to though.'

A smile flickered on her face. 'Do you always ask permission before hacking into someone's emails?'

'Of course,' he said, smiling back at her. 'It'd be rude not to.'

Imogen nodded. 'Well, if you can get into them . . . yeah, please, go ahead.'

'OK,' he said. 'I'll get working on it as soon as I can and I'll let you know what I find.'

'Thanks, Cal,' Imogen said.

'No problem.' He glanced at his watch again then looked at me. 'I've got to meet someone at five, John. Do you want me to drop you off back at my place to pick up your car before I go, or are you staying here for a while . . .? John?'

'Yeah, sorry,' I said distractedly, looking up from the floor. 'I'll pick up my car later on, if that's OK.'

'Yeah, of course.' He turned to Imogen. 'And if there's anything else I can do . . . well, you know, just let me know.'

She nodded.

'See you later then,' he said to both of us.

Imogen thanked him once more and waved him goodbye as he left the room, but I was already staring down at the floor again, unable to keep my eyes off a broken picture frame lying face up on the floor. There wasn't much left of it. The glass was smashed, the thin silver frame broken and bent out of shape, and all that remained of the photograph that had been in the frame was a two-inch raggedy strip on the right-hand edge showing a heat-scorched image of a man's smiling face . . . or at least, half a smiling face. The left side of his face, and most of his body, had been burned away with the rest of the photo. But I knew the photograph. I'd seen it countless times. I knew that the smiling man was my father.

'John?' Imogen said. 'Are you all right?'

'Yeah,' I said, without looking up. 'Yeah, I'm just . . . hold on a second . . .'

The flickering memory was clearing now . . . the memory of Leon telling me something . . . it was there, in the burned photograph. It was there. It was . . .

October 2009.

It was October 2009 and Leon was telling me to remember the picture . . .

It all came back to me then.

I'm in Leon's study, talking to him about the Anna Gerrish case. I need his advice. Mick Bishop has become involved in the case and I want to find out as much about him as I can. Leon helps me, telling me what he knows about Bishop, showing me what a vicious man he can be, and warning me to watch out for him. After a while, Leon begins to tire. His illness is starting to take hold of him now. I tell him to get some rest, thank him for his help, and then head for the door.

Just as I reach it though, Leon says to me, 'You see this picture, John?'

I turn round and see him looking up at a framed photograph on the wall. It's a picture of Leon and my father, taken shortly before my father died. They're together at a barbecue somewhere – red-faced in the sun, drinks in their hands, both of them smiling broadly at the camera.

'If ever you have any questions, John,' Leon says, 'and I'm not here to answer them . . . just remember that picture.'

I look at him. 'What do you mean?'

He smiles wearily. 'You're a detective . . . you'll work it out when the time comes.'

I'd had no idea what he was talking about then, and I'd never really thought about it since, but now, as I stood there gazing down at the burned photograph, I could hear Leon's voice in my head – *if ever you have any questions, John, and I'm not here to answer them . . .*

He wasn't here.

. . . just remember that picture.

I stared at the ashes of my father's smile . . .

. . . you'll work it out when the time comes.

I couldn't work it out. I didn't understand it . . .

'John?'

. . . it was just a picture.

'John?'

I looked up at Imogen.

'What's the matter?' she said. 'What are you doing?'

'It's the picture . . .' I muttered, gazing down at it again. 'That one there . . . the framed photograph . . .'

'What about it?'

'Leon told me to remember it.'

'What?'

I quickly explained everything to her then, and when I'd finished she asked me what I thought he'd meant.

'I don't know,' I admitted, bending down to pick up the broken frame. I turned it over, examining the back, but there was nothing there. No inscription, no message. As I turned it over again, the burned scrap of photograph slipped out of the frame. I caught it before it dropped to the floor. I studied it closely, front and back, but again there was no clue as to the significance of the picture.

'Where was it taken?' Imogen asked.

I shrugged. 'Nowhere special, as far as I know. Just a barbecue somewhere . . . I've no idea where.'

'Was anyone else in the photograph?'

I shook my head. 'Just the two of them.'

'And they were just drinking beer and smiling at the camera?'

'Pretty much, yeah.'

'Are you sure it's the same photograph? I mean, Dad had quite a few photos on his wall—'

'It's the same one,' I said firmly.

'How do you know?'

'It's the only photograph I've ever seen of my father smiling.'

Imogen put her hand on my arm, and for a moment or two we just looked at each other, silently sharing our sadness, then she took her hand away, rubbed her eyes, and let out a long and weary sigh. 'Christ, John,' she said. 'I don't understand any of this. I mean, what the hell's going on here?'

'I don't know.'

She sighed again, and I saw her glance up at the window. 'We probably ought to get going,' she said. 'It's going to be dark soon. We don't want to be stumbling around here in the darkness.'

'Yeah,' I agreed, still transfixed by the picture frame.

'Are you hungry?'

I looked at her. 'Sorry?'

'Do you want to get something to eat?'

'Uh . . . yeah, OK. Yeah . . . I could eat something.'

She nodded at the frame in my hands. 'Are you bringing that with you?'

'Do you mind?'

'Nope. I was kind of hoping you would.'

10

After we'd left Lexden Vale, Imogen decided that she wasn't really up to eating out anywhere – she didn't want to be around other people, she said – so instead of stopping off at a restaurant somewhere we drove straight back to her place. Her flat was on the ground floor of a low-rise apartment complex in the recently built dockyard development area south of the river. She'd been living there for just over a year, having sold the house she'd shared with her ex-husband, and this was the first time I'd seen it. As with most new dockyard developments, the housing was aimed quite unashamedly at the higher end of the market, and although a lot of the buildings were a little too sterile for my liking, a little too modern and clean, it wasn't hard to see the attraction of living here. The private parking, the river views, the excellent security – CCTV, alarms, push-button locks. And if Imogen's flat was anything to go by, the apartments themselves were equally impressive – spacious, pristine, modern, bright. I actually felt a bit out of place when Imogen first showed me in, a feeling that reminded me – with some coincidence – of the embarrassment and intimidation I'd felt when I was a seventeen-year-old kid visiting the Mercers' house. The feeling didn't last long this time though, and it wasn't quite as unsettling, but as she showed me into the flat, and I looked around at the seemingly vast expanse of the open-plan room, with its polished floorboards and its bright white walls, and its stunning array of floor-to-ceiling windows . . . I momentarily felt that I really didn't belong here again. It was too clean for me, too spotless, too shiny. It made me feel like a tramp.

Then Imogen said, 'Yeah, I know . . . it's a bit much, isn't it? But I'm planning on dirtying it up a bit, you know, make it a bit more *homely*.'

I looked at her. She was smiling.

'I'll make us something to eat in a minute,' she said. 'Do you want a drink first?'

'Yeah, why not?'

And after that I started feeling OK again.

We avoided talking about the fire at first. I don't know if we did it on purpose – an unspoken agreement to put all the confusion and distress to one side for a while – or if it just happened that way. But whatever the reason, I think we both needed a break from the mind-frazzling stuff, and it felt pretty good just sitting there talking about other things for a change. Imogen had opened a bottle of wine and settled herself down in a huge white leather settee, and I was sitting in a matching white leather armchair drinking cognac, and it all felt very comfortable. She didn't even mind me smoking in the flat. The smell of cigarette smoke reminded her of her father, she said. Which came as some surprise to me, as I'd never known him to smoke.

'He used to have a couple of cigarettes every day when I was little,' she explained. 'One at lunchtime, and one in the evening.'

'Really?'

She nodded. 'I can still remember the smell of it on his clothes.'

'And you liked it?'

'Yeah.' She looked at me, watching as I lit a cigarette. 'Does Bridget let you smoke in the house?'

Imogen had never met Bridget, but she knew we were living together, and I'd told her a little bit about her. 'I smoke in my flat,' I said, 'but not in Bridget's.'

'You're still in separate flats then?'

'Yeah.'

'And that works?'

'It seems to.'

She nodded quietly, sipping wine. 'So it's still all going OK?'

'Yeah, it's good . . . I mean, we don't really *do* very much. We go out for a drink now and then, a meal sometimes, take the dog out for a walk, but most of the time we just stay in and . . . I don't know. Watch TV, listen to the radio, read books . . .' I grinned. 'Pretty wild, eh?'

'Sounds all right to me.'

'It is . . . I like it.'

'Good,' she said. 'I'm happy for you.' She drained the wine from her glass, then picked up the bottle and poured herself another. 'I'll get us some food in a minute . . . really, I promise.'

'No rush,' I told her.

She passed me the bottle of cognac. 'Help yourself.'

I refilled my glass, took a sip, and puffed on my cigarette. 'How's everything going with you?' I asked her, realising immediately what a stupid and insensitive question it was. 'I mean, apart from all this, you know, the fire and everything . . .' I shook my head. 'Sorry, that was a really idiotic thing to say—'

'No, it's all right . . . really, it's fine.' She drank more wine. 'Actually, since I started running the company my social life has been virtually non-existent. I'm either at the office all day or away meeting clients, and I rarely get home before eight or nine, and by then I'm too tired to do anything.' She smiled at me. 'I can't even find the energy to watch TV. I usually just have a bath, a few glasses of wine, and go to bed.'

I sipped from my glass, enjoying the smooth heat of the brandy. 'Is the business still doing OK?'

'I wouldn't say it's doing OK, but we're just about holding up. A lot of our regular clients have really cut back on their spending, so we're not getting the number of jobs we used to, but that doesn't mean we're not busy. In fact, we're having to put in even more hours now to chase down whatever work there is.'

'Right . . .' I said, nodding thoughtfully. 'So you don't just sit around in your office all day, drinking coffee and smoking cigarettes, hoping something's going to turn up?'

She laughed. 'Is that how you're dealing with the economic downturn?'

'Yeah, pretty much . . .'

'Is it working?'

'That all depends.'

'On what?'

'Your definition of "working".'

I told her about Jamaal Tan's murder then, summarising Ayanna's story and telling her everything that had happened so far, up to and including Hassan Tan's blunt refusal to talk to me that morning. By the time I'd finished I was more convinced than ever that Ada had been right all along, and I should never have gone anywhere near the case. There was clearly *some*thing going on, but now that I'd talked it through, and I'd heard myself talking it through, it was fairly obvious that it was going to take a lot of hard work and a lot of hard time to get to the bottom of things. Which would have been fine if I was getting paid . . . and the police weren't so heavily involved . . . and Mick Bishop wasn't lurking around in the background. And besides, I had more important things to do with my time now. Two good people were dead, possibly murdered . . . the least I could do was try to find out what had happened to them.

'So what's next?' Imogen said.

'Sorry?'

'The case . . . the one you just told me about. What are you going to do next?'

'I don't know,' I said, shaking my head. 'I might just give up on it, to be honest.'

'Really?'

I looked at her. 'What would you do?'

'I wouldn't have taken it on in the first place.'

'Well, yeah, but Mercer don't take cases like this—'

'I wouldn't have taken it on even if we did.'

'All right,' I sighed. 'Let me put it another way. What would you do if you were in my place?'

She grinned. 'Same answer. I still wouldn't have taken—'

'If you *had* taken it on then.' I gave her a look. 'What would you do if you were in my place and you had taken the case?'

'I'd wish I hadn't.'

'Honestly?'

She nodded. 'It's just not worth it, John. As far as I can see, there are only two possible outcomes, neither of which is going to do you any good. Number one . . .' She held up a slightly unsteady finger. 'DI Lilley isn't lying, and they really have got Jamaal's killer in custody for a different murder, and all they're trying to do is make sure the case they have against him isn't jeopardised—'

'Do you think that's likely?'

'No. But it's not impossible. And if it is the truth, however unlikely, and you keep nosing around asking questions about Jamaal, you're going to end up in a shitload of trouble.'

'Right,' I said, stubbing out my cigarette. 'And what if Lilley *is* lying?'

'Then they're covering up the murder for another reason.'

'Such as?'

'I've no idea. But whoever's behind it – and I think we both know who we're talking about – they're going to do everything they can to stop you uncovering it, aren't they? And, again, that's going to be bad news for you, John. Really bad news.'

I drank some more brandy. 'You don't think Lilley's behind it then?'

'Do you?'

I shook my head. 'It's got to be Bishop.'

'Exactly.' She poured more wine into her glass and took a long drink. The bottle was almost empty now. 'Dad really *hated* that fucker,' she said coldly, staring into space. 'He utterly despised him. And he never forgave him for what he did to your father.'

'I know . . .'

I'd never forgiven him either.

Leon and my father had always known that Mick Bishop didn't just bend the rules, he broke them. He broke the law. He hurt people, humiliated people, corrupted people. I'd personally seen him kill a man in cold blood. But although my father was well aware of Bishop's criminality, he'd never actually been in a position to prove it until January 1992, when he'd come into possession of a video showing Bishop and two other police officers torturing a drug dealer and robbing him of five kilos of cocaine. After passing the video and other incriminating information to his immediate superior, DCI Frank Curtis, my father was subsequently accused of fabricating evidence and making false statements against a fellow officer in a deliberate attempt to ruin his career. Three weeks later, while suspended from duties pending a full investigation, £25,000 in cash and two kilos of cocaine were 'discovered' in my father's station locker, and conclusive evidence was produced of his inappropriate relationship with an eighteen-year-old girl called Serina Mayo who'd recently been a key witness for the prosecution in the high-profile trial of a serial paedophile.

Two days later, while my mother was visiting her sister

for the day, my father locked himself in his office at home, drank most of a full bottle of whisky, and shot himself in the head.

In a suicide note addressed to my mother, he categorically denied the allegations of corruption, insisting that the cocaine and cash had been planted in his locker, and that he suspected DI Bishop and possibly DCI Curtis of colluding in a plot to discredit him. But he didn't deny that he'd been having an affair with Serina Mayo.

I'm so sorry, Alice, he wrote to my mother. *I don't know how it happened or why. It just happened. It was, quite literally, an act of madness.*

My mind was drifting in a cloud of brandy now, and as Imogen carried on talking about her father, her saddened voice soft and quiet, I found myself floating back through the years, lost in a haze of time-blurred images . . .

October 2009, I'm back in Leon's study again, and he's opening his laptop and tapping keys and he's saying to me, 'Corruption is a crime, John. It's not just a breach of trust, a bending of the rules, an abuse of power . . . it's a crime. A corrupt police officer is a criminal, it's as simple as that. And Bishop . . . well, come over here and look at this, see for yourself.' And as I get up and go over to his desk, Leon angles the laptop so we can both see the screen . . . and at first I can't quite make out what I'm looking at, but when I lean in and half-close my eyes I realise it's a stilled image from a poor-quality video. Four figures are on the screen: a man tied to a chair, another two men standing behind him, one of them with a baseball bat in his hand, and Bishop . . .

I look at Leon. 'Is this what I think it is?'

He nods. 'It's a copy of the CCTV video that your father gave to DCI Curtis, the one that shows Bishop and the others torturing the man in the chair.'

'Shit,' I say quietly, looking back at the screen.

'You don't need to see all of it,' Leon says. 'And I'm sure you know what happens anyway, but I just wanted to let you see what Bishop is capable of . . . are you ready?'

I nod.

Leon taps the keyboard and the video starts up. Bishop is standing in front of the man in the chair, and as the video begins, I see him leaning down and yelling violently in the man's face. There's no sound, so the yelling is silent, but there's no mistaking the fury in his voice. The man in the chair is screwing his eyes shut and stretching his head back in a vain attempt to get away from Bishop, but Bishop just keeps on screaming at him . . . and then suddenly he stops . . . and with no hesitation at all he draws back his arm and punches the man viciously in the face. The blow is so hard that the man – still tied to the chair – tumbles sideways to the floor. The two other men immediately pick him up again, and while they're doing that, I see Bishop lighting a cigarette. He takes a few hard puffs on it, says something to the man, now upright in his chair again, and as the man begins shaking his head in wild-eyed fear, Bishop calmly steps forward and spears the burning cigarette into his right eye.

'Jesus Christ,' I whisper as Leon stops the video.

'And that was only the beginning of it,' Leon says, pressing more keys . . .

. . . and now Leon is closing the laptop and saying to me, 'That's how it works with Bishop. He gets something on you, something he can use against you . . . and once he's got it, you're his for life, whether you like it or not. You'd be amazed at how many people he's got in his pocket – police officers, criminals, politicians, businessmen . . . he's a very powerful, and very dangerous, man.'

Leon smiles at me then, a sad and weary smile that seems to take an awful lot out of him. 'And listen,' he mutters. 'Listen . . .'

His eyes are closing even as he speaks to me.

I turn quietly and start to leave. But just as I get to the door, I hear him speak to me again.

'You see this picture, John?' he says.

I turn round and see him looking up at a framed photograph on the wall. It's a picture of Leon and my father, taken shortly before Dad died. They're together at a barbecue somewhere – red-faced in the sun, drinks in their hands, both of them smiling broadly at the camera.

'If ever you have any questions, John,' Leon says, 'and I'm not here to answer them . . . just remember that picture.'

I look at him. 'What do you mean?'

He smiles again. 'You're a detective . . . you'll work it out when the time comes.'

I shake my head. 'I don't understand—'

'You know, John,' he says vaguely, 'there's something I've been meaning to ask you for a long time . . . something I've been thinking about . . .'

'Leon,' I say. 'I really think you should get some rest now—'

'You see, what I can't understand, what I've never been able to figure out . . .' He looks at me, his entire body quite still. 'When your father killed himself in his room . . . why did he lock the door?'

'What?'

'It doesn't make sense, does it? If you're going to kill yourself, why make a point of locking the door first? What purpose does it serve?'

'I don't know . . .' I say, confused. 'I've never really thought about it . . .'

He smiles distantly. 'Perhaps you should.'

'Are you trying to say—?'

'I'm sorry, John,' he mutters, his eyes beginning to close again. 'Would you mind asking Claudia to come up here? I think . . . I think I'm . . .' He sighs hard. 'God, I'm so fucking tired.'

'John?'

. . . November 2009, I'm sitting with Serina Mayo in the front room of her small terraced house. She's thirty-seven now, but she looks older. Dyed black hair, pulled back tight and tied in a ponytail. Thin lips, her eyes heavily made up, her mouth set hard in a permanent scowl. It's a harsh face, dark and brittle, the skin lined and cracked like the varnish on a dusty old portrait. It's the face of a once beautiful woman who's suffered too much, too young.

She's talking to me about my father.

'. . . it was always hard to tell with Jim,' she says. 'He suffered quite badly from depression, and some days it got so bad that he could barely even talk, but even then . . .' She shakes her head. 'I don't know, there was just something *about him, a strength, an inner belief . . . he just never struck me as the kind of man who'd kill himself.'*

'John?' Imogen repeated. 'Are you all right?'

I shook the memories from my head and looked over at her. 'Yeah, sorry,' I said, lighting a cigarette. 'I was just . . . it's nothing. Sorry, it's been a long day.'

'Yeah, tell me about it,' she said, smiling ruefully and sipping more wine. I glanced at the bottle and saw that it was empty. Part of me knew that I ought to go now. No more drinking, I'd had enough. It was time to call a taxi, go home, go back to Bridget . . . go to bed, sleep off the brandy. Start again tomorrow.

'What do you think's going on, John?' Imogen said tearfully. 'Honestly, tell me what you think.'

I hesitated for a moment or two, gazing over at the window, seeing distant lights twinkling dully in the winter-black night . . . then I reached for the cognac bottle, refilled my glass, and turned back to Imogen.

'I think we have to wait,' I told her. 'We don't know if the fire was deliberate yet, we don't really know *any*thing—'

'We know someone took Dad's hard drives.'

'Yeah, but—'

'And we know that Lisbie was lying.'

'No, we don't. Not yet anyway. All we've got at the moment is a bunch of stuff that doesn't make much sense. It doesn't necessarily mean anything.'

She shook her head. 'You don't believe that.'

'Maybe not. But until we can actually prove anything—'

'And how are we going to do that?'

'Like I said, we wait.'

'For what?'

'For Cal, for a start. Let him check Leon's emails, see if he finds anything.'

'What if he doesn't?'

I looked at her. 'Have the post-mortems taken place yet?'

'They were scheduled for today, but there was some kind of hold-up and they've both been put back to tomorrow morning.'

'OK,' I said quietly. 'What time in the morning?'

'I don't know,' she muttered, trying not to cry.

'Sorry, Immy,' I said. 'But we need to find out—'

'I know,' she mumbled, sniffing back tears. 'I know . . . I'm just . . . it's hard . . .'

I didn't say anything for a while, I just sat there quietly, drinking and smoking while Imogen stared blankly at the floor, twisting a knotted tissue in her hands, sniffing and snuffling . . . and I didn't know what to do. Should I go over and comfort her, put my arms around her, hold her tight . . .? Or should I go home? Go back to Bridget, go to bed, sleep off the brandy, start again tomorrow . . .?

'Listen, Imogen,' I started to say. 'Maybe it'd be best if—'

'God, look at the state of me,' she said suddenly, sitting up straight and rubbing her hands. 'I'm filthy . . . my hands are *black*.' She looked at me. 'I've probably got crap all over my face, haven't I?'

'Just a bit,' I admitted, studying her face and realising that it was a bit of a mess. Black smudges everywhere, tear stains, smeared make-up.

'I need a shower,' she said, getting unsteadily to her feet. 'Do you mind?'

'Well—'

'I won't be long. Couple of minutes, OK? And then I'll *definitely* get us something to eat.'

'OK,' I said, smiling at her.

'Just make yourself at home,' she said, waving her hand around, her upper body circling slightly. 'I'll be back in a minute . . .'

She headed off across the room, trying too hard to walk steadily, and I saw her stumble slightly over a low step that led up to a door at the far end of the room. She opened the door and went inside, leaving the door open behind her. The room was dark for a second or two, then a soft red light snapped on, revealing the interior of her bedroom. White walls, a king-size bed, another floor-to-ceiling window. I heard another door opening, then the sound of running water . . . and all of a sudden I realised that I could see Imogen's half-naked reflection in the night-blackened window. She was standing in the bathroom doorway, getting undressed . . .

I couldn't help staring for a moment or two, captivated by her pale-skinned figure, but then I made myself look away. It wasn't right. I picked up my brandy glass, went over to the window, and gazed out into the night.

11

I called Bridget while Imogen was in the shower. There was no answer from our home number, and when I tried her mobile I got her voicemail message. I guessed she was driving, probably on her way back from the pet shop. I left a quick message, telling her I'd be back in an hour or two and that I'd already eaten so she shouldn't wait for me, then I sat down in the armchair, drank some more cognac, and wondered what the hell I was doing. Why had I just lied to her? Why had I told her I'd eaten when I hadn't? What was the point of that?

I lit a cigarette and thought about it for a while, trying to work out if I'd meant to lie to her. And, if so, why? Had I simply assumed that Imogen *was* going to make us something to eat in a minute, in which case it wasn't really a lie, or was it just that I hadn't really known what to say to Bridget and I'd said something, anything, just for the sake of it? And if that was the case, why hadn't I known what to say?

It didn't make sense.

I didn't make sense.

Sometimes I wonder if I've ever grown up.

'Ah, fuck it,' I muttered, looking around, trying to remember where I'd put the broken picture frame.

I was a bit drunk, that was all. Too much cognac on an empty stomach.

I was just a bit drunk.

The picture frame was on a glass coffee table beside the armchair. I went over and picked it up, took it back to the armchair, and sat there staring at it. The room was quiet, just the muffled splash of the shower from the bathroom and the faint drone of an aeroplane passing by overhead, and I could hear the blood and alcohol pumping through my veins. A hollow roar was rushing through my head, like the sound of an old washing machine in an empty basement.

I closed my eyes.

. . . you see this picture, John?

. . . if ever you have any questions . . .

. . . remember . . .

. . . remember . . .

. . . you'll work it out when the time comes . . .

I opened my eyes.

The floor tilted.

I waited for it to steady itself, then looked down at the picture again. The seared remains of my father's smiling face looked back at me . . . Jim Craine . . . *he just never struck me as the kind of man who'd kill himself . . .*

But he had.

I picked up the scrap of photograph, rubbed my eyes, and studied it closely. There was very little to see. The background was blurred – a smudge of green that could have been anything, a hedge, a bush, a tree . . . and something grey, possibly a wall. And that was about it. A bit of smiling face, something green, and something grey. It didn't tell me anything.

I carefully placed the scrap of photograph on the arm of the chair, took a sip of brandy, and picked up the broken picture frame. It was rectangular, about nine inches by seven. A plain silver-coloured frame, of no great quality, fixed to a metal backing. The frame itself was twisted and buckled, the top right-hand corner no longer joined, but the backing seemed reasonably intact. I turned the frame over and studied the back. It was scorched and blackened, the metal slightly bowed, but there was no serious damage. I tapped it lightly with a fingertip. It rattled. I tapped it again, a little harder, and it rattled again, a little louder. I turned the frame over, held it to my ear, and tapped the front of the backing – once, twice – trying to pinpoint where the rattle was coming from. It didn't sound like a loose bit of the frame – it somehow seemed more solid than that – but I couldn't figure out what else it could be. I gave it a gentle shake – it didn't rattle. A harder shake. Still no rattle. I took hold of the loosened bit of frame in the top right-hand corner and gave it a sharp tug. It came away from the backing with just a faint crack, and the bottom of the frame peeled away with it. I quickly snapped off the rest of the thin metal frame, dropped the bits to the floor, and stared down at the frameless metal backing in my hands. It was obvious now that the frame had been glued to the backing – the hardened remains of the glue were still visible – and that the backing itself wasn't just a sheet of thin metal, it was two sheets of thin metal, joined together.

I tapped it again.

It rattled.

The sheets were joined with four lightweight rivets, one in each corner. One of them was loose. There was a very slight gap between the two sheets. I tried to prise them apart with my fingernails, but the gap was too small. I couldn't get any purchase. I looked around the flat, searching for something to use as a lever . . . a knife, fork, nail file, anything. Nothing. I got to my feet . . . too fast. Blood rushed to my head, the room started spinning, and I had to sit down again.

I lit a cigarette and waited for the whirling to stop.

The shower was still running. Imogen was taking a long time. I glanced over at the open door, looking for her reflection in the bedroom window, telling myself that all I was doing was making sure she was OK. But the glass was all steamed up now, so I couldn't see if she was OK or not, and I knew in my heart that I was lying to myself anyway. Of course she was OK. She was just taking a shower. And I was just a drunk-eyed pig.

I got up, more slowly this time, and went over to the kitchen in the corner of the room. Everything looked brand-new and unused – the marble countertop, the porcelain sink, the sleek wooden cupboards and drawers. I started opening drawers, found the cutlery, and picked out a slim-handled table knife. Placing the metal sheets on the counter, I held them down with one hand, jammed the knife between the two sheets with the other, and levered it up. The loose rivet popped out, widening the gap, and then all I had to do was shove my fingers between the sheets, grab hold of both edges, one in each hand, and give them a good hard yank. My first effort didn't quite work. The rivets held, but only just. I took a deep breath, held it for a second, and yanked again, and this time the rivets popped out, scattering across the countertop, and the sheets came apart in my hands.

My heart was beating hard now, and I could feel the tingle of adrenaline racing through my blood as I closed my eyes for a second, breathed in slowly, breathed out again, then opened my eyes and gazed down at the two metal sheets. There was nothing attached to either of them, and as far as I could see, nothing had been lodged in between them. Nothing had fallen out. No notes, no messages. The sheet in my left hand was blank, just a dull grey rectangle with fire-blackened edges, but the one in my right hand . . .

I looked closer.

Scratches . . . there were marks scratched into the metal. Crudely scratched lettering, a word, gouged out with a penknife, or maybe a screwdriver . . . and beneath the letters . . . was that a drawing, a picture of something? I couldn't see well enough, the light was too dim. I looked around, found a light switch and turned it on. A fluorescent spotlight snapped on in a canopy over the counter. I leaned in, held the metal sheet in the light . . . and now I could see it all.

'Shit,' I whispered.

The scratched lettering at the top of the sheet read:

J.
Remember?

And below that was a roughly scratched picture of a flower. It looked like the work of a child – a ragged ring of imperfect petals perched on top of a stick-like stem. Despite the crudity of the drawing, it was quite clearly some kind of flower, but if it hadn't been for the jagged little triangles scored up and down the stem, I'd never have guessed what kind of flower it was supposed to be.

The triangles were thorns.

The flower was a rose.

Remember?

Yellow roses . . .?

What about roses? Yellow roses . . . do you think they'd be suitable?

Yellow roses in a granite vase . . .

'Christ, Leon . . .' I muttered, staring at the drawing. 'What the fuck . . .?'

I was back in the armchair again when I heard Imogen calling out to me from the bathroom. I'd been sitting there for the last ten minutes or so, smoking and drinking, studying Leon's picture, trying to work out if it meant what I thought it meant . . . and then, when I'd heard the shower stop running, I'd started to think about Imogen. What was I going to tell her about the drawing? Should I tell her everything? Should I tell her about the roses at my father's grave? Should I tell her what I was beginning to think? Or should I keep my thoughts to myself for a while, wait until I'd checked things out first . . .?

'John!'

There was no real panic or alarm to her voice, but she wasn't just calling out casually to me either. She sounded concerned . . . apprehensive.

'John!' she called out again. 'Can you come here a minute, please?'

I got up and hurried over to the bedroom.

'Fuck it,' I heard her say.

'What is it, Im?' I said, stepping through the open door. 'Are you all right?'

She was standing at the bedroom window, her hands cupped to the glass, peering out into the darkness. She was wearing a black silk dressing gown and her hair was glistening wet.

'I thought I saw someone,' she said, still staring through the window.

I went over and stood beside her. 'Where?'

'Over there,' she said, pointing to her right. 'By the fence. I saw something move, a glint of something, and then I saw a face . . . or I thought I did anyway.'

I wiped steam from the window, cupped my hands to the glass and looked out. There was very little light, just a pale orange glow from somewhere above, and all I could make out in the dimly lit darkness was a narrowish strip of lawn, about ten yards wide, with a high brick wall on the right-hand side and a low decorative fence running along the far edge. There was no sign of life anywhere.

'What's on the other side of the fence?' I said.

'A steep grass bank . . . it leads down to the footpath along the river.'

I carried on looking for a while, scanning the lawn, the area around the fence, but I didn't see anything. No face in the dark, no glint of anything, no movement. I turned to Imogen again. Her eyes were glazed, her brow furrowed, and she seemed more confused than concerned now, not quite sure if she was making a fool of herself or not.

'I'm sorry, John,' she said quietly. 'It was probably nothing—'

'I'll go and check outside,' I told her. 'Just to make sure, OK?'

She shook her head. 'There's no need—'

'It's no trouble,' I said. 'How do I get out?'

She showed me to a back door at the side of the kitchen and I went out into the orange-tinged darkness. It was a bitterly cold night, the air misted with feathery white flecks of ice, and when I took a deep breath to clear my head, the frozen air ripped into my lungs like a knife. I squeezed my eyes shut for a moment, cursing the cold, and when I opened them again the night sky was spinning.

I lit a cigarette and waited for the sky to settle down.

I was drunk, that was all.

Nothing to worry about.

Just drunk in the cold night air.

I raked my fingers through my hair, breathed in and out a couple of times – not too deeply this time – then I pulled my penlight from my pocket, turned it on, and started looking around in the sodium-lit gloom. The light, I realised, came from a small domed lamp fixed to the top of the wall, just below the roof of the building. I couldn't understand what purpose it served. It was too dim to see by, and it certainly wasn't bright enough to provide any real security. All it seemed to do was glaze the darkness with a chemical light that made everything look slightly eerie. The green-tinted whiteness of the frosted grass was tinged with a violet-blue glimmer. The powdery white efflorescence on the high brick wall had a yellowy-grey glow to it, the bricks themselves were orange, and the black of the night all around the lamp was a dull grey blur of nothing much at all.

There was a wrought-iron gate about halfway along the brick wall, padlocked shut, and when I checked round the corner of the flat, on the left-hand side, I saw an identical layout in the garden of the flat next door – another narrow lawn, another brick wall, another wrought-iron gate. I quickly shone the penlight around, just to make sure that no one was there, but I didn't bother checking the gate. It didn't make any difference if it was padlocked or not – although I guessed it probably was – because both the brick walls were open at the far edge of the lawn, so if someone wanted to get in, a padlocked gate wasn't going to stop them. All they'd have to do was follow the brick wall down to the far end of the lawn, step around it and hop over the decorative fence.

I went over to the fence and shone the torch down the steep grass bank. It was a fairly severe drop down to the river, perhaps fifty feet or so, and I wouldn't have wanted to try climbing up it, but it certainly wasn't impossible. Streetlights lit up the pale-grey ribbon of the footpath at the foot of the slope, and in the spread of the lights I could just make out the green-black slick of the river snaking along towards the gloom of the old dockyard buildings over to my right. Way across the other side of the river, perhaps half a mile to my left, on the south side of Riverside Business Park, I could see lights shining in the windows of a building

161

that I was pretty sure had to be Juno's. I gazed across at the distant lights, wondering idly who I might see if I was close enough to see in through the windows – Hassan Tan, Curt Dempsey, Mick Bishop . . .?

I shook my head – why was I even thinking about them? – and turned my attention back to the footpath below. It was separated from the bank by a six-foot-high metal fence, the top of which was strung with razor wire, and I guessed it was probably secure enough to deter a casual intruder. But if someone really wanted to get over it . . .? Again, it was by no means impossible.

But even if someone had managed to clamber over the fence and climb the steep grass bank, and even if they had been spying on Imogen, they weren't around any more. The path was deserted, the grass on the bank was undisturbed. Whatever Imogen had seen – if indeed she'd seen anything – it was gone now.

I took a final drag on my cigarette, flicked it over the bank, then went back inside.

Imogen was waiting for me in the kitchen, cradling a half-empty glass of wine in her hand. The freshly opened bottle on the counter beside her was about three-quarters full, so I guessed she'd already had a glass while I was out in the garden. She was looking pretty drunk now – her eyes unfocused, her body swaying – and it pained me to see her like that, it just wasn't *right* for her. But I knew – I *know* – that nothing in grief is right or wrong. Nothing makes sense, and nothing has to make sense.

Death rips you up, tears you apart, it becomes you . . . it burrows down into your soul, and once it's there, you know – you *know* – there's nothing left. So what does it matter what you do? As long as you think it's helping you, then it's helping you. Right or wrong doesn't come into it. You just do what you do. And if Imogen was drinking herself senseless to escape her pain, that's what she was doing, and whatever I felt about it was of no consequence at all. Not that I was in any position to judge her anyway. I'd been doing what she was doing, and to a far greater extent, for the best part of twenty years. Who was I to say it wasn't right?

'Did you see anything?' Imogen asked me, her voice slightly slurred.

'There's no one out there,' I told her, rubbing the cold from my hands. 'It was probably just a cat or something—'

'God, I'm such a fucking idiot,' she said, shaking her head. 'I'm sorry, John . . . really. I feel so stupid—'

'Hey,' I said gently, putting my hand on her arm. 'It's perfectly all right, OK? You thought you saw something, that's all. It's no big deal.'

'Yeah, I know, but—'

'Don't worry about it,' I said, smiling at her. 'All right?'

She just looked at me for a moment, her head wavering, her eyes trying to focus, then suddenly she frowned and grabbed my hand. 'You're *freezing*,' she said, holding my palm to her cheek. 'God . . . your hand's like *ice*. Come here, let me warm you up.' She pulled me towards her, putting her arms round my back and squeezing me tightly. 'Just hold me, John,' she said quietly. 'Please . . .'

As she pressed herself against me, and I gave her a tentative hug, I suddenly realised that her dressing gown was open and she was naked underneath. I froze for a moment, seized in a whirl of confusion – *does she know her gown's open? should I tell her? did she undo it on purpose?* – and then I felt her taking hold of my hands and guiding them inside her gown, pressing them to her naked skin, and she whispered in my ear, 'Relax, John . . . it's all right. Just hold me . . .'

I could feel my heart beating hard, my flesh tingling.

'No, Imogen,' I said quietly, taking my hands away. 'No, I can't . . .'

'Yes, you can. I know you want to . . .' She moved her hips. 'I can feel it . . .'

'No,' I repeated, easing away from her. 'I don't think we should—'

'Why not?' she said, stepping back from me.

'You know why.'

She just stood there then, her gown wide open, staring defiantly into my eyes, daring me to look at her. I held her gaze. There was no unpleasantness in her eyes, no anger or mockery, she was simply offering herself to me – nothing more, nothing less. She wanted physical intimacy. My body wanted it too, but my head and my heart knew better, and as I moved towards her and carefully retied her dressing gown, I could feel all the tension draining out of me.

I was doing the right thing.

Imogen didn't do anything to stop me. She didn't move, didn't say anything, she just stood there, half-smiling at me as I covered her up, and then, as I stepped back again and looked into her eyes, she started to giggle.

'Sorry,' she said, putting her hand to her mouth, trying

not to laugh. 'It's not funny . . .' She gave a little snort. 'I think I'm a bit drunk.'

I smiled at her.

She wiped her nose, grinning at me. 'It was worth a try though, wasn't it?'

I sighed, not knowing what to say.

She nodded, staring at me . . . and then, quite suddenly, she made an odd little gulping noise, looked down at the floor, and burst into tears. 'Fuck, John . . . I'm *so* sorry. Really . . . I mean, God, what's the fucking *matter* with me? Jesus *Christ* . . .'

'It's all right,' I said, putting my arm round her.

'No, it's fucking *not—*'

'Come on,' I said. 'Let's go and sit down, OK?'

'I'm sorry,' she sobbed. 'I just . . . I just . . .'

'It's OK,' I said, guiding her over to the settee. 'Just sit down a minute, all right?'

'You're not going anywhere, are you?'

'I'm right here.'

'Please don't leave me, not tonight. Please . . .?'

I sat her down, went over and poured myself a glass of brandy, took a long drink, then went back over and sat down beside her. Glancing up at a clock on the wall, I was surprised to see that it was gone eight o'clock. Bridget would be wondering where I was. I'd call her as soon as I'd got Imogen settled down a bit, I told myself, taking another good slug of cognac. Ten minutes, fifteen at the most . . . I'd call her.

I could feel the haze of alcohol heat rising up inside me now, the golden warmth of the brandy glowing in my heart . . .

165

It felt good.

Like an old friend.

We didn't talk much for the next hour or so, we just sat
there together on the settee, Imogen half-dozing, crying
quietly every now and then, while I just drifted off into a
comfortable state of semi-consciousness. I smoked a few
cigarettes, kept my glass topped up, mulling things over in
the back of my mind as I gazed through the window at the
sodium-lit snowflakes dancing in the dark. I can't remember
what I was thinking about. I was just drifting, floating
around in my head, and that was fine with me.

At one point I had to get up to go to the bathroom, and
as I leaned forward to push myself up off the settee,
Imogen's eyes opened suddenly and she said, with some
panic, 'What are you doing? Where are you going?'

'It's all right,' I told her. 'I'm just going to the
bathroom.'

'Oh,' she said, relieved and a little embarrassed. 'OK . . .
sorry.'

When I came back, she was sitting up straight with a
glass of cognac in her hand. 'I thought I'd join you,' she
said, raising the glass and taking a big sip. She swallowed,
squeezed her eyes shut, and coughed. 'It's nice, isn't it?'

'Very nice,' I agreed, lighting a cigarette.

She refilled her glass, drank far too much in one go,
coughed again, put the glass down, then slumped back into
the settee and closed her eyes. After just a few seconds, she
began breathing heavily, her mouth half-open, her breath
rasping sleepily in her throat. I sat there smoking my cigarette

and sipping brandy, wondering why I hadn't called Bridget yet. I could have called her while I was in the bathroom. But I hadn't. Why not? I didn't know. I looked down at Imogen. She'd sleep all night now, I imagined. She was pretty out of it. *I'll finish this cigarette*, I told myself, *then take her into the bedroom, get her into bed, make sure she's covered up, and then call a taxi and get myself home . . . she'll be fine. She won't even know I've gone.*

I poured myself another inch of brandy.

Just one more . . .

'Hey,' Imogen muttered.

I looked at her, surprised to see she'd woken up.

'What's going on?' she mumbled, looking around.

'Nothing,' I told her, putting out my cigarette. 'Listen, Im, I think you should get off to bed—'

'Why does it have to hurt so much, John?' she said suddenly, looking up at me. 'I mean, what's the point? Hurting doesn't help anyone, does it? It doesn't do me any good, it doesn't help Mum and Dad . . . it doesn't help anyone, does it?'

I didn't really want to talk to her about it, and I'm not sure that I meant to, but as I leaned back and lit another cigarette, and she rested her head on my shoulder, I just started telling her stuff . . . and the odd thing about it was that, as far as I was aware, it was stuff that I'd never even thought about before.

'Maybe it's an evolutionary thing,' I found myself saying. 'I mean, it all boils down to the same thing in the end, doesn't it? You know, life and death, survival . . . making sure your genes carry on. Maybe grief is just a kind of doomsday mechanism, and its only real purpose is to protect our genetic future. We *have* to hurt when our loved ones die, because the more we hurt, the harder we'll try to keep them alive. And keeping them alive – our offspring, partners, family – means keeping our genes alive. And that's what it's all about. You know, keeping our genes in the game. That's all we're here for.' I puffed on my cigarette, thinking about what I'd just said, wondering if it made any sense, and whether I actually believed it or not. 'And the pain has to be real,' I went on, 'the threat of grief, the threat of its torment . . . it has to be real, and it has to be seen to be real, or the mechanism itself is toothless.' I nodded contentedly, quietly pleased with the argument. 'What do you think, Im?' I said, looking at her. 'Imogen?'

She was asleep.

'Fair enough,' I muttered, smiling to myself. I drank off the last of my cognac, stubbed out my cigarette, and gently shook Imogen's shoulder. 'Imogen? Come on, Im, wake up . . .'

'Nuhh . . .' she mumbled.

I gave her another shake. 'Come on, you need to go to bed now.'

'Mmm?' she said, half-opening her eyes.

'Bed,' I repeated, taking her hand and starting to pull her up.

'Yeah . . . OK . . . just a sec . . .' She rubbed her eyes, yawning. 'What's the time?'

'Bedtime, come on.'

I helped her to her feet, put my arm round her waist, and started walking her across the room.

'We're going to bed now?' she muttered, smiling dopily at me.

'No, *you're* going to bed now.'

'Uh-uh,' she said, with an exaggerated shake of her head. 'You said you'd stay with me . . . you promised—'

'No, I didn't—'

'But I can't—'

'Careful!' I said, steadying her as we went through into the bedroom. She'd swayed away from me, almost stumbling into the wall.

'Sorry . . .'

'It's all right,' I said, leading her over to the bed. 'You're OK, you just need to—'

'*Please* don't go, John,' she said, turning suddenly to me. 'I really don't want to be on my own tonight. Please . . .?'

'There's nothing to worry about,' I told her. 'There's no one outside—'

'It's not that . . . it's just . . . I just need you to be with me.'

'I can't, Imogen. I'm sorry. I really have to go—'

She looked at me. 'You don't *have* to.'

'Yeah, I do.'

She moved closer, keeping her eyes fixed on mine. 'Just call her,' she said quietly, putting her hand on my arm. 'Tell her you're working late.'

'No—'

'Why not? What harm can it do? She'll never know—'

'No, but I will.'

'We don't have to *do* anything,' she went on. 'I promise . . . I just . . .' Her hand tightened on my arm. 'Please, John? Just stay with me . . . just for tonight . . .'

Her voice was trembling now, and I could feel her hand shaking. She was very pale too, and her eyes . . . they didn't look so good. She was frightened, I realised, genuinely scared of being left on her own. She looked so desperate, so vulnerable . . .

Fuck, I thought to myself. *Fuck it.*

'I can stay for a while, OK?' I heard myself say. 'I can't stay all night, I really can't, but—'

'Thank you,' she said simply, leaning forward and kissing me. 'You won't regret it.'

'We're not going to do anything, remember?' I said firmly. 'I'm just going to stay here—'

'I know,' she said, smiling. 'Don't worry. I won't seduce you.'

'I'm not joking, Imogen. If you start—'

'I won't start anything. I promise.'

'Right . . . well, get into bed then. I need to make a phone call. I'll be back in a few minutes.'

'Yes, sir,' I heard her say as I went back into the main room, closing the door behind me. And I thought I heard her stifle a little giggle too. As I crossed over to the settee and helped myself to more cognac, I couldn't help wondering if I'd just been taken in, played for a fool . . . but then I remembered the fear in her eyes, the desperation, and I knew she hadn't been faking that. And the rest of it, the flirting and joking . . .? She was drunk, messed up, emotionally fucked . . . it didn't mean anything. And even if it did, what did it matter? Right or wrong didn't come into it. She was doing what she had to do, and whatever I felt about it was of no consequence at all.

I lit a cigarette, took out my phone, and called Bridget.

'Hey, Bridge,' I said quietly when she answered. 'Sorry I didn't call before, I got caught up with something.'

'That's all right,' she said. 'Are you OK?'

'Yeah, you?'

'Fine, just a bit tired. One of those days, you know . . .'

'Listen,' I said, 'I can't talk for long, I'm kind of in the middle of something. I don't know how long it's going to take—'

'Is this the thing about the murdered boy?'

'Not exactly. It's just something . . . well, I'll tell you about it later, OK? It's a bit complicated—'

'Yeah, OK. No problem.'

'I'll probably be at least another couple of hours or so, maybe a bit longer, it just depends . . .'

'It's all right, John,' she said, a smile in her voice. 'Just come home when you can . . . I'll be here, don't worry.'

'Yeah,' I said, utterly sick of myself now, 'yeah, I know. Don't wait up for me though, OK?'

'I will if I want to.'

I closed my eyes. 'I've got to go, Bridge. See you later.'

'Yeah, see you, John.'

The line went dead.

'Fuck,' I said to the empty room. 'Fuck, shit, *fuck* . . .'

I hated myself, hated myself even more *for* hating myself. I hated the cheating, the lying, the excuses for cheating and lying – *I'm just trying to do the right thing, I can't leave Imogen right now, but I don't want to hurt Bridget either, and it's not as if I'm doing anything wrong with Imogen, I'm only . . .*

171

'Only what?' I asked myself, filling my glass with brandy. 'You're only what?'

I drank half the glass down in one.

Retched a little, coughed.

Said 'fuck' again.

I lit a cigarette, sucking the smoke deep into my lungs, and went over to the window. The snow had stopped. The lights across the river were still shining in the darkness. A glint of something caught my eye, a faint movement at the far end of the lawn ... I cupped my hands to the glass, peered out, and saw a pair of glowing eyes moving across the lawn. Sodium eyes ...

I laughed.

It was a cat.

I finished off the brandy, refilled the glass, put out my cigarette, and went back into the bedroom.

The light was still on – a warm red light glowing in a black glass lampshade – and Imogen was lying face up on the bed. She was sleeping. Her dressing gown was on the floor. She was naked. I walked quietly over to the bed, put my drink on the bedside table, and sat down carefully beside her. She stirred slightly, wriggling her head, then settled again. She was lying on top of the duvet, and I couldn't see any way of getting her under it without either waking her up or lifting her up. I decided it was best to wake her.

'Imogen?' I said softly, leaning over and touching her shoulder. 'Hey, Imogen?'

She woke with a start, staring up at me with confused eyes, and then, with a sleepy smile of recognition, she reached up and pulled me down towards her.

'No, Immy,' I said, trying to pull back. 'Hold on—'

She kissed me, her arms tight around my neck.

I pulled away, breathing hard. 'Just get into bed, Imogen, OK? Sit up a minute—'

'OK . . .' She sat up, smiling, and wrapped her legs around my waist.

I stared at her. 'You said you wouldn't do this.'

'I was lying.'

I shook my head. 'Please just get into bed.'

'Only if you come with me.'

'All right,' I said.

'Really?'

I nodded. 'Get in.'

She frowned at me for a moment, not sure whether to believe me or not, then slowly unwrapped her legs from my waist, rolled over to one side, pulled the duvet back, and rolled under it. 'Now you,' she said, folding back the duvet to let me in.

'I just have to go to the bathroom first,' I said, getting to my feet.

'Don't be long.'

I picked up my drink, crossed over to the bathroom, opened the door and went inside. I didn't put the light on. I closed the door, locked it, and sat down on the toilet. I don't know how long I sat there – ten minutes, perhaps, maybe fifteen – but it was long enough to smoke a couple of cigarettes and finish the glass of brandy. And by the time I went back out again, Imogen was fast asleep.

I went over to the window to close the blinds, but they were controlled by some kind of push-button mechanism on the wall, and after squinting drunkenly at it for a minute or two, I still had no idea how it worked.

I left the blinds open and went back over to the bed. Imogen was lying on her side now, her knees drawn up to her chest, and she was sleeping deeply at last. I sat down on the edge of the bed and let out a long sigh of relief. Now I could go home. She'd be all right now . . . she'd sleep till late in the morning, wake up with an aching head, and with a bit of luck she wouldn't remember anything.

I took my phone out, opened Google, and started looking for a local taxi number. My eyes were really heavy, tired and drunk, and my legs felt like two lumps of lead. I sat back and rested my head on the pillow, taking care not to wake Imogen, and I swung my legs up onto the bed. Google was still trying to load. I turned it off, waited a moment, then turned it back on again. Now I couldn't get a connection at all.

I yawned.

I was *really* tired.

I closed my eyes for a moment . . . then opened them again.

I breathed out. Glanced at my phone. Still nothing.

I closed my eyes again, just for a moment . . .

12

The first thing I noticed when I woke up was the light. It wasn't right. The bedside lamp was still on, but instead of glowing warmly in the darkness, it had the lifeless light of a lamp left on in the daylight. Daylight . . .

'Oh, no,' I muttered, rubbing my eyes and squinting over at the window. '*No . . .*'

The light wasn't exactly streaming in through the glass, and the snow-clouded skies were so heavy and dark that for the briefest of moments I tried to convince myself that it was still night-time after all, but my hope lasted less than a heartbeat. I could see the lawn outside, frosty-green in the daylight, and away in the distance, over to my right, a glint of a pale winter sun peeking through a gap in the clouds . . .

The sun . . .

Daylight.

'*Shit!*'

Wide awake now, and starting to panic, I glanced quickly at the alarm clock on the bedside table. The display read 08.17.

I froze for a moment then, suddenly aware of something else that wasn't right. My skin . . . I could feel the softness of the duvet on my skin. I looked down. I wasn't wearing anything. And I was in the bed . . . not sitting on it, not even lying on it. I was lying *in* it. And I was naked. And so was Imogen, lying next to me, her bare arm draped over my hips.

'Jesus *Christ*,' I whispered, cautiously removing her arm. Her eyelids flickered, she grimaced slightly, made a quiet little snorting sound, then breathed out a breath of stale wine, rolled over, and went back to sleep. I stared at her, desperately trying to remember now – had we done anything? had we slept together? why was I undressed? when did I get undressed? why had I got into bed? *when* had I got into bed? – but my mind was blank. The last thing I could remember was sitting on the bed, trying to open Google on my phone, closing my eyes for just a moment, and then . . . nothing. I had no recollection at all of what I'd done during the night. Not so much as a hint. I must have been drunker then I'd thought, pass-out drunk . . . but the strange thing was, I didn't really have much of a hangover. A bit of a throbbing head, a tightness in my chest, a touch of nausea . . . I mean, I didn't feel great, but compared to hangovers I'd had in the past, this was nothing.

Not that that helped. I still couldn't remember anything. And whether I'd done anything or not with Imogen, I'd still spent all night with her . . . and Bridget had still spent the night on her own.

I scrambled out of bed then, found my clothes – they were in a pile beside the bed – and got dressed as quickly as I could. I hurried out of the bedroom, taking my phone from my pocket as I went, and crossed over to the settee and sat down. I was just about to hit Bridget's speed dial key when I suddenly realised that I hadn't given any thought to what I was going to say to her. I paused, thinking about it, automatically reaching into my pocket for a cigarette. *You were working*, I told myself, lighting the cigarette. *You were on a stake-out, waiting in your car outside someone's house, a fraud suspect, hoping to get a photo of them . . . and you fell asleep*. I puffed on my cigarette, nodding satisfactorily to myself. It wasn't much of a story, but it would do. I squeezed my eyes shut for a moment, forcing the clench of self-loathing from my mind, and tried to compose myself. I could hate myself later. Right now, I just had to put things right. I opened my eyes, took a deep breath, and called Bridget's mobile.

After a heart-pounding ten rings or so, it switched to voicemail. *Hi, this is Bridget Moran, please leave a message.*

I waited for the beep, then said, 'Hey, Bridge, it's me. I'm *really* sorry . . . I just fell asleep last night. I was on a stake-out, in my car, and . . . I don't know, I must have just dozed off. I hope you weren't too worried. Anyway, I'll try you at the shop now, but . . . well, just call me as soon as you can, OK?'

The pet shop didn't open until nine, but Bridget liked to get there early so she could get everything prepared in advance – the animals, the cages, the cash, whatever. She was usually at the shop by 8.15 at the latest. It was 8.35 now. She should be there . . . but if she was, why hadn't she answered her mobile? Too busy, probably. But then . . .

I put out my cigarette and lit another.

Why hadn't she called me?

Even if she hadn't been overly concerned about my whereabouts last night – and I would have expected her to be a *bit* worried, at the very least – why hadn't she called me when she'd woken up this morning? Even if she'd slept in her flat, she must have realised I wasn't home. So why hadn't she tried ringing me? I checked the missed calls on my phone. There were seven, most of them from Cal or Ada, none from Bridget.

I called the pet shop.

Bridget's recorded message came on after just a few rings. *This is Hey Pets, your local pet store. We can't answer the phone at the moment, but if you'd like to leave a message and a contact phone number after the tone, we'll get back to you as soon as possible. Thank you!*

'Are you there, Bridge?' I said. 'It's me, John . . . pick up if you're there, please, I really need to talk to you.'

While I waited for a response, another thought struck me. Maybe she wasn't working at the shop today? I closed my eyes, trying to remember if she'd worked the day before . . . but for a moment or two I couldn't even remember what day it was now. Was it Friday today? Or Saturday? It was Saturday. Yes, it was definitely Saturday. But then I realised that it didn't matter what day it was, because I still couldn't remember if Bridget had worked the day before or not.

'Sarah?' I said into the phone. 'Hey, Sarah, are you—?'

The recording beeped and the line went dead.

I tried our home number. There was no answer, and we don't have an answering machine at home, so I couldn't leave a message.

I was beginning to worry about Bridget now. Where was she? Why wasn't she answering the phone? Had something happened to her? It did occur to me that she might be avoiding my calls on purpose, punishing me for staying out all night without getting in touch with her . . . but Bridget wasn't like that. She'd make sure I was OK first, find out why I hadn't come home before getting angry about anything. And she didn't know anything anyway. She didn't know where I was, who I was with, what I might or might not have done . . . she had no reason to be angry with me.

Well, she did . . . but she didn't know it.

I looked down at my mobile. There were six unopened text messages waiting for me, and it was highly unlikely that any of them were from Bridget – she doesn't like texting – but I checked them anyway. Three were from Cal, two were from Ada, and one was spam. I glanced at the email icon on the screen. I had five emails. I nearly didn't bother looking at them – why would Bridget email me? – but I was almost out of options now, and before I took things any further, I thought I might as well check them, just in case.

I opened my email box and scanned the inbox, dismissing the first four items almost immediately. Two book recommendations from Amazon, a final subscription reminder from the Association of British Investigators, and an urgent tax query from George Salvini, my accountant. But the fifth email . . . that was different. I didn't even glance at the sender's address, all I could look at, all I could *see*, was the subject heading. Six simple words, screaming out

179

at me from the screen, hammering blunt nails into my heart. I closed my eyes, praying for the words to go away, but when I opened my eyes again they were still there.

johnny and imogen hot sex pix!

It's hard to describe how I felt as I sat there staring at the screen – numb, sick, empty, confused . . . words aren't enough. I just didn't want it to *be* . . . whatever it was. I wanted it gone, never to have been. I wanted it out of my head. Those words . . . God, I could hardly bear to even look at them. But I couldn't stop looking, staring . . . hoping . . . it *could* just be a coincidence, couldn't it? Just a spam thing, no different to a million other spam messages, only this one just happened to include the names Johnny and Imogen. It wasn't impossible, was it? No one ever called me Johnny, did they? No one who knew me anyway. So maybe . . . maybe . . .

Maybe nothing.

I turned my attention to the sender's address. It was listed as *krubcr91346@alam.com*. It meant nothing to me.

I knew I had to open the email, if only to check the remote possibility that it wasn't as bad as I thought, but I had a terrible feeling that once I opened it my world was going to come tumbling down. So it wasn't easy, and it took me a while to actually do it – sitting there with my mobile in my hand, my thumb hovering over the screen, my hand trembling, my mouth bone dry . . . but eventually, after several failed attempts, I finally just did it.

'Fuck it,' I said, jabbing my thumb at the screen.

It wasn't as bad as I thought.

It was a whole lot worse.

There was no message with the email, no text at all, just four instantly recognisable photographs. They weren't very good quality – a bit grainy, poorly lit, taken at night with no flash – and they reminded me of the voyeuristic pictures of unsuspecting celebrities that the gutter press love to print – lovers kissing on a beach, or in a hotel room, their indiscretions captured by a smirking paparazzo with a telephoto lens. The photos in the email didn't show any celebrities though, they showed a somewhat weary-looking man in his early forties, dressed in a crumpled black suit, and a very beautiful black-haired woman in various states of undress. I doubted if these pictures had been taken by a paparazzo, but whoever had taken them had definitely used a telephoto lens. I knew that because I knew where they'd been taken from. It was obvious. I'd been there myself, last night. I'd stood at the far end of the garden, searching for what I'd thought was a figment of Imogen's imagination. I'd seen the flat from the end of the garden, I'd seen in through the curtainless windows, so I knew the photographs had been taken from out there. And I knew that the moments they captured had happened. I remembered them. They *had* happened. Of course, the photographs themselves didn't tell the truth of those moments, they told a different story altogether, and I knew – with a heavy heart – that it didn't matter how distorted that story was, because the camera never lies, does it?

The first picture showed us embracing in the kitchen. Imogen had her arms round my back, I was holding her, and it was quite clear that her dressing gown was undone. We were still in the kitchen in the next photograph, but we weren't holding each other any more. This one showed Imogen standing in front of me, her gown wide open, staring into my eyes, and I was just looking back at her. I was almost sure that I'd been staring into her eyes at the time, but that's not how it looked in the photo. It looked like I was gazing quite openly, if not hungrily, at her body.

The third photo showed Imogen kissing me in the bedroom. I was still dressed, but she was naked. She was lying on her back on the bed, pulling me down towards her, her arms round my neck, kissing me on the mouth. A split second later I'd pulled away and told her to get into bed, but of course there was no record of that. But there was evidence, in the last photograph, of the moment just after I'd told her to get into bed when she'd sat up, smiling, and wrapped her bare legs around my waist. And once again, because I hadn't immediately pushed her away, the picture gave the impression that I was perfectly happy with the position I was in. Who wouldn't be? I mean, there you are, sitting on a bed with a naked woman wrapping her legs round you . . . you're not going to push her off, are you?

Shit, I thought, lighting another cigarette. *If anyone sees these . . .*

And that's when I spotted it. A name, an all-too-familiar name in the details at the top of the email.

Subject: *johnny and imogen hot sex pix!*
Date: *19/01/2012 04:18:26 GMT Standard Time*
From: *krubcr91346@alam.com*
To: *jcrainepi@aol.com*
CC: *bridgetmoran876@aol.com, bridgetheypets@aol.com*

Now I knew why Bridget wasn't answering her phone. She'd seen the photographs. She did have a reason to be angry with me after all . . . she had reason enough to never want to see me again.

I stared blindly at her name on the screen . . . *bridgetmoran876@aol.com*

It was nine o'clock in the morning.

My world was tumbling down.

13

Imogen was in a pretty bad way when I woke her up. Hungover and sick, dazed, confused . . . she could barely even talk at first.

'Whassit . . .? No . . . *gaah* . . . *shee* . . .'

'You have to get up, Imogen,' I said firmly. 'I need to talk to you.'

'Wasstime?'

'It's just gone nine. Come on—'

'Shit,' she said, squeezing her eyes shut. 'Fucking *hell* . . .'

'Listen to me, Im,' I said. 'This is important—'

'God, my fucking head—'

'Please, Imogen. Just listen to me a minute.'

The tone in my voice got through to her, and she propped herself up, rubbed her eyes, and looked at me.

'I know you don't feel well,' I said. 'But something's happened, and I need to talk to you about it.'

'What? What's happened?'

'Get dressed,' I told her. 'I'll make you some coffee. And don't be long.'

While she was getting dressed, I put the kettle on and went out into the garden. Last night's snow lay thick and icy on the ground, covering the lawn in a pristine white blanket, so even if the photographer had left any telltale signs behind, I wasn't likely to find them. But I crunched my way across the lawn anyway, shivering in the cold morning air. When I reached the little fence above the bank, I stopped for a moment or two and took a quick look around, but there was nothing to see. I went over to the far end of the brick wall on the right, stopped again, then turned round and looked back at the flat. I was fairly sure that this was where the photographer had been hiding, probably just behind the wall, or off to one side, a little way down the bank. I edged behind the wall and looked back at the flat again. The angle seemed about right, the view of the windows from here roughly the same as that in the pictures. I looked down and gazed around the snow-covered ground, searching for anything that might prove me right – cigarette ends, footprints, chewing-gum wrappers . . . but if there was anything there, it was hidden beneath the snow.

I looked back at the flat again. Imogen was at the kitchen window, gulping down a glass of water. As she lowered the glass, ran her fingers through her hair, then frowned and put her hand to her forehead, I suddenly realised that I was watching her now just as the photographer had watched us both last night, and for the first time since I'd seen the pictures I began asking myself questions. Why would anyone want to take pictures of us? Who were they? And why send the photos to me and Bridget? What was the point of that? And, what's more, how did they know about me and Bridget?

It didn't make sense.

Unless I was missing something . . .

It just didn't make any sense at all.

I realised that Imogen was looking back at me through the window now, squinting painfully, shielding her eyes against the light. I nodded at her, and half-heartedly raised my hand, but I couldn't muster a smile. My world was fucked, her parents were dead, possibly murdered, and now I was about to go in there and show her the tawdry contents of an email entitled *johnny and imogen hot sex pix!*

What was there to smile about?

She didn't say anything as I explained everything to her, she just sat there quietly, listening intently, but I could see the colour draining slowly from her face, and when I finally opened the email and passed her my phone, and she stared in stricken silence at the pictures on the screen, I thought she was going to be physically sick. Her mouth dropped open and she leaned forward a little, putting her hand to her chest . . . then she closed her mouth, swallowing something down, and stifled a retch . . . and then finally she closed her eyes and began shaking her head from side to side, slowly and deliberately, groaning and cursing under her breath. I gave her a few moments, then reached over, gently took the phone from her hands, closed the email, and put the phone in my pocket.

'*God*, John . . . *Jesus*,' she muttered, still shaking her head. 'I don't know what to say . . . I can't . . . I've never felt so fucking . . . I mean, shit . . . fucking *shit*!'

'It's all right—'

'No, it's *not*. I mean, how *could* I? How could I be so fucking—?'

'It doesn't matter.'

'Of *course* it fucking matters! Look at what I *did* . . . it's dis*gust*ing. It's fucking *awful* . . .' She turned suddenly to me. 'Oh, Christ, John . . . what about Bridget? If she sees—'

'I think she already has.' I lit a cigarette. 'The email was copied to her, and she's not answering my calls . . . so, you know . . .'

'Oh, John,' Imogen sighed. 'I'm sorry . . . I'm *so* sorry . . . God, what was I *thinking*?'

'You were drunk,' I said simply.

'That's no excuse.'

'You don't need an excuse. All I'm saying is you were really drunk, that's all. You hadn't eaten anything, you were emotionally confused, grieving for your mum and dad—'

'Yeah, right,' she said bitterly. 'I was so full of grief that I spent the night getting pissed out of my head and acting like a whore.' She angrily shook her head. 'Very fucking *touching*.'

'There's no point dwelling on it,' I said. 'It happened, it's done, forget about it.'

'That's easy for you to say.'

'No, it's not,' I said, looking at her.

She looked back at me for a moment, slowly realising what I meant, then she sighed and shook her head again. 'This is worse for you than it is for me, isn't it? A lot worse.'

'Well, it's not great for either of us—'

'No, but it doesn't really make any difference to me if anyone else sees the pictures, does it?' She shrugged. 'I wouldn't like it, obviously, but it wouldn't be the end of the world . . . I mean, it wouldn't change anything. It wouldn't hurt anyone else.' She looked at me. 'But it's different for you, isn't it?'

'Yeah.'

'Sorry, John . . .'

'It's not your fault.'

She smiled sadly. 'It's me in the pictures, and that's all Bridget needs to know.'

I nodded.

'What are you going to do?' she said.

'I don't know . . . find her, talk to her, try to explain—'

'I'll talk to her.'

'What?'

'If I tell her what really happened . . . I mean, if I tell her that it was all me, and that you—'

'God, no,' I said, shaking my head.

'But—'

'Look, Imogen, I know you're only trying to help, but this is something I've got to sort out myself. All right?'

'Yeah, of course . . . if that's what you want.'

'It is.'

'OK . . .' She looked at me for a few moments, thinking about something, then she lowered her eyes and gazed at the floor. 'Did anything else happen last night?' she asked awkwardly. 'I mean, did we . . . you know?'

'I don't think so.'

She raised her eyes to me. 'You don't *think* so?'

'I was pretty drunk myself,' I admitted. 'All I can remember is sitting beside you on the bed last night, fully dressed, and the next thing I knew it was eight-thirty in the morning and I was in bed with you, and my clothes were on the floor.'

'But you can't remember if we—?'

'I can't remember anything.'

While she thought about that, rubbing the back of her neck and staring out of the window, I found myself thinking about the photographer again. They had to know me, I realised . . . or know *of* me, at least. They knew my email address. They knew about me and Bridget. They knew her email addresses, home and work. They knew she worked at the pet shop . . .

'It doesn't really matter, does it?' Imogen said.

'What doesn't?'

'If neither of us can remember if we slept together or not, and no one else can possibly know . . . well, that kind of makes it a non-thing, doesn't it?'

'A non-thing?'

'Not true, not false, not anything. Nothing.'

'Until one of us remembers. Then it becomes something.'

She nodded. 'Well, yeah . . .'

'Or if someone else *does* know.'

She looked at me.

'Check your emails,' I said.

She pulled a mobile from her pocket and started pressing keys. While she was doing that, I took out my phone and tried calling Bridget again. I rang her mobile, our landline, the pet shop . . . no one picked up. I put my phone away and turned back to Imogen. She was still pressing keys.

'Found anything?' I asked her.

She shook her head. 'Just the usual stuff.'

I sighed. 'That's what I don't get . . .'

'What do you mean?'

'Well, I'm just trying to understand the reasoning, you know . . . why would someone take pictures of us? I mean, I could understand if they were trying to blackmail one of us, or both of us, but the whole point of blackmail is to use whatever you've got on someone as a threat. You know, if you don't give me what I want, I'll send these pictures to your girlfriend. But there's no threat here, is there? They didn't ask me for anything, they just sent the photos to Bridget.'

'So we're not being blackmailed.'

I shook my head. 'And if it was just some pervert, some random weirdo with a voyeurism fetish, why bother sending the pictures to me? And how would he know who I was anyway?'

Imogen nodded. 'A perv might get a kick out of sending the photos to me.'

'But they haven't been sent to you.'

'No . . .'

'Just to me and Bridget.'

Imogen frowned. 'Why?'

'I don't know. I mean, that's what I can't work out. What's to gain from sending the pictures to Bridget? All it does, as far as I can see, is fuck up our relationship.' I looked at Imogen. 'Why would someone want to do that?'

'And how did they know you were here? Did you tell anyone you were coming here?'

'I didn't know I was coming here. Did you tell anyone?'

She shook her head. 'We must have been followed, John. Someone must have followed us from Lexden Vale.'

'Unless they were already here.'

She looked at me. 'But this isn't about *me*, is it? It's about you.'

'We don't know that.'

'We don't know anything.'

I lit a cigarette. 'We'd better start finding out then, hadn't we?'

'How?'

It was a good question. The trouble was, I didn't really have any answers. Apart from trying to trace the address the email was sent from, which I was pretty sure Cal could do, I couldn't think of anything else we could do just then. And besides, all I really wanted to do now was sort things out with Bridget. Or try to, at least.

'Have you got somewhere else you can stay for a while?' I asked Imogen, glancing at my watch.

'Why?'

'We don't know who was out there last night, do we? It's unlikely they'll come back again now that they've shown their hand, but I still don't think you should stay here on your own.'

Imogen shook her head. 'I'll put one of my people outside for a couple of nights, just to be on the safe side. But I'm not going anywhere, John. No one's going to force me out of my own home.'

'One of your people?' I said, trying to lighten the tone. 'Is that what you call them now, "your people"?'

She didn't smile back. 'You know what I mean.'

I nodded, wishing I hadn't said anything.

'You should get going,' Imogen said. 'You need to find Bridget.'

'I'll call a taxi—'

'No need,' she said. 'I'll drive you. I have to go into the office anyway.'

'I don't think that's a good idea. If Bridget sees me with you—'

'I'm not stupid, John. I mean, I'm not going to drive up to your house and park right outside, am I? Give me *some* credit . . .' She paused, almost managing a smile, but not quite. 'I don't suppose I deserve much credit, do I?'

While Imogen got ready to go – looking for her car keys, going to the bathroom – I went over to the coffee table, picked up the backing of the picture frame, and looked again at the words and the picture scratched into the metal. I hadn't got round to telling Imogen about it, and as she hadn't mentioned it, I guessed she hadn't seen it. I wondered if I should tell her about it now, but I quickly decided against it. She had enough to worry about as it was.

As she came out of the bathroom, and I slipped the metal sheet inside my jacket, a vague thought flashed through my mind: *what if all this is somehow connected? the fire at Leon's, the missing hard drives, the cryptic message, the emailed photographs of Imogen and me . . .?*

'Are you ready?' Imogen said, putting on her coat.

No, I thought, my mind turning to Bridget. *No, I'm not ready at all.*

'Yeah,' I said, 'let's go.'

14

The silence of an empty house is unmistakeable, the lack of presence hangs in the air like a shroud, and as soon as I opened our front door and went inside, I knew that Bridget wasn't there. I still had to double-check of course, but it didn't take long. A quick look in my flat, a brief glance out the back, then upstairs to Bridget's flat. Sitting room, bathroom, bedroom . . . all empty. I was just about to leave her bedroom when her open laptop caught my eye. It was on her dressing table, surrounded by the usual clutter of Bridget's stuff – make-up, perfume, jewellery . . . pots of this, tubes of that. I went over to the table, hesitated for a second, then reached down to the laptop and hit the return key. A quiet beep sounded, lights flashed, and Imogen's naked body appeared on the screen, smiling as she wrapped her legs round my waist . . .

It looked even worse on the laptop. Bigger, clearer, more realistic. But most of all, worst of all, it was *here* – on Bridget's laptop, on her dressing table, surrounded by *her* stuff . . . and she'd had to sit here, on her own, looking at it . . . looking at *that* . . .

I wanted to scream.

I wanted to throw the laptop against the wall, smash it to pieces, stamp on it, obliterate it, wipe those awful images from the face of the earth . . . I wanted to make them *gone*. But I knew they could never be gone now. Bridget had seen them, they'd be in her eyes for ever.

I turned off the laptop, went downstairs, went into my front room and put the metal backing from the picture frame in a drawer. I went into the kitchen and filled a glass from the tap, drank it down, then left the house and headed back up to the top of the street where Imogen was waiting for me in her BMW.

It was ten to eleven. The skies were low, the light dim and heavy, and the snow on the pavement was a dirty brown mush.

Hey Pets is situated halfway down Market Street on the west side of the shopping precinct. It's a strictly pedestrianised area of town, so Imogen dropped me off at a bus stop in the High Street, right next to a little lane that cuts through to the precinct.

'I can't wait for you here,' she said, glancing in the rear-view mirror, 'but if you give me a call when you need picking up—'

'Thanks,' I said, unbuckling my seat belt, 'but I'll be all right now.'

'You sure?'

I nodded, looking at her. 'Don't forget to let me know when you get the post-mortem results, OK?'

'Christ,' she said quietly, 'I almost forgot about that.'

'Will you be OK?'

'Yeah . . .' She breathed in. 'Yeah, I'll be fine. I'll call you as soon as I know anything.'

I nodded. 'And don't go home on your own.'

She tried a smile. 'I'll take one of my people with me.'

'Take a good one.'

'They're all good.'

'And let me know if anything happens, anything at all.'

'Yeah.'

'Right . . . well, I'd better get going.' I hesitated. 'I don't know when I'll get the chance to see you—'

'Don't worry about me,' she said, waving her hand. 'Just do whatever you've got to do, you know . . . put things right.'

There was an awkward little moment between us then, neither of us sure how to say goodbye after everything we'd been through. Could we still hug each other? Was a friendly kiss on the cheek still acceptable? The awkwardness was broken by the sudden angry blare of a horn as a bus pulled up behind us, almost ramming into the back of the BMW. The driver leaned out of his cab and yelled, '*It's a bus stop, wanker. Get out of the fucking way!*'

I grinned quickly at Imogen, said, 'See you later,' and got out of the car. As I hurried across to the pavement, I heard the bus driver calling out, '*Hey, HEY! What's the fucking matter with you? Can't you see it's a—?*' and then I heard Imogen's voice yelling back at him, cutting him off. '*Yeah, yeah, it's a bus stop . . . there's no need to shit your pants about it. I'm going, OK?*'

The quiet smile this brought to my face didn't last very long, and by the time I'd reached Market Street it wasn't even a distant memory. In fact, I was so sick with fear now, so eaten up with the prospect of having to face Bridget, or of finding out that she wasn't there, that it was difficult to imagine ever smiling again.

The street wasn't too busy – the New Year's sales were over, no one had any money left – but I was barely aware of the rest of the world anyway. I was locked away inside my head – thinking, dreading, hoping, remembering . . . and as I approached the pet shop, passing the boarded-up windows of an old-fashioned hardware store that had recently gone out of business, a particular memory suddenly came back to me.

It was the day I'd visited Bridget at the pet shop for the first time, just over two years ago. A cold Saturday afternoon in October. It had been raining all day, but as I'd made my way down Market Street, it was just beginning to ease. In the distance, patches of clear blue sky were breaking through the purple-grey blanket of cloud. The street was busy, but not so busy that I couldn't keep walking in a straight line, and it wasn't long before I found myself standing outside the pet shop, smoking a cigarette, wondering what the hell I was doing there. Why was my heart beating so hard? Why was my blood racing? And why did I have a tiny black planet spinning around inside my chest, whipping out threads of adrenaline? I'd stood there smoking my cigarette and staring at the ground, not knowing why I was there. Then I'd put out my cigarette and begun walking back the way I'd come . . . but after three or four steps I'd stopped, turned round, and gone back.

I couldn't help it, I remembered now. I'd felt sixteen years old again – stupid and pure, a blue-eyed animal, wanting and needing only this moment . . .

And here I was again, I realised, standing outside the pet shop, smoking a cigarette, not knowing what I was doing . . .

Nothing much changes, does it?

Same feelings, different causes.

Or maybe not so different . . .?

I put out my cigarette and went into the shop.

There were no customers inside, and no sign of Bridget. Sarah was there, kneeling down on the floor, stacking tins of dog food onto a shelf, and when the bell over the door sounded, she stopped what she was doing and looked over her shoulder at me. Expecting to see a customer, she began to smile, but the welcome in her eyes turned sour the instant she recognised me, and I knew then that she'd either seen the photos or Bridget had told her about them.

We looked at each other for a moment, not saying anything, and I breathed in the smell of the pet shop. It was a smell I never tired of: straw, hay, fish tanks, the rubbery tang of dog toys, the fresh leather scent of collars and leads . . .

Sarah placed a tin of dog food on the shelf and got to her feet. She was only slightly older than Bridget and me, somewhere in her mid- to late forties, but she'd always had an air of stuffiness and maturity about her that belied her age. She didn't look particularly old – fresh, freckled skin, an attractive face, reddish-brown hair cut in a bob – and she didn't dress like an older woman – she usually wore jeans and a jumper, as she was today – but there was just something about her that had always reminded me of a killjoy older sister. She'd known Bridget a long time, and they were very close friends, but Sarah and I had never really liked each other. We got on OK, we tolerated each other, but that was about it.

'Bridget's not here,' she said to me now, her voice as cold as her eyes.

'Where is she?'

'She doesn't want to see you.'

'Where is she?' I repeated, glancing over at a door at the back of the shop. The door led through into a combined storeroom/kitchen, and beyond that a narrow wooden staircase. The stairs gave access to a small flat upstairs – sitting room, bedroom, bathroom. Sarah had used the flat for a while after she'd split up with her husband, but it had been empty for some years now. I didn't think Bridget was up there. The flat was a bad place for her . . . for both of us. We'd been through a terrible experience up there a few years ago, something that had scarred us both, and as far as I knew she hadn't set foot in the place since.

'Is she upstairs?' I said to Sarah.

'I told you, she's not here.' She gave me an ugly look. 'How *could* you, John? How could you *do* that to her? I mean, good *God*—'

'It's nothing to do with you, Sarah. All I want—'

'You've ruined everything. You know that, don't you?'

'Look,' I sighed, trying to stay calm. 'I just want to talk to her, OK? Explain what really happened—'

'Oh, I think Bridget knows what happened. I mean, it's not as if . . . hold on, where do you think you're going?'

'Upstairs,' I said, walking past her.

She didn't say anything, didn't try to stop me, and I knew in my heart I was wasting my time. Bridget wasn't here. But I went upstairs anyway, checked the dusty little sitting room, the bedroom . . . still haunted with memories . . . the bathroom. She wasn't there. I went back downstairs.

'Satisfied?' Sarah sneered.

'Listen,' I said to her. 'Tell Bridget I'm sorry, but it's not what it looks like. Tell her I just want a chance to explain, that's all. After that . . . well, it's up to her. I'll do whatever she wants.' I looked hard at Sarah. 'Have you got that?'

She didn't reply, she just stood there, her arms crossed, glaring at me.

As I left her standing there and headed for the door, I could hear the birds fluttering softly in their cages, and the fish tanks bubbling quietly, and I wondered if I'd ever be here again. I opened the door, pausing for just a moment to savour the sounds and smells for perhaps the final time, and then I stepped out into the cold morning air and shut the door behind me.

I didn't bother looking for Bridget any more. She could be anywhere – at her sister's place in Devon, at Sarah's house, at a hotel somewhere – and despite Sarah's loathing for me, her understandable disgust at what she thought I'd done, I was reasonably sure she'd pass on my message to Bridget. And then . . . well, the way I saw it, Bridget would either give me a chance to explain or she wouldn't. And in the meantime, I might as well carry on living, doing what I do . . . no matter how fucking pointless it was.

*

I called Cal on my way to the taxi rank in the High Street, letting him know that I was on my way over to pick up my car. 'And if you've got time,' I added, 'there's a couple of things I need to see you about.'

He had plenty of time, he told me. And he had a few things to see me about too.

I waited until I was in the back of the taxi before calling Ada. Despite our lack of business, we still kept the office open on Saturday mornings, so I knew Ada would be there. I didn't really need to call her, but I hadn't seen her for a while as I hadn't been into the office, but most of all it stopped me from having to talk to the taxi driver.

'Anything I need to know?' I asked her.

'Well, if you answered your fucking phone now and then—'

'I've been busy,' I said.

'Doing what?'

'This and that . . .'

'Ayanna Osman keeps calling. She wants to know if you're making any progress.'

'If she calls again, tell her I'll ring her on Monday.'

'*Are* you making any progress?'

'Not really.'

'I told you, John. You should have listened—'

'Yeah, yeah, I know. Anything else?'

'Not that I can think of . . .'

'What, nothing?'

'A couple of enquiries on the website . . .'

'What kind of enquiries?'

'Someone's looking for a job, if you're interested. They've just left school, got four GCSEs, and they're *very* quick to learn.'

'Great.'

'Yeah, and someone else wanted to know if we offer reduced rates for people on benefits. I replied to that one.'

'Tactfully, I bet.'

'Told them to fuck off and get a job.'

I laughed.

'And George Salvini needs to see you about the tax. Says it's urgent.'

'Can't you deal with it? I thought you'd given him everything he needs anyway.'

'Yeah, but now he needs to know how you're going to pay.'

'What do you mean?'

'We're almost broke, John. We don't have enough money to pay the tax.'

'Shit.'

'That's why George needs to talk to you.'

'Yeah, all right . . . I'll sort it out next time I see him.'

'What are you doing now?'

'I'm on my way to Cal's. He's helping me out with a couple of things.'

'Is everything OK, John?'

'Yeah . . .'

'You sound a bit frazzled.'

'It's just . . . just stuff, you know.'

'Stuff?'

'Yeah, I'll tell you all about it when I see you.'

'Don't let it fester.'

'Right,' I said, smiling to myself. 'I'll bear that in mind.'

Cal was hyped up on something when I got there, jabbering away like a lunatic, buzzing around all over the place, and from the look of him, and the state of his flat – it looked like a typhoon had just blown through it – I guessed he'd been up all night working on something.

'What are you on?' I asked him as he showed me in and sat me down.

'D'you remember Barbarella,' he said, 'the acrobat . . .? She lived here for a while. We had a bit of a thing . . .?'

'The bendy girl?'

'Yeah.'

'How's that going?'

He shrugged. 'Haven't seen her for ages. She went to France, I think, got a job in a burlesque show or something. But it turned out she's got a twin sister, Celeste, and when Barb moved out Celeste moved in—'

'Celeste?'

'Yeah.'

'Is she bendy too?'

Cal grinned. 'She's *just* like Barbarella . . . I mean, they're *exactly* the same.'

'Like twins,' I said.

'Well, yeah . . . except Celeste's not an acrobat, she's a chemist.' He laughed. 'A fucking chemist, can you believe that? And she gets this stuff sometimes, you know . . . synthetic stuff? And most of it's legal too.'

'You mean like mephedrone, stuff like that?'

'Fuck knows what it is. I just take it.'

'Is it good?'

He looked at me. 'You wouldn't like it.'

'Why not?'

'It fucks with your brain.'

'That's what drugs are supposed to do.'

'Yeah, but this stuff . . .' He looked at me. 'I mean, it's not a good idea to take it if you're a bit . . .'

'A bit what? Unstable?'

He smiled awkwardly. 'I didn't mean—'

'Or am I just too old for your fancy new drugs?'

He grinned. 'You can try some if you want.'

'Have you got anything else? Any old-fashioned drugs?'

'Like what? Opium?'

'I'd prefer a bit of speed.'

He lit a cigarette, puffed thoughtfully on it, and blew out a stream of smoke. 'I thought you were being a good boy these days?'

I gave him a look. He stared back at me for a moment, his eyes like saucers, then reached into his pocket.

'It's sulphate,' he said, passing me a wrap. 'But it's really strong, so don't take too much.'

'Thanks,' I said, taking the wrap from him. I opened it up, pinched out a little onto the back of my hand, and snorted it. It kicked in almost immediately, lighting me up with a brain-bursting surge that nearly blew my head off. '*Fuck!*' I gasped, sniffing hard. 'Jesus *Christ!*'

'I told you,' Cal said.

'Shit . . .'

203

'You all right?'

I nodded, wiping snot from my nose. 'Got anything to drink?'

He hesitated for a second, concerned for my welfare, as he always was, but he didn't say anything, just crossed over to a drinks cabinet, took out a crystal tumbler and a bottle of Johnny Walker Black Label, and brought them back over to me.

'Thanks, Cal,' I said, pouring a few inches into the glass.

'You look like shit, John,' he said.

'Thanks again.'

'You know what I mean.'

I nodded, taking a good long drink, sighing as the whisky went down . . . and just for a moment everything felt OK. Everything and nothing . . . all at once. Like a golden dream. I lit a cigarette and leaned back, blowing smoke at the ceiling, savouring what I knew would never last.

When Cal began telling me what he'd found out, it took me a while to work out what he was talking about. He just started rambling on about people he'd spoken to, and what they'd told him, pacing around all over the place as he talked, and it wasn't until he mentioned something about the Somali community that I remembered what this was all about. I'd asked Cal to look into the local gangs for me. He was going to find out what he could about the gangs and . . . what else was it? Something else to do with the Jamaal Tan case . . ?

I couldn't remember. It was a long time ago. Yesterday . . .

Yesterday was a long time ago.

'. . . and there's been a Somali community at Redhills

for years,' Cal was saying. 'Most of them came over in the early nineties when all that shit was going on in Somalia, you know, the war and everything, but the gang stuff is all pretty recent. Most of the gang kids come from families who moved here from London. There's not that many of them yet, and they're still not major players or anything, but they're getting there. And they don't mess around, you know? They can be really nasty fuckers if they need to be.'

'What are they into?'

'Whatever they can get at the moment. Skunk, Es, ketamine . . .'

'Crack?'

Cal shook his head. 'Not really. The Chinese have still got most of the crack and heroin trade. There's two Chinese gangs, both based across the river, but although they're separate outfits they work together most of the time, so they're pretty strong. And they've got a lot more manpower than the Somalis.'

'Are they fighting each other?'

He frowned. 'It's hard to tell . . . there's definitely been *some* trouble between them – a few stabbings, kids getting beaten up, stuff like that. And some of it sounds pretty vicious. But I also heard that they struck some kind of a deal for a while, a partnership . . .'

'The Chinese and the Somalis?'

He nodded. 'It didn't last very long, apparently. But the guy I was talking to said he wouldn't be surprised if it happened again. The Chinese don't want a war, the Somalis want in on the big stuff . . .' Cal shrugged. 'It kind of makes sense to join forces.'

I nodded, feigning interest. Cal had clearly put a lot of work into all this, and his eagerness to impress with his findings was so ardent that I didn't have the heart to tell him that I just wasn't interested any more. And besides, it was kind of nice just sitting there, half-listening to him, not really thinking about anything. It was a welcome change.

'Did you find out if Jamaal was involved with the gangs?' I asked him, refilling my glass.

Cal waggled his hand – maybe, maybe not. 'He hung around with them sometimes, both the Somalis and the Chinese, and he probably did a bit of running for them now and then, maybe even a bit of small-time dealing, but – as far as I can tell – that was about it.'

'Did he buy his own stuff from them?'

Cal nodded. 'He'd have to . . . anyone using crack or heroin round here gets their stuff from the Chinese. Not directly, of course, but that's where it all comes from. And even if you do find another source . . . well, if the Chinese find out you're buying from someone else, they don't just put your new supplier out of business, they put you out of business too.'

'So maybe Jamaal was buying from someone else, and the Chinese found out.'

'It's possible,' Cal said. 'But they don't usually fuck about when they hurt people. They just hurt them. Jamaal was sexually assaulted, wasn't he?'

I nodded. 'Raped.'

'I don't think the Chinese would do that. Some of the Somali kids can be pretty brutal, but . . .' He shook his head. 'I don't know. I'm only guessing about all this . . . anyone could have done it, I suppose. I mean, Chinese, Somali . . . they're all just people, aren't they? And people can do anything, wherever they're from.'

'That's true.'

'There's one thing I *am* pretty sure about though.'

'What's that?'

'Whoever killed Jamaal, it wasn't the guy that Lilley told you about, the one they've already got in custody.'

That was the other thing I'd asked him to look into. I remembered now . . . we'd spent some time talking about which areas of the case we needed to focus on, and eventually we'd decided to concentrate on two separate angles: the local gangs, and the story about the killer who was already in custody.

According to Cal, his name was Kassim Mukhtar. He was twenty-four years old, unemployed, and he lived on the Redhills estate. He was arrested on 13 November last year and charged with the murder of a nineteen-year-old man called Johnson Geele. Three days earlier, Geele had been attacked outside a pub called The Wyvern, a notorious trouble spot in the Quayside area of town. Despite suffering multiple stab wounds, Geele survived long enough to name his attacker, and Mukhtar was arrested and taken in for questioning the day after the attack. Geele died from his injuries on 12 November, and Mukhtar was subsequently charged with his murder.

'No one in the pub saw anything, of course,' Cal said, 'so the prosecution don't have any witnesses, but they've got a knife with Mukhtar's prints on, and forensics found traces of Geele's blood on his trainers, so I can't see him getting away with it.'

'Was it a gang thing?' I asked.

Cal shook his head. 'Mukhtar runs with the Somalis, and he's pretty high up, but everyone I've talked to says this was just a fight over nothing. Geele dissed Mukhtar about something, or Mukhtar thought he did . . . you know what it's like. Geele probably just looked at him the wrong way, or bumped into him at the bar or something . . .'

'So Mukhtar killed him.'

Cal nodded. 'But he didn't kill Jamaal Tan.'

'Who says he did?'

'Lilley did—'

'No, he didn't. All he said was that they knew who the killer was, and they already had him in custody for another murder. Lilley never gave me a name.'

'Right, sorry,' Cal said, 'I forgot to tell you that bit . . .' He paused for a moment, lighting a cigarette, then went on. 'I went through the police and court records for the last twelve months and pulled out all the murder cases investigated by Hey CID. I narrowed down the list to cases that haven't come to trial yet, then narrowed that down to cases in which the suspect is still in custody, and that gave me three names. One of them's a seventy-two-year-old woman who's alleged to have put rat poison in her husband's tea. I discounted her. Then there's that case that was in all the papers a while ago, the guy who ran over his wife's boyfriend . . . remember that?'

I nodded. 'The really fat guy . . . he'd drunk two bottles of vodka or something.'

'Yeah, and I didn't think he fitted the bill.'

'And the third one was Mukhtar?'

'Correct.'

'And he does fit the bill?'

'I can't see how it could be anyone else, John. Based on what Lilley told you, the suspect he's claiming to have killed Jamaal has to be Kassim Mukhtar.'

'And why don't you think he did it?'

'Because Mukhtar wasn't even in Hey when Jamaal was killed.' Cal pulled a sheet of paper from his pocket and unfolded it. 'This is a printout from the custody record at Bethnal Green police station.' He glanced at me, quietly pleased with himself, then looked back at the printout. 'On 27 August last year,' he said, 'the date Jamaal Tan was murdered, Kassim Mukhtar was being held in a cell at Bethnal Green. He was arrested on suspicion of possession of a controlled drug at 3.15 a.m. on 26 August. He was then held for questioning for an initial twenty-four hours, subsequently extended to thirty-six hours, and he was finally released without charge at 14.20 on 27 August.' Cal looked up at me. 'Jamaal's body was found at six o'clock that morning.'

'So Kassim Mukhtar couldn't have killed him.'

'Nope.'

'Lilley was lying.'

'Yep.'

'Do you think Lilley knows that Mukhtar couldn't have done it?'

Cal shrugged. 'I doubt it . . . I mean, why would they try to frame him if they knew he had a cast-iron alibi?

And we don't even know if they are trying to frame him, do we? For all we know, Lilley just made the whole thing up to keep you quiet.'

I lit a cigarette and gave it some thought . . . not a lot of thought, admittedly, and it only really interested me in a purely abstract sense. It was a puzzle, something to think about for a few minutes, nothing more. It didn't *concern* me.

'What do you think?' Cal asked.

I drank more whisky. 'You've done a really good job, Cal.'

'I know that. But what do you think about—?'

'Did you get anywhere with Leon's emails?'

He looked at me for a moment, surprised by the sudden change of subject, and maybe a little disappointed too, but he didn't stay down for long. He had cyber stuff to tell me about now. I could see the joy in his spaced-out eyes.

There are various methods of deleting unwanted emails, most of which don't actually delete them at all, they just put them somewhere else, or write over them. And even if a computer's hard drive is removed and destroyed, the user's email account can still be accessed. All you need is their email address and password.

'And if you don't know their password,' Cal explained, 'it still doesn't matter. I mean, it helps to have it, obviously. It makes things a lot quicker. But if you know what you're doing, cracking a password is a piece of piss.' He looked at me. 'But that wasn't the problem. The problem was . . . once I'd got Leon's password, which took me all of two minutes, I couldn't find any trace of his account.'

'What do you mean?'

'It's really hard to explain . . .' He shook his head. 'I've never come across anything like it before. I mean, I've hacked into accounts that have been closed down, but this was different. This was . . . I don't know. It just wasn't *there* any more. It was like there was a totally blank space where Leon's email account should have been.'

'So you couldn't check anything?'

'There's nothing *to* check. It's all gone . . . everything. Believe me, if there was anything to find, I would have found it. But there's nothing left, absolutely nothing . . . and that's really weird. I mean, even *I* couldn't hack into an account and delete it without leaving *some*thing behind. You always leave something behind – either tiny remnants of what used to be there, or minute traces of your presence, byte-sized cyber footprints . . .' He shook his head again. 'It's virtually impossible to leave no trace at all.'

'Who could have done it then? I mean, if it's that unusual—'

'It's scarily unusual, John. That's what I'm trying to tell you. Whoever did this, they're not only seriously good, but I can't see how they could have done it using commercially available equipment.'

'What does that mean?'

Cal grinned. 'They must have used a *really* big computer.'

'And what does that mean?'

'Well, all kinds of organisations use computing systems powerful enough to do something like this – laboratories, universities, research facilities – but I think it's more likely, all things considered, that this was some kind of spooks operation. I mean, it's the kind of thing they do, and they've got the equipment to do it—'

'Spooks?' I said. 'Are you sure?'

He shrugged. 'Spooks, cops . . . it's hard to tell the difference these days. You've got your counter-terrorism units, SOCA, MI5, JIC, GCHQ, Special Branch . . . and that's just the ones we know about. They're all spooky bastards, John, and they're all over the fucking place.'

'But why would anyone like that want to wipe Leon's emails?'

'For the same reason they took his hard drives.'

'There was something on them they didn't want anyone else to see.'

Cal nodded. 'Proof of something, probably.'

'Like what?'

'Who knows? Something Leon was working on, something he'd found out, something he'd stumbled across . . .' He looked at me. 'Whatever it was, someone was desperate to keep it quiet.'

'Desperate enough to kill him?'

'Why bother taking his hard drives and wiping his emails if you're *not* going to kill him? They'd have to, wouldn't they? Otherwise he'd talk.'

I nodded slowly, sipping whisky. 'And Claudia too . . . if they killed Leon, they'd have to kill her.'

'And then burn the house down to make it look like an accident . . .'

'And get rid of any forensic evidence.'

'Exactly,' Cal said.

I lit a cigarette and smoked it quietly for a while. There

was little doubt in my mind now that Leon and Claudia had been murdered, and that their killer, or more likely killers, hadn't acted on the spur of the moment. The whole thing had to have been planned – the fire, the hard drives, the emails . . . the fire investigator's lies, the decorating stuff, the sleeping pills – it was a complex operation. Professional, resourceful, coldly efficient . . . a crime carried out with such skill and precision that it was virtually impossible to prove.

But they'd missed something.

They'd missed the rose . . .

Leon's rose. His message to me.

Whoever they were, however fucking professional they were, they didn't know about that. No one did. And I aimed to keep it that way.

'Listen, Cal,' I said, pulling out my mobile, 'I've got to get going in a minute, but I need you to check something else for me.' I glanced down at my phone and opened my emails. 'It's an address,' I told Cal. 'An email address . . . I need to find out who sent me something.'

'No problem,' he said, holding out his hand for my phone. 'Let me see.'

I hesitated. 'You don't have to do it right now—'

'It won't take a minute.'

'Can't I just give you the address and get going?'

'Well, yeah, but . . . what's the matter?'

'Nothing. I'm just a bit late for something, that's all. I really do have to get going.'

He smiled. 'You're no good at it, John.'

'No good at what?'

'Lying.'

'I'm not lying . . . I'm just . . .' I sighed, looking at him. He was still smiling at me. 'It's kind of awkward,' I said. 'A bit embarrassing.'

'You know me, John,' he said. 'I'm the soul of discretion.'

I gave him a look.

He stopped smiling. 'Is it important?'

'It might be.'

He nodded. 'You can just leave me the address if you want, and I'll see what I can do. If it's a straightforward trace, it won't be a problem. But if it's anything more . . . I mean, if the sender doesn't want to be found, I'm going to need the actual email.' He looked at me. 'It's up to you, John. I'll do whatever you want.'

I thought it over for a second or two, but I already knew what I had to do. I sighed again, opened the email, and passed the phone to Cal.

15

I should have known that Cal wouldn't be bothered by the photographs of Imogen and me, and once I'd got over the initial embarrassment of sharing them with him, I felt kind of stupid for having any doubts in the first place. He was a bit surprised by the pictures, of course, but he certainly wasn't shocked – it takes a lot more than a few risqué photos to shock Cal – and when I told him what had really happened, he just accepted it without so much as a raised eyebrow. No questions, no criticism, no judgement. But although the photographs themselves didn't bother him, there was a lot about them that did, and as he went over to a worktop and sat down, plugged my mobile into one of his laptops and began downloading the email, I could see the concern growing in his eyes.

'Do you think Bridget will believe you when you tell her nothing happened with Imogen?' he said, staring at the laptop screen.

'I don't know . . . what do you think?'

'Well, *I* believe you . . . but I'm not your girlfriend.'

'Why do you believe me?'

His fingers skipped rapidly over the keyboard. 'You don't have any reason to lie to me.'

'I don't have any reason to lie to Bridget,' I said, going over to stand behind him.

'Yeah, but you would if you *had* fucked Imogen.'

'Christ, Cal . . .'

'What? That's what it's all about, isn't it? Whether you fucked her or not.' He grinned. 'What do you want me to call it? Making *lurve*? Sleeping together.' He leaned forward and studied something on the screen. I leaned forward too, but all I could see was a nonsensical stream of numbers and letters. 'Do you want me to find out where she is?' Cal said.

'Bridget?'

He nodded. 'I can trace her mobile if you want. It won't take long.'

'No . . . thanks, but I think I'll just wait for her to get in touch.'

'OK, but if you change your mind . . .' He leaned back, frowning at the laptop. 'Shit, this is fucking odd.'

'What?'

'Well, the email itself, for a start. I mean, it's obviously a fake, sent via a disposable and anonymous account that's been set up using a series of proxy IP addresses, but it just doesn't look like any fake account I've ever seen, and I've tracked down thousands of the fuckers. I've actually created quite a few myself. They're not all identical, of course, but the differences between them are mostly superficial. Underneath it all, they all share the same basic structure.' He lit a cigarette. 'But this one is totally different. It doesn't look the same as the rest, it works differently, and it's much *much* harder to trace.'

216

Cal pressed a key on the laptop, bringing up a map of the world. 'This is a simplified schematic of a trace,' he said, pointing out a network of black lines connecting dozens of red spots in dozens of different countries. 'It's not a true representation of the actual tracking process, but it gives you an idea of what a trace on a normal anonymous account looks like. The software tracks the account from proxy server to proxy server, following the false trails all over the world, until eventually it comes up with a genuine originating location. It can take hours, even days sometimes, but there's always a pattern to the data you're getting back, and you can usually tell from the pattern how close you're getting to the target.' He hit another key, and another map of the world came up, but there was no network of lines and spots on this one, just a single red mark surrounded by a tangled circle of overlapping lines. 'This is the trace on your email,' Cal said. 'And as you can see, it's nothing like the other one. It's nothing like *anything* . . .' He shook his head. 'It's fucking weird, John. That's what it is.'

The location of the circled mark was somewhere in the middle of the Atlantic Ocean.

'Is there anything there?' I asked Cal.

'Fuck knows . . . I doubt it. I mean, there shouldn't be anything there. And even if there is, it's not telling me anything. I'm getting no data from the trace, it's not taking me anywhere. It's not going anywhere.'

'Does that mean you can't track it?'

'Pretty much, yeah. I can try a few other things, and you never know, they might work . . . but from what I've seen so far, I'd be very surprised.' He looked at me. 'This is as good a cyber wall as I've ever seen, John.'

'As good as the removal of Leon's emails?'

'On the same level, yeah.'

We looked at each other, both thinking the same thing. Same level, same kind of job, same family targeted. Leon's emails anonymously wiped, his daughter's privacy anonymously invaded.

'It's got to be connected,' Cal said.

'Yeah . . . but how do *I* come into it? The pictures were emailed to me and Bridget, no one else.'

'Not that you know of.'

I nodded. 'But why send them to us? What does it achieve?'

'It threatens your relationship.'

'Yeah, but what does that achieve?'

'It worries you, unbalances you.'

'I'm not unbalanced.'

He glanced at the tumbler in my hand. 'It's not even midday yet and you've already had four or five whiskies and a good snort of speed . . . that's hardly the behaviour of a well-balanced man, is it?'

I glared at him. 'What are you trying to say?'

'There's no need to get snotty with me, John, I'm not having a go at you. I'm just thinking out loud, you know . . . I mean, just think about it. Leon and Claudia are murdered, their house deliberately burned down. You meet Imogen at the house, you go inside and poke around, you go back to her place. Next thing you know, incriminating pictures of you and Imogen are emailed anonymously to

218

your girlfriend.' Cal looked at me. 'If I'd killed Leon and Claudia, and I thought you were nosing around too much, it might occur to me to send you a little warning. You know, this is what we can do, this is how easily we can fuck you up . . .'

'But they couldn't have known anything was going to happen at Imogen's place, could they? No one even knew I was going there, let alone what might happen.'

'If you're following someone, do you know what's going to happen?'

'Well, no . . .'

'You might be *trying* to get something on the person you're following, proof that they're faking an industrial injury or something, but you don't know you're going to get it, do you? You just keep following them, keep watching them, and hope that something happens.'

'Christ,' I muttered, shaking my head.

'Well . . . we could be wrong. I mean, it's possible . . . we could be completely mistaken about everything.'

'Yeah, and I *could* win this year's Most Well-Balanced Detective Award.'

We carried on talking for a while, batting things around, trying to come up with some answers, but we didn't really get very far. Cal said he'd keep looking into the emails, try out some different approaches, and I told him there were a couple of things I had to check out. I didn't tell him what they were, and he didn't ask.

'I'll let you know if I find anything,' I said as he showed me out of the house.

He nodded. 'Are you all right to drive?'

'Why shouldn't I be?'

'You've had a few drinks, John.'

'I drive better when I'm drunk.'

'You couldn't drive any worse.'

I smiled. 'I'll be all right.'

'Keep your eyes open, OK?'

'Yeah.'

'And try not to get into any more compromising positions with naked ladies.'

I didn't *feel* too drunk to drive, especially after another big snort of speed, but I knew I was well over the limit, so I started off driving as inconspicuously as I could – not too fast, not too slow . . . not *too* anything – but after a while, when the speed kicked in, I began to wonder if I was driving *too* inconspicuously, and that was such a distracting notion – how the hell do you drive in a not *too* inconspicuous manner? – that in my confusion I almost went through a red light. So I gave up trying to be unnoticeable.

'Don't think about it, for Christ's sake,' I told myself. 'Just fucking drive.'

I didn't see anyone following me, and I'd been keeping my eyes open from the moment I'd left Cal's house, but I knew that didn't necessarily mean anything. If I was being followed by someone who knew what they were doing, I probably wouldn't spot them anyway. So I didn't take any chances.

When I got to Stangate and turned off into the steep little lane that leads up to St Leonard's church, I pulled in at a passing-point about halfway up the lane, stopped the car, and turned off the engine. It was a narrow lane, barely wide enough for two cars to pass, and from where I was parked I could see the junction behind me. I lit a cigarette, adjusted the rear-view mirror, and waited.

After five minutes, only one person had driven past, a tweedy old woman in a blue Citroën estate. Ten minutes later, she passed me again, heading back the way she'd come, this time with an Afghan hound in the back of the car. I gave it another five minutes, passing the time by smoking cigarettes and trying to figure out the story behind the tweedy woman and the dog – was it hers? where had she just been to get it? why had it been there? had someone been looking after it for her? – and then I got out of the car, took another good look around, and started walking up the hill.

The skies were still dark and heavy, the air cut with an icy chill, and a white wind of sleet was blowing across the fields beyond the church. As I opened the church gate and headed round the back to the graveyard, I suddenly thought – for no reason at all – that I wasn't going to see what I expected to see. The feeling just took hold of me that something here was going to be different today – changed, moved, disturbed . . . not the same as the last time. It was the kind of feeling that flutters in your heart, unknown and uncalled for, beyond any rational control. But as I weaved my way along the gravel paths between the grave-stones, nothing seemed out of place, and when I reached the far side of the graveyard and stopped in front of my parents' graves, everything looked just as it should – the wooden bench, the matching granite gravestones, standing side by side, the grey granite vases of flowers, white irises for my mother, yellow roses for my father. The flowers were three days older than the last time I'd seen them, and the snow and ice had taken their toll – the frost-ravaged petals almost gone, the limp stems wilting sadly in the vases. As I brushed sleet from the bench and sat down, I realised that without Leon's care the graves would soon become wild and overgrown, the flowers rotted to nothing, and I promised myself, there and then, that I wasn't going to let that happen. It wasn't as if it was much of a chore, was it? A trip out here once a month to tidy things up and refresh the flowers . . . I could do that, couldn't I?

I *would* do it.

I lit a cigarette.

The smoke blew away in the cold white wind, taking my promise with it.

I sat there for a while, finishing my cigarette, then I got to my feet, turned round, and looked out over the graveyard and the church. There was no one in sight. I hadn't heard any approaching cars while I'd been here, and there was no sign of any vehicles in the lane beyond the church. As far as I could tell, I was on my own.

I went over to my father's grave, looked around once more, then crouched down in front of it. The granite vase had a perforated metal lid for holding the flowers in place. I removed the almost-dead stems, lifted off the lid, then angled the vase towards me and looked inside. There was a foam block at the bottom, a green cube, about four inches square. I reached into the vase and pulled it out. It

222

was one of those absorbent foam blocks that flower arrangers use to hold flowers in place and keep them watered. I turned it over in my hand. A section had been cut out from the bottom half of the cube, about three inches square, and some kind of package had been jammed inside the resulting space. A small black plastic package, wrapped with waterproof parcel tape. It was a tight fit, and I had to break an edge off the foam block to remove it. I studied the package for a while, examining it, feeling it, gently squeezing it, but it was wrapped so well that there was no way of telling what was inside. I stood up, went back over to the bench, looked around again, then sat down and got to work on the package.

It took me a while to get the tape off – picking at it with my fingernails, trying to find a loose edge – but I got there in the end. And then I started unwrapping the black plastic sheeting itself. It was a single sheet of polythene, probably cut from a bin-liner, and it had been wrapped so many times around whatever lay inside that by the time I'd almost finished unravelling it I began to wonder if there was actually anything inside.

But there was.

At the heart of the layers of black polythene wrapping was a small clear-plastic bag with an airtight seal, and inside the bag was a memory stick. I opened the bag and carefully tipped the small white stick into the palm of my hand. It was an 8GB Sony flash drive. It didn't look like much – a slim chunk of white plastic, no more than an inch and a bit long, with one end slightly tapered and the other end edged with a strip of clear plastic . . . it didn't look like much at all. But as I closed my hand around it and glanced over my shoulder again, I knew that it could be everything.

If ever you have any questions, John, and I'm not here to answer them . . .

Before leaving, I put the foam block and the wilting yellow roses back in the vase, and replaced the vase at the base of my father's gravestone. Then I slipped the memory stick back in the plastic bag, put the bag in my pocket, and headed back to the car.

I took a few basic precautions on the way back to Hey – making four right turns in a row, driving down a couple of no-through roads – but I knew in my heart that I was probably wasting my time. Even if I was being followed, whoever was following me was bound to know where I lived, and where I worked, and where the people I knew lived and worked, so even if I did shake them off, it didn't really make any difference. They'd still know where to find me. I did consider going somewhere else to see what was on the memory stick – an Internet café perhaps, or maybe the library – but I was cold and wet, and the speed was wearing off, and I needed a drink . . .

I needed to go home.

The house was still draped in its empty silence when I got back, the hallway cold and gloomy, the post uncollected on the floor. I hadn't really expected Bridget to be there, and there was no good reason she should be, but I couldn't help hoping . . .

Hoping against hope.

She wasn't there. Of course she wasn't there.

I went into my flat, turned on the gas fire, and changed into some dry clothes. A quick visit to the bathroom, then I went back into the bedroom, picked up my laptop, and took it into the front room. The house was cold, the windows dragged with snow, the room greyed in the dead winter light. I poured myself a stiff drink, took the bottle and glass over to the settee in front of the fire, sat down, and turned on the laptop. While it was booting up, I snorted two pinches of sulphate, chased the speed down with whisky, and lit a cigarette.

Now I felt OK . . .

Ready for anything.

Everything and nothing . . .

Another golden dream.

They might never last, but you can always find another.

I fished Leon's memory stick from my pocket, took it out of the bag, and slotted it into the laptop.

There were three files on the flash drive: two Word files and an audio file. One of the Word files was named *1PASSWORD*, the other one *2JOHN*, and the audio file was called *3PATH*. I opened the *1PASSWORD* file.

It read simply: Password for 2JOHN = the man who kidnapped his own dog.

Wilson Charteris, I thought immediately, smiling at the memory. Charteris was one of my very first clients. A wealthy man who'd fallen on hard times, and lost most of his sanity in the process, he'd hired me to find his missing dog, a black labrador called Duke, who he claimed had been kidnapped. It didn't take long to solve the case as it turned out that Wilson Charteris was a lot crazier than I'd thought, and he'd actually kidnapped Duke himself. I'd found the dog in the basement of Charteris's house, gnawing happily on a bone. And Charteris had still paid me.

I closed the *1PASSWORD* file and double-clicked the one named *2JOHN*. When the password request came up, I typed in *CHARTERIS*, and the file opened. I paused for a moment, taking a drink, then began to read.

Hello John,

I don't know why I picked Charteris. I was trying to think of a password, something that only the two of us would know, and he suddenly just popped into my head. I haven't thought about him in years. I wonder if he's still alive?

Talking of which, I won't be alive if you're reading this. That's the plan anyway. I don't know how long I have left at the moment, but I don't expect to last much more than another six months or so. When the time comes, and hopefully I'll know when it's coming, my intention is to give you every-thing I have before I go. In which case, you'll never need to read this. If the cancer takes me suddenly, and I don't get a chance to discuss things with you, I've already left instructions for you with Claudia. She has a clue to another password that will give you access to my files, but in order to secure her safety, I've told her nothing of what

I've been doing, and I'd ask you to do the same.

So much for my natural death.

But if you are reading this, John, it's almost certain that my death was unnatural (how strange it is to be talking about my own demise in the past tense!). It may be the case that I fall victim to a straightforward murder, but it's far more likely that my death will be made to look like an accident. Or quite possibly suicide. An accidental death is always possible, of course, so I can't rule out that possibility, but whatever it looks like, John, however accidental it appears, it will almost certainly be murder. And as to suicide, I can assure you, quite categorically, that if my death looks like suicide, it's been faked.

Just as your father's was.

I had to stop reading then. My breath had caught in my throat, and for a few numbing moments I couldn't seem to do anything about it. Couldn't let it out, couldn't breathe it in . . . I couldn't swallow. There was nothing there. I forced myself to move, straightening my back and raising my head, tearing my eyes from the shock of the words on screen . . . *suicide, it's been faked. Just as your father's was*. . . and with an involuntary jerk of my neck, I suddenly gulped down a lungful of air.

I sat there for a few seconds, breathing in through my nose – which seemed to help calm me, for some reason – and once my heart had begun to slow down, I refilled my glass, took a few measured sips, and turned my eyes back to the screen.

That's what this is all about, John. Your father. As you know, I've always had my suspicions about Jim's suicide, but for a long time that's all they were, unfounded suspicions. I had no proof that he didn't kill himself. Indeed, every piece of evidence supported the verdict. He left a note. He admitted to the affair with Ms Mayo. He was under investigation for corruption. The pathologist's findings were consistent with suicide. And, of course, he'd suffered from depression for most of his life. There was nothing to suggest his death was anything but suicide. But I knew Jim better than anyone. We worked together for many years, we were close friends for many years. He was like a brother to me. And I knew in my heart that he would never take his own life.

I think I might have told you once that I couldn't understand why your father had locked his office door before shooting himself. That never made sense to me. Why would he lock the door if he was going to kill himself? What purpose could it serve? Alice wasn't at home, so there was no chance of him being disturbed. And he would have known that a locked door wouldn't have kept her out of his office when she returned, it would only have served to alarm her. Why would Jim want to alarm her before she'd even found his body? And as for the theory that a suicide victim will lock the door in order to warn their loved ones of the shock that awaits them . . . well perhaps, in some cases, that's true. But I've always felt, deep in my heart, that Jim would never have locked that door.

And for a long time my heart was all I had to go on.

But over the last five years or so I've had a lot of spare time on my hands, a lot of time to think about things, to ask questions, make enquiries, to prove my suspicions. And although I still don't have incontrovertible proof that Jim was murdered, I have enough circumstantial evidence to put it beyond doubt. Whether that evidence is strong enough for a realistic prospect of conviction after all these years, that's another question. But your father was murdered, John. There's no question about it. Mick Bishop killed him. Jim was about to reveal something that would bring Bishop down, so Bishop decided to get rid of him. He shot him dead, placed the gun in his hand, locked the office door from the inside, and went out through the window. I still don't know for sure how he got Jim to write the suicide note (and there's no doubt that Jim did write it), but for a man like Bishop it wouldn't have been difficult.

The evidence is all there, John. Everything you need to know is in the files on my computer. There are no hard copies. Paper is too fragile, and too insecure, for information of this nature. And I've also decided not to make duplicates of the computer files. This means, of course, that the original files are the only files, and if they're lost or stolen or destroyed, the information they contain can't be retrieved. Which pains me to imagine, I have to admit. But the alternative is even more painful to imagine, because the more copies there are, the more chances there are of the files falling into the wrong hands, and if that were to happen, the consequences could be disastrous. Innocent people could suffer, perhaps lose their lives. And I'm not going to let that happen.

I can only hope I've made the right decision. But if not, the audio file 3PATH is my insurance. If all the other files have been destroyed or stolen, you'll still have this one, and while the evidence it contains is absolutely central to everything, it poses no threat to the innocent. You'll understand when you listen to it.

One last thing, John. I've taken every possible precaution over the years to keep Bishop from getting wind of my enquiries. Of course, I knew from the start that I couldn't keep everything from him, but as long as he thought I was just a cancer-ridden old man, bumbling away in the dark, asking the odd irritating question, I was reasonably sure he wouldn't bother me. But it goes without saying that if he does get to know what I have on him – and we both know there's very little he doesn't get to know – he won't think twice about dealing with me in the same way he dealt with your father. What he does with me is neither here nor there

– I've been ready to die for a long time – but you need to be very careful now, John. Once I'm gone, you're all that's left, the only one who knows.

Make sure you keep it that way.

And do what you have to do.

It's tempting to ask you to send my regards to Claudia and Imogen, but I mustn't. And you mustn't. Just promise me you'll stay in touch with them. They're both very fond of you, and it gives me great comfort to think of my three favourite people spending time together long after I've gone.

And now I must stop, John. I'm very tired.

Live on for me, my friend.

Leon.

16

How are you supposed to feel when something you've believed and accepted for twenty years turns out to be a lie? Your heart has been shaped by this falsehood, you've measured your life against it, and now, in a trice, it's gone. It never happened. For twenty years you've been labouring under the sick illusion that your father took his own life, and now the illusion has been revealed for what it always was. You father didn't take his own life, his life was taken from him. His life was stolen. How the hell are you supposed to feel about that?

Relieved? Liberated? Outraged?

Sad?

Sorry?

Can you convince yourself that in the end it doesn't matter how he died, because dead is dead, and that's all there is to it? No. What you feel is beyond you. You can only ever feel what you feel, what you are. That's all you have. And as I sat there reading through Leon's message again and again, coldly digesting every single word, all I had in me was a drowning emptiness, a void, a tameless desire to kill.

I could drink for ever now.

Pour it into my heart.

I filled my glass, drank it down, and opened the audio file.

After a few seconds of muffled noise – amplified knocks and clonks, the sound of a microphone being adjusted – Leon's voice crackled out from the laptop speaker.

Interview with Dr Gerald McKee, 7 August 2010. McKee is the forensic pathologist who carried out the post-mortem on DI James Craine in 1992. The following recording was made without McKee's knowledge, at his home, using a hidden recording device.

There was silence for a moment or two, then a hiss came from the speaker, fading up into a vague rumble of background noise, and I heard Leon's voice again.

Thank you for agreeing to see me, Dr McKee. I appreciate your—

I didn't agree to see you, Mr Mercer. You threatened me, remember?

Yes, well—

I don't take kindly to threats.

You're welcome to call the police if you feel threatened, Doctor. You're on very good terms with DCI Bishop, I believe? Perhaps you'd like to speak with him before we take this any further.

There was a pause then, and I could picture Leon looking calmly at McKee, waiting for his reaction.

I can give you five minutes, McKee said, trying to sound confident, but failing. *Five minutes, and then I want you out of here. Do you understand me?*

Perfectly.

You'd better sit down, I suppose.

Thank you.

I heard the sound of a chair being moved, footsteps, a door being closed . . . more footsteps. Then,

So what's this all about, Mr Mercer? And I'd appreciate it if you'd come straight to the point. I'm a very busy man, as you know. I don't have time—

Darren Feeney, Leon said bluntly.

I'm sorry? McKee said after too long a pause. *Darren who?*

In December 1990, Darren Feeney was charged with the rape and murder of a sixteen-year-old girl called Ciara Reed. Feeney was twenty-one at the time, a known drug dealer. Ciara was his younger sister's best friend. Feeney didn't deny having sex with Ciara, but he claimed it was consensual, and he categorically denied having anything to do with her death. When the case came to trial, Feeney was convicted almost entirely on the basis of forensic evidence provided by the pathologist who carried out the post-mortem on Ciara's body. Does that jog your memory, Dr McKee?

It was a long time ago. I can't be expected to remember every single—

You told the court that the injuries to Ciara's body were consistent with her being raped.

Yes, but—

And that the cause of death was asphyxiation, which in your opinion was the result of a pillow being held over her face.

I was asked by the prosecution—

And you further stated that DNA evidence retrieved from the scene proved beyond doubt that Darren Feeney was responsible for both the rape and the murder of Ciara Reed.

Silence.

But Ciara wasn't raped, was she, Doctor?

Another silence.

And she wasn't murdered either.

I couldn't have known—

You would have known if you'd done your job properly. A sober pathologist would have known that a certain degree of bruising is not inconsistent with consensual sexual intercourse. A pathologist without a pethidine addiction would have noticed that Ciara Reed had a congenital heart defect—

There's no proof—

She had a defective heart. Fact. She had a high level of MDMA in her system. Fact. You got it wrong. Fact. And the reason you got it wrong is that you performed the post-mortem while under the influence of alcohol and self-prescribed painkillers.

No.

Yes, Dr McKee. And because of your criminal ineptitude, Darren Feeney was sentenced to life imprisonment for a crime he didn't commit. And three months into his sentence, he was attacked by other inmates and stabbed to death in his cell.

This is all pure conjecture—

I have a copy of the General Medical Council's 1999

investigation into your alcohol and drug abuse, and I have a copy of the second post-mortem report on Ciara Reed that DI Bishop requested shortly after your initial examination. As you know, this report has never been published, but you've seen it, and you know that if it ever gets out, your career would be over. And that's why Bishop has had you in his pocket for the last twenty years. You do what he tells you, and you have a life. You stand up to him, you're finished.

I heard McKee sigh.

What do you want from me? he said wearily.

I'm going to ask you some questions, and you're going to answer them. If I'm satisfied you're telling the truth, that'll be the end of it. I'll walk out of here and you'll never see or hear from me again. But if I'm not satisfied, if I think you're lying to me, I'll send all the evidence I have against you, including the second post-mortem report, to the relevant authorities and every newspaper in the country. Is that clear?

How do I know you won't do that even if I do tell you the truth?

You don't.

Are you asking me to trust you?

You need to understand something, Doctor. I don't like you. In fact, I find you singularly repulsive, and nothing would give me greater pleasure than making sure you never work again. I can do that right now, right this second.

I heard the muffled sound of movement, then something beeped, and Leon continued.

This phone holds copies of everything I need to ruin your career. I've already written an accompanying email detailing the extent of your corruption, and as you can see, the email is addressed and ready to send. All I have to do is press a button, and that's it. You're finished. Disgraced. And with a bit of luck, you'll end up facing criminal charges and a custodial sentence. Now, do you understand that, Dr McKee?

Yes . . .

You don't ask me any more questions, is that clear?

Yes.

And you understand that if I'm not satisfied with your answers to the questions I'm about to ask you, I won't hesitate to send this email.

I understand.

Good. Let's get on with it then. First question. In 1992 you performed the post-mortem examination on the body of Detective Inspector James Craine. Is that correct?

Yes.

You remember it?

Yes.

You stated in your report that the cause of death was a single gunshot wound to the head. Correct?

Yes.

You also stated that, in your opinion, the wound was self-inflicted. Is that right?

Yes.

On what evidence did you base this judgement?

The nature of the gunshot wound . . . it was a contact

*wound, which is often consistent with suicide. There
was both gunpowder residue and traces of the victim's
blood on DI Craine's right hand. And his were the
only fingerprints found on the gun.*

Anything else?

The victim left a suicide note.

Did you see it?

I was aware of it.

Did you see it?

No.

*Were there any significant injuries to DI Craine's
body that you failed to include in your report?*

I'm not sure I understand—

Yes or no, Doctor?

There was some bruising . . .

Where?

Around the neck, the upper arms.

Fresh bruising?

I believe so.

*Did you form an opinion as to the cause of this
bruising?*

*It's possible he may have been involved in a struggle
of some kind.*

It's possible?

Yes.

Did you mention this possibility in your report?

No.

Why not?

Silence.

Dr McKee? Do you understand the question?

Yes . . .

Then please answer it.

I think you know—

I didn't ask you what you thought, Doctor. I asked you why you failed to mention the bruising in your post-mortem report. You have two seconds to answer the question. One—

Bishop told me to ignore it.

DI Bishop?

Yes.

Detective Inspector Michael Bishop?

Yes.

He told you to ignore the bruising on the neck and upper arms of DI Craine's body?

Yes.

And that's why there's no mention of any bruising in your post-mortem report?

Yes.

Why did DI Bishop ask you to lie about your findings?

I didn't lie, I just—

Answer the question.

McKee sighed. *He said it was a very sensitive case, and it was in no one's interests to muddy the waters.*

What did you take that to mean?

I honestly didn't know.

Did you ask him to explain?

No.

You just did as he asked.

Yes.

239

Why?

You know why.

Say it.

Another heavy sigh. *He threatened to reveal oversights from a previous post-mortem examination.*

Ciara Reed's post-mortem?

Yes.

Which you carried out.

Yes.

And by oversights you mean the gross errors you made that led to a serious miscarriage of justice and the subsequent death of Darren Feeney?

More silence.

I'll take that as a yes, Leon said after a while.

You have no idea—

Did I ask you a question?

No.

So why are you talking?

I was only—

You don't speak to me unless I ask you a question. Have you got that?

Yes . . . sorry.

Now the bruising on DI Craine's neck and upper arms – could that have been caused by him being forcibly held down in a chair?

It could have, yes.

By how many people?

That's impossible to say.

More than one?

Very probably.

OK, last question. In your expert opinion, Dr McKee, given what you've just told me, is it possible that James Craine was shot to death by a person or persons unknown, and his murder made to look like suicide?

There was another long pause then, just the sound of breathing in the recorded silence, and eventually McKee answered quietly: *Yes, it's possible.*

Thank you.

Click.

And that was it. End of interview.

There was nothing else on the file.

After I'd played it back, stopping here and there to replay certain sections, I filled my glass, lit a cigarette, and played it all the way through again. Then, with the afternoon light beginning to fade, and snow falling silently on the street outside, I shut down the file, closed my eyes, and thought long and hard about what I'd just heard.

It didn't prove anything. And it definitely wouldn't be admissible as evidence in a criminal prosecution. In fact, on its own, with nothing to substantiate it, the recording had virtually no evidential standing at all. All it was, in essence, was a recording of two men talking. There was no proof that one of them was Dr Gerald McKee. And even if it could be proved, it was quite clear that his admissions were made under threat, and would almost certainly be retracted. And what had he admitted to anyway? Some unexplained bruising on my father's neck and upper arms, the *possibility* that he hadn't committed suicide . . .?

No, it didn't prove anything at all.

But Leon would have known that. And I knew it was Leon on the tape, and I knew Leon Mercer. Leon was the most honest man I've ever known. If he said it was McKee on the tape, it was McKee. If he said my father's suicide was faked, it was faked. And if he said Mick Bishop killed him, I knew that was so.

I didn't need proof.

I'm not a police officer. I'm not a judge. I'm not bound by the niceties of law. My justice is mine.

It was just gone four-thirty when Imogen called. I was sitting in the dark, the curtains closed, the whisky bottle almost empty. Vaporous shadows from the light of the gas fire were ghosting across the walls, and as I reached out for the ringing phone, a car rolled down the street outside, and just for a moment the shadows changed shape as the passing headlights swept across the curtained window. I waited for the gas-fire ghosts to return, then answered the phone.

'The post-mortem results have just come through,' Imogen told me, her voice calm but empty. 'Mum died from smoke inhalation, Dad from either smoke inhalation or the blunt force head injury he suffered when he fell, or possibly a combination of both.'

'Who gave you the results?' I asked her.

'The Coroner's office. They called me about five minutes ago.'

'Did they go into any more detail?'

'Not really. I'll get a full written report at a later date—'

'Will that include toxicology tests?'

'I don't know, I didn't ask. I was a bit . . . well, I wasn't really thinking straight, you know.'

'Yeah, of course.' I lit a cigarette. 'I don't suppose they told you who carried out the post-mortems, did they?'

'No. Does it matter?'

'It might.'

'Why?'

'I don't want to say too much on the phone, Imogen, but I think you're right about the fire.'

'It wasn't an accident?'

'None of this was an accident.'

'How do you know? Have you found something? What have you—?'

'Not on the phone, OK?'

'I need to know, John.'

'I know you do, and I promise I'll tell you everything as soon as I can. But I need you to do something for me first.'

I heard her take a breath, forcing herself to be patient. Then, 'All right, what do you want me to do?'

'Call the Coroner's office and ask them for the name of the pathologist who carried out the post-mortems.'

'What if they won't tell me?'

'Make them tell you . . . threaten to sue them, break down in tears, make them feel sorry for you . . . whatever it takes.'

'OK.'

'Text me the name when you've got it.'

'OK. Anything else?'

'Tell the Coroner you want second post-mortems on both the bodies. You want them carried out as soon as possible, and by a pathologist of your choice.'

'Christ, John,' she said quietly.

'You'll need to get your solicitor to instruct an independent pathologist, but we can sort that out later. All right?'

'Yeah, it's just a bit . . .'

'I know, but it has to be done, Imogen. Trust me. Call the Coroner's office now.'

'OK. Will I see you later?'

'Where are you going to be?'

'At the flat.'

'I'll come round when I can.' I was just about to end the call when something occurred to me. 'Do you know what happened to Leon's mobile?' I asked Imogen.

'What do you mean?'

'He would have had it with him that night, wouldn't he? Either in his pocket or somewhere in his study.'

'I suppose so . . .'

'So what happened to it?'

'The fire happened to it, John. I mean, if it was in his pocket, there wouldn't be anything left of it. And if it was somewhere in his study, and it wasn't destroyed in the fire . . . I don't know. Maybe it's still there. But I would have thought one of us would have seen it when we were looking around the other day.'

'Yeah, you're probably right,' I said.

'I could ask around, if you think it's important. The

police might have it, or maybe someone at the Coroner's office might know—'

'No, don't bother,' I said. 'It was just a thought. It's not worth wasting any time over.' I glanced at my watch. 'It's quarter to five, Im. You'd better make that phone call.'

Even if Leon's mobile hadn't been destroyed in the fire, it would almost certainly have been destroyed by his killers. And even if they'd missed it, and it had somehow survived the fire, the phone was hardly likely to still contain the incriminating evidence that Leon had used to threaten McKee, the 'copies of everything' he'd mentioned on the tape. And for all I knew, Leon might have been bluffing anyway, and there never had been any evidence stored on his phone. So I knew there was next to no point in trying Leon's mobile now. But I also knew, from hard-earned experience, that next to no point isn't quite the same as no point at all.

So I tried his number anyway.

It went straight to voicemail: *This is Leon Mercer, please leave a message.*

A dead man's voice.

I finished off the whisky, stuffed more sulphate up my nose, then put on my coat and stumbled out into the snow.

17

Wyre Street at six in the evening. The snow falls steadily, muting the sounds of the city, and the smell of cheap food lingers in the air. It's the time of day that doesn't know what to do with itself. Too early for going out, too late for going home, the night is neither here nor there. The town dozes, resting after another long day, readying itself for the chaos of the night to come. The sleeping street isn't empty, but it might as well be. The misplaced souls who people this time are as formless as shadows – shuffling aimlessly from place to place, passing the time, just passing by, looking in shop windows at things they don't want but wouldn't mind having. They don't belong anywhere. Not even here. No one belongs to this time.

It doesn't take long to walk from my house to my office in Wyre Street – half an hour, forty minutes – and I'd quite happily leave my car at home every day if I could. I like walking. And I hate driving. I don't like cars, I don't like what they do to people. But I can't do my job without a car. As someone once said to me, it's not as if you can chase after the bad guys on a bus, is it?

But although that night was a good night for walking – the snow-covered streets refreshingly unfamiliar – I didn't leave my car at home out of choice. I'd been drinking all day, the roads were icy, and I'm a bad enough driver at the best of times. It wasn't a difficult decision to make.

I'd walked the long way round – along through the subways and pathless embankments that criss-cross the bypass roundabouts and junctions, right on Eastway, then right again down the hippy-shop backstreets that run parallel to the High Street – and now I was almost there, heading down Wyre Street, passing the shuffling shadows, approaching the nondescript entrance to my office building. There were no lights showing in my office windows, so I guessed Ada had already left, and the offices on the second floor had been empty for months, so they were dark too. But I wasn't surprised to see the lights on in George Salvini's ground-floor office. George is always working. Long nights, weekends . . . he's never out of his office.

As I took my office keys out of my pocket and stepped up to the front door, George was just coming out. Dressed as ever in a tailored suit, silk tie, and polished leather shoes, he had an unlit cigarette in his mouth and a slim gold lighter in his hand.

'John!' he said, smiling as he saw me. 'What a pleasant surprise.'

'Hey, George. Working late again?'

He lit his cigarette. 'Busiest time of the year, my friend. Last-minute tax returns, piles of receipts to go through, you know how it is.'

I nodded.

'Which reminds me,' he said, blowing out smoke. 'You and I need to discuss your financial situation.'

'Yeah, I know.'

'It's serious, John.'

I smiled. 'Money's always serious.'

He fixed me with a stern look. 'We really do need to talk quite urgently. If we don't—'

'How about Monday?' I said.

'Now would be better.'

I shook my head. 'Now's not a good time for me, George.'

'I'm here all weekend.'

'Monday morning,' I told him. 'I promise.'

He sighed. 'Very well. What time should I expect you?'

'First thing.'

'Eight o'clock?'

I laughed.

'Nine o'clock then,' he said.

'Make it ten, and you've got yourself a date.'

He shook his head, smiling. 'And you wonder why the economy is failing?'

'Nope,' I said, patting him on the arm and heading through the door. 'Can't say I give it much thought.'

I don't keep very much in my office safe – I don't usually have very much worth stealing – but although the information on Leon's memory stick was of no financial value, and as far as I was aware no one else knew about it anyway, I wasn't taking any chances. So after I'd downloaded the files to my PC – and emailed them to Cal as a back-up – I went over to the wall safe and opened it up . . .

And that's when the sick illusion of my father's death came back to me.

I hadn't forgotten about the gun in my safe – I could never forget it – but it was only when I saw it that I suddenly realised it wasn't the same any more. There was no physical change. It was still the same 9mm semi-automatic Beretta it had always been, and it still looked how it had always looked, and it was still in exactly the same place as I'd left it . . .

But it wasn't the same gun.

Not any more.

I'd always known it as my father's gun, the weapon he'd used to take his own life, but as I reached into the safe and picked it up, it not only meant something entirely different to me now, it felt entirely different too. It wasn't my father's gun any more, it was his murder weapon. And that changed everything. It changed the gun's history, *our* history: all the times I'd held the Beretta to my own head, wondering how it would feel to pull the trigger . . . the times I'd used it on others . . . the time Mick Bishop had used it to shoot his own brother . . .

They'd all become part of the illusion now.

And I didn't know what to do with that.

I put the memory stick in the safe, locked it, then took the Beretta over to my desk and sat down. I opened up the bottom drawer and took out a dusty glass and a half-full bottle of Teacher's. I wiped the glass, filled it, held it up to the light for a moment, then took a long drink. Almost immediately the ache in my bones began to ease. I lit a cigarette and gazed down at the gun in my hand . . .

A police officer named Cliff Duffy had given it to me nearly twenty years ago after I'd helped him out with a potentially career-threatening problem. I wasn't a PI at the time, but Duffy had worked with my father for many years, and he'd always had a lot of respect for him, so I was happy enough to do him a favour. When he'd asked me if there was anything he could do in return, I've never really understood what prompted me to ask him if he could find out what had happened to my father's gun, and if possible get hold of it for me, and I'm still not exactly sure how he did it, but he did. And having the gun had meant something to me. I don't know what. It had just somehow meant something to me. And what's more, I'd used it. I'd taken a life with it. And in doing so the gun had become part of me. It had become mine.

And the illusion didn't change that, I realised now.

It might not be my father's gun any more, but it was still mine.

My gun.

My history.

My justice.

It was a far from rational conclusion, and I wasn't even sure what it meant, but it satisfied me for now.

I thumbed the catch on the pistol grip and slid out the magazine. Fully loaded, it held fifteen rounds. I began emptying the magazine, removing the shells one by one and placing them on the desk in front of me. There were ten rounds left, as I knew there would be. I reloaded the magazine and slipped it back into place, racked a round into the chamber, and was just about to return the pistol to the safe when I heard footsteps coming up the stairs.

I sat still and listened hard.

Whoever it was, they were on their own, they weren't trying to cover the sound of their steps, and they weren't in any great hurry. They were just coming up the stairs . . . nice and steady . . . *tump, tump, tump, tump* . . . passing the second floor now, on the way up here . . . *tump, tump, tump, tump.* . . the steps getting louder . . .

I slipped off the safety catch and held the Beretta out of sight in my lap.

Tump, tump, tump, tump . . .

They'd reached the third floor now and were coming along the hallway.

My office door was open, I could see through into the main office. I could see the pebbled glass panel of the office door, its faded black lettering – *John Craine Investigations* – and now I could see the shadow of a man on the other side of the door. He paused for a moment, not moving at all, just standing there, and then his head moved, his shoulders dipping slightly as he reached for the handle, and the door eased open.

Leon once told me that Mick Bishop was nowhere near as one-dimensional as he liked people to think, and that in his own twisted way, he was a very complicated and highly intelligent man. And as I watched Bishop entering my office that night, it was easy to see what Leon had meant. He came in confidently, but not without caution, pausing for just a moment in the half-open doorway, taking a quick

251

look round, before stepping into the main office and closing the door behind him. It only took him a second or two to scan the office, determine it was empty, and glance through the doorway at me, but even as his eyes met mine, I'd already seen enough to know that he hadn't changed one bit. He was the same Mick Bishop he'd always been – self-assured, nerveless, totally in control of himself and the situation. And it struck me then, with a touch of envy, that the notion of territory meant nothing to him. Wherever he was – your home, your workplace, anywhere at all – Mick Bishop believed he had a God-given right to be there.

'Evening, John,' he said casually, crossing the main office towards me. 'Catching up on your paperwork?'

'How did you get in here?' I asked as he entered my office.

'Your queer friend downstairs . . . what is he, Greek or something?' Bishop pulled up a chair and sat down opposite me. 'Anyway, he let me in. Very accommodating.'

'Make yourself at home,' I said, slipping the Beretta under my thigh.

Bishop gave me a tight little smile.

I lit a cigarette and poured myself a drink. 'Do you want one?' I said to him.

He stared at me, a look of indifferent curiosity in his eyes. 'Why do you do it?'

'What?'

'Drink so much.' He shook his head. 'I mean, what do you get out of it?'

I didn't answer, I just took a long drink and gazed back at him over the rim of the glass. He didn't seem to have aged over the last two years or so. He had to be in his late fifties or early sixties by now, but there was no trace of grey in his wiry black hair, no dullness to his cold dark eyes. The quarter-inch scar on his jaw still highlighted the hardness of his mouth, and his skin was as plastic-white as ever. He was dressed in a dark-blue blazer with silver buttons, a pale-blue shirt with a white collar, and a crimson tie pinned with a thin gold chain.

'What do you want?' I asked him.

He shrugged. 'I was just passing by, saw the lights in your office window, thought I'd drop in for a chat.'

'Right.'

'What?' He half-smiled. 'You don't believe me?'

I glanced at my watch. 'I'm kind of busy at the moment. I don't really have time for—'

'Did you enjoy the fight?'

'What?'

'The boxing at Juno's the other night . . .' He cocked his head, giving me a look. 'You know, I'd never have taken you for a fight fan, John.'

'And why's that?'

He shrugged. 'Oh, I don't know . . . I just wouldn't have thought it was your kind of thing.'

'Yeah, well,' I said, looking at him. 'We all have our hidden depths, don't we?'

He smiled. 'There's no depth to me, John. You should know that.'

'Right. You're just a good honest copper, trying to do his job.'

'That's me.'

'Of course it is,' I said, looking at my watch again.

'You're overdoing it,' Bishop said.

'What?'

'The busy-man act . . .' He shook his head. 'Christ, John, what do you think I'm going to do? Realise you're busy, say sorry, and walk out of here? Even if you were busy, which you're patently not, do you really think I'd give a shit?'

'All right,' I said, stubbing out my cigarette. 'Why don't you just tell me what you want?'

'I want to know what you were doing at Juno's, for a start.'

'What if I don't want to tell you?'

'I'll arrest you, take you down to the station, and ask you again.'

'On what charge?'

'Suspicion of murder, GBH, possession of a controlled drug—'

'Murder? What murder? What are you talking about?'

'I told you once before, John, I can do whatever I fucking like. I could have you arrested on suspicion of terrorism and get you locked up for a month if I wanted to. I don't need a reason, I can just do it.' He sniffed. 'And even if I did need a reason, I've got more than enough to take you in.'

'Like what?'

'Like that psycho you beat to death on Hale Island a couple of years ago. What was his name again? Gallow or something? Harrow?'

'Garrow,' I breathed, my heart shocked cold. 'His name was Ian Garrow. And he deserved everything he got.'

'I'm sure he did. In fact, I know he did. But unfortunately the law doesn't recognise your right to decide who lives and who doesn't. It's a shame, I know, but there you go.'

I lit a cigarette, staring down at the desk, trying to dismiss the memories of Hale Island from my mind. I didn't regret killing Ian Garrow, and I certainly didn't feel bad about it, I just didn't want to remember it. Standing over his groaning body, void of all natural emotion, pounding a heavy steel bar into his head . . . hammering it down as hard as I could, over and over again . . .

'And there was that other one too,' Bishop said. 'The biker you brained at the caravan park, the one who was fucking your sister.'

I looked up.

Bishop was smiling. 'You know he's in a wheelchair now, don't you? Just sits there all day dribbling and moaning . . . I don't suppose he even remembers what you did to him. Or maybe he does. Not that it matters. The fucker can't talk, can he?'

I drained my glass, refilled it, and drank some more.

Bishop watched me for a moment, quietly shaking his head, then he sniffed again and said, 'Look, I don't have a problem with what you did down there. I know SOCA and Customs had their reasons for keeping it all quiet, and that's fine with me. All I'm saying is that just because they've buried it, that doesn't mean it's gone away. If I need to dig it all up again, I can do it.' He snapped his fingers. 'Just like that.' He stared at me. 'Do you understand?'

I stared back at him, not saying anything.

'So,' he went on, 'now that we know where we stand, let's try again, shall we? What were you doing at Juno's on Monday?'

As I paused for a moment, thinking things through, I felt my phone buzzing in my pocket. I pulled it out and glanced at the screen. There was a text from Imogen. I opened it up and read: *mum&dad's pathologist ws dr gerald mckee. ok?* I stared at the name for a second or two, then looked across at Bishop.

'Everything all right?' he asked.

I closed the text, put the phone back in my pocket, then leaned to one side, pretending to adjust my seat, and nudged the Beretta into a more comfortable position under my thigh. I picked up my glass, took another sip of whisky, and looked across at Bishop. 'I think you probably know what I was doing at Juno's,' I said.

'Why don't you tell me anyway.'

I shrugged. 'I was there to see Hassan Tan.'

'Why?'

'I was looking into his brother's murder and I wanted to talk to him about it.'

Bishop nodded. 'So you've been hired to investigate the Jamaal Tan killing, is that right?'

I lit a cigarette. 'I was asked to look into it.'

'Who asked you?'

'Ayanna Osman, the boys' aunt. She came to see me, told me about Jamaal, and asked if I could do anything to help. She seems to think the police aren't doing their job properly.'

'And you agreed to help her?'

'I told her I'd see what I could do.'

'And then what?'

'I went to Juno's and tried to see Hassan after his fight, but that didn't work out too well, so then I made an appointment with DI Lilley and asked him a few questions about Jamaal.' I looked at Bishop. 'As I'm sure you know, Lilley told me all about Kassim Mukhtar, and that's when I realised I was wasting my time.'

Bishop was very good at keeping a straight face, and if I hadn't been watching him so closely I probably wouldn't have noticed the momentary widening of his eyes when I mentioned Kassim Mukhtar. He covered it up pretty well, blanking his face again almost immediately, but when he cleared his throat and sniffed again I knew I'd given him something to think about.

'So what are you saying?' he said cautiously. 'You're *not* investigating Tan's murder any more?'

I shrugged. 'There's no point, is there? You've already got the man who did it, and it looks like he's going down for the pub killing anyway, so as far as I'm concerned, that's it.'

'What about Ayanna Osman?'

'What about her?'

'Have you told her about Mukhtar?'

I shook my head. 'Not yet.'

'Are you going to?'

'I don't know . . .' I looked at him. 'Is that why you're here? You want to make sure I don't tell her about Mukhtar?'

He laughed, a derisive little snort. 'You can tell her whatever you want. Make something up, tell her the truth . . . either

257

way, she probably won't believe you.' He tapped the side of his head. 'She's a damaged woman, John. You know that, don't you? I mean, it's not surprising given what she's been through, even if only half of it's true.' He arched his eyebrows at me. 'I don't know what she told you about herself and her family, but whatever it was, I wouldn't put too much faith in it if I were you. The poor cow doesn't even know she's making things up most of the time. She lives in the fucking clouds.'

Now who's overdoing it? I thought to myself, looking at him. 'So if you're not worried about keeping Mukhtar's name out of it,' I said, 'what *are* you worried about?'

'Who said I was worried about anything?'

'This isn't a social call, is it?'

He smiled tightly. 'I just wanted to make sure you understood the situation, John. Ayanna Osman doesn't want to draw attention to herself, she's too paranoid about getting deported, so even if you do tell her about Mukhtar, she's not going to start shouting her mouth off to anyone. But how do I know that you're not?'

'Why the hell would I?'

'You tell me.'

I laughed, shaking my head. 'Are you *serious*? Is that really what this is about?'

'I want Mukhtar put away,' he said, staring coldly at me. 'And I'm not going to let you or anyone else do anything that might jeopardise his conviction. If rumours start getting out that Mukhtar was involved in the Tan killing, even if they are only rumours, the whole fucking case could collapse. So, yes, I am serious.'

I shook my head again. 'I already told you, all I did was take a quick look into things, and now I'm done with it. There's nothing in it for me, there never was. I didn't even get paid for the few hours I spent on it in the first place. All I got out of it was bruised bollocks and a visit from you. So why in God's name would I want to waste another single breath on anything to do with Jamaal Tan or Kassim Mukhtar? I don't want *any*thing to do with either of them. I wish I'd never fucking heard of Jamaal Tan.'

Bishop nodded slowly, seemingly satisfied.

I sighed, outwardly weary of it all.

But inside I was satisfied too.

I thought, and hoped, that that was it. We'd played our stupid games, got what we wanted from each other, and now it was over. Bishop had reasserted his control over me, reminding me of his reach and power, and I'd done my best to convince him that I had no interest whatsoever in the death of Jamaal Tan. We were both satisfied with each other's lies, and that, I assumed, was the end of it.

But as I waited for Bishop to make a move – putting out my cigarette, sipping more whisky, lighting another cigarette – it didn't take long to realise that he had no intention of going anywhere. He was just sitting there, staring blankly at me, barely moving at all, as settled as a reptile on a rock in the sun.

I sighed again, genuinely tired of it all now, and poured myself another drink.

'You didn't answer my question,' Bishop said as I raised the glass to my lips.

I swallowed whisky. 'What question?'

'Why you drink so much,' he said, eyeing the glass in my hand. 'What *do* you get out of it?'

'I don't get anything out of it,' I told him. 'It gets something out of me.'

He nodded, feigning interest, but I knew he didn't care. He was just biding his time, talking for the sake of it, asking questions out of habit. The only thing that interested him was the game. Not the pieces. And that's all anyone was to him, a piece in the game. A pawn, a rook, a knight . . . a counter, a card, a Monopoly dog. What *makes* a piece doesn't matter, does it? An ivory pawn does exactly the same as a plastic one. All that matters about pieces is what can be done with them.

'I was sorry to hear about Leon,' Bishop said.

'Yeah,' I said quietly. 'I bet you were.'

He shrugged. 'Well, I'll admit that we didn't always see eye to eye—'

'He hated your guts, for Christ's sake. He fucking despised you.'

Bishop smiled. 'Hate's not such a bad thing, you know. At least it means something.'

I shook my head. 'All it means is he hated you.'

'Maybe so . . .'

'There's no maybe about it.'

He shrugged again. 'Look, John, I understand how you feel—'

'No, you don't.'

A flash of irritation crossed his eyes, but it only lasted a moment. He sniffed, composing himself, and looked me in the eye. 'How's Imogen doing?'

'Both her parents have just died,' I said, holding his gaze. 'How do you think she's doing?'

He nodded. 'It must be very hard for her.'

I just stared at him.

He said, 'You know her fairly well, don't you?'

I said nothing.

'Look,' he said, 'we've both been there, haven't we? We've both lost family to a violent death, we've both suffered the shock and grief that comes with it—'

'You *were* your brother's death.'

'It makes no difference, believe me. Death is death, no matter the cause. Grief doesn't recognise culpability.'

'Christ,' I said, shaking my head in disbelief.

'All I'm trying to say,' he went on, 'is that you need to keep an eye on her.'

'What?'

'Imogen. Right now she needs someone to look after her, someone who knows what she's going through. Do you understand what I'm saying?'

'I don't care what you're saying. What I don't understand is why you're saying anything at all.'

'I'm trying to give you some advice.'

'Right . . . and why would you want to do that?'

He paused for a second, looking impassively at me, then said, 'I'm given to understand that Imogen may have some concerns about the fire at her parents' house. Is that right?'

'Concerns?'

'Doubts, suspicions . . .'

'What makes you think that?'

'She's been in contact with the Coroner's office, asking

questions about the pathologist and requesting second post-mortems. And someone from Mercer Associates has been making enquiries about the fire officer in charge of the investigation . . .'

As Bishop was telling me this, I was struggling to keep the surprise from my face. How the hell had he found out about Imogen's phone call to the Coroner's office so quickly? And how did he know she'd been checking out the fire investigator when I didn't even know about it myself? I stared at him, mentally shaking my head, and realised he was still talking. I pulled myself together and zoned back in.

'. . . and I know for a fact that she's spent quite some time looking around the house, both on her own and with you and Cal Franks. It's also been brought to my attention that someone's been sniffing around after Leon's computer and email records, and it's not hard to guess who that might be.' He stared back at me for a moment, letting his words sink in, then carried on. 'Now maybe I'm wrong, maybe I'm just jumping to conclusions, but it seems to me that what we have here is a grieving individual who can't, or doesn't want to, accept the truth.'

'The truth?' I said.

Bishop nodded. 'It was an accident, John. Simple as that. A tragic accident. I admit we'll probably never know the exact cause of the fire, and perhaps there are one or two questions that still need answering, but from all the evidence I've seen, and all the experts I've talked to, there's absolutely no doubt that the fire was an accident.'

'You're sure about that?' I said, looking him in the eye.

His gaze never wavered. 'One hundred per cent.'

'So why does it matter if Imogen is looking into things?' I said. 'If she's not going to find anything, what's the problem? It can't do any harm, can it?'

Bishop took a deep breath, let it out slowly, and leaned forward in his chair. 'Have you heard of the term "noble cause corruption"?'

'Yeah,' I said. 'It's an excuse bent coppers use to justify their crimes.'

He smiled humourlessly. 'That's one interpretation. Personally, I prefer to think of it as bending the rules for the sake of the greater good. But whichever way you look at it, we both know it happens. It always has, and it always will. Because for every police officer, no matter how clean they might be, there'll come a time when the rules stop them from doing what they know to be right. Perhaps they'll be investigating the rape and murder of a ten-year-old girl, and they'll have a suspect, and they'll know without doubt that he did it, but they'll also know that he's going to get away with it because the evidence they have is inadmissible due to a chain-of-custody error. So what are they going to do? Let him go? Send him back out onto the streets to rape and kill another little girl? Or are they going to find a way round the rules – bend them, break them, rip them apart – and do whatever it takes to lock the sick fucker away?'

'Nice speech,' I said, sarcastically clapping my hands. 'Very noble indeed.'

His face darkened, his shoulders tensed, and just for a moment I thought he was going to lunge at me. But even as I lowered my hand to the side of my leg, resting my fingers on the grip of the pistol, I saw him regain control of himself. The rage left his eyes, his shoulders relaxed, and with a steadying breath he nodded to himself and settled back in the chair.

'You think you know it all, don't you?' he said calmly. 'You really think—'

'Are we done here?'

'What?'

'Are we finished? I'm tired . . . I've had enough—'

'No,' he said coldly, 'we're not finished. I'll tell you when we're fucking finished.'

'All right then,' I said wearily, reaching for my cigarettes, 'so let's just get on with it, shall we? No more speeches, no more bullshit, just say what you've got to say, then fuck off and leave me alone.'

18

There wasn't much I could have done even if Bishop had admitted to killing my father and murdering Leon and Claudia – I still would have had nothing to prove his guilt – but people like Bishop never admit to anything. The truth to them is a foreign concept. They lie as a matter of course, even when they don't need to. It's how they survive. So I wasn't overly surprised when Bishop started spinning me a story that seemed at first to have nothing to do with Leon's death, and even less to do with the truth, and I knew there was no point in trying to stop him. This was his play, his move, and I had to let him make it whether I wanted to or not.

'The first thing you've got to understand, John,' he said to me, 'is that things were very different in the eighties. When I worked with Leon and your father at Hey CID, the job was all about catching villains and putting them away, and everything else was secondary. There were no targets to meet, the paperwork wasn't unbearable, we didn't have to worry about getting sued all the time. There was no such thing as human rights back then. There was no PACE, no compensation culture, no CCTV cameras filming your every move—'

'Ah, the good old days,' I said, rolling my eyes. 'Ford Capris, kipper ties, forced confessions, false convictions . . .'

Bishop shook his head. 'I'm not wallowing in nostalgia here, John. I'm not saying things were better back then, I'm just telling you how it was. I deal in facts, not feelings, and the simple fact is that the world has changed over the last thirty years.' He shrugged. 'It's nothing new, of course. The world's always changing, but as long as you accept that that's the way it is, and you realise there's no point in trying to hold on to the past, it doesn't really make any difference. The thing is though, although you can't live in the past, you can't escape from it either. It's always there. And unlike everything else, the past never changes. It *can't* change. Our histories are set in stone, John. What's done is done.' He looked at me. 'You of all people should know that.'

'What's your point?' I said, sipping whisky.

'Secrets,' he said simply, staring hard at me. 'That's my point. Secrets from the past. We've all got them – you, me, your father, Leon . . . none of us are innocent. We all have buried sins.' He paused for a second to let that sink in, his eyes never leaving mine, and just for a moment, as his head turned slightly and the dark light from the window crossed his face, I thought I saw something that spoke of things to come. I thought I saw the bones beneath his skin. 'The thing about buried sins though,' he continued, 'is their nasty habit of being dug up. It doesn't always happen, of course, and even when it does . . . well, most of the time it doesn't really matter.' He shrugged. 'I mean, who cares about age-old sins? Most of them have no real consequence, do they? But sometimes . . .' He paused again, leaning forward to emphasise his point. 'Sometimes, when secrets are unearthed, the consequences can be very real indeed.'

He took a breath and leaned back. 'And that's why Leon's past is best left buried, John. There were certain things he did as a police officer that very few people know about, and if they were to come out now . . .' He shook his head. 'Well, let's just say it would cause a lot of damage.'

'Are you seriously trying to tell me that Leon Mercer was dirty?'

He sighed. 'I've already told you, John. Things were different back then. The job was different. If you judged what we did in the eighties by today's standards, every single one of us would come out dirty.'

'No,' I said, shaking my head. '*You* would, because you've always been corrupt, and I'm sure there were plenty more like you. But Leon was a good cop, a good man—'

'I'm not saying he wasn't. And I'm not saying that I'm a saint either, by the way. I know exactly what I am. But it's not only people like me who cross the line, good men do it too.' He looked at me. 'Your father was a good man, wasn't he?'

My heart went cold. I couldn't speak.

Bishop shrugged. 'It was simple lust that did for him, of course. But it just goes to show—'

'My father was innocent. You know that.'

Bishop frowned. 'He was fucking an eighteen-year-old girl, John. He was fucking the victim of a serial paedophile, a key witness for the prosecution in his own case. You call that *innocent*?'

'That's not how it was—'

'And what about the £25,000 and the two kilos of coke we found in his locker?'

'You put it there.'

'Really?'

'You set him up.' *And then you killed him*, I wanted to add. *You went to our house, you shot him in the head, you made it look like suicide. You not only murdered my father, you took away everything he was.*

'I know it must be hard for you,' Bishop said. 'But eventually you're going to have to accept the truth about your father. And that doesn't mean you have to think badly of him. He just made a mistake, that's all.'

I stared at him, hating every cell in his body.

'All right, listen,' he said, looking at his watch. 'A lot of things happened in the eighties that everyone would rather forget, and I'm not just talking about Hey CID. It was a bad time for the force as a whole. The Met was dirty from top to bottom, the Flying Squad was out of control, even the anti-corruption units couldn't be trusted. Everything was a fucking mess. And everyone got dragged into it . . . *every*one. Good or bad, it made no difference. If you were a police officer, you were part of it. And Leon was a major part of it.' Bishop looked at me. 'Do you know what a ghost squad is?'

I shook my head.

'It's an elite covert squad of specially picked officers whose job is to root out corruption at the highest levels. The idea really took hold in the early nineties when officers working in official anti-corruption units were found to be investigating themselves, but ghost squads in one form or another had been around for a long time before then. The one that Leon became part of originated in the early eighties, and as far as I know it was still in operation when he retired.' Bishop looked at me. I don't know if he was expecting some kind of reaction, but if he was, he didn't get it. I lit a cigarette, avoiding his gaze, and poured more whisky into my glass.

Bishop carried on. 'Leon spent years working in the shadows, and because most of what he did was off the record, he didn't have to follow the rules. He could use phone taps, bugs, illicit payments . . . whatever it took to get the job done. So he knew everything there was to know about everybody. He was privy to all their dirty secrets, from the lowliest DC's false expense claim to the Deputy Commissioner's six-figure pay-off. He knew it all, John. Do you understand what that means?'

It doesn't mean anything, I said to myself. *Because none of it's true.*

'I'll tell you what it means,' Bishop went on. 'In the first place, it means that most of the rumours about Leon's squad were probably true, and that in the end they had so much power and control, and so little accountability, that most of them really did become even more corrupt than the dirty cops they were supposed to be catching. And while you might think that bent cops deserve whatever they get, the reality is that the conviction of any corrupt police officer automatically casts doubt on every case they've ever worked on, and that means that every villain they've ever locked up will have a good chance of getting their convictions quashed. So the price you pay for nailing one dirty cop is the possible release of every piece of shit they've ever put away – murderers, rapists . . . you name it.' Bishop looked at me. 'And lastly, even if Leon did keep his hands clean back then, he not only had the goods on just about everyone, he took it all with him when he retired.'

'What do you mean?' I asked, suddenly interested. 'What did he take with him?'

'Before he left,' Bishop said, 'Leon went through every case he'd ever worked on, official and unofficial, and made copies of everything. Files, records, statements, tapes . . . everything.'

'How do you know that?'

'It doesn't matter how—'

'And why would he do it anyway?'

Bishop shrugged again. 'Who knows? Maybe he thought he needed some insurance. Or maybe he just knew how much it was worth. And that's the whole point. The information he took isn't just worth a lot, it's incredibly sensitive. In fact, it's even more sensitive now than it was back then, because a lot of the officers Leon was investigating at the time are either Chief Constables or Commissioners now, or they've left the force altogether and moved on to bigger things. Some of them are MPs, some are Lords, others are executive directors of multinational companies . . . they've become people with influence. And the last thing any of them need is the revelation of their long-buried secrets.' Bishop took a deep breath and let it out slowly. 'Now do you see what I'm getting at?'

I shook my head. 'It doesn't add up.'

He sighed. 'What doesn't?'

'If Leon had all this information, and he had it for

twenty-odd years, how come he never used it? Did he ever blackmail anyone?'

'Not as far as I know.'

'Did he ever threaten to reveal anything?'

'No, but—'

'And why haven't you done anything about this before now? Why is it only a problem now that he's dead?'

'You've just answered your own question,' Bishop said, a touch of irritation in his voice. 'It wasn't a problem before now *because* he didn't do anything with it. And it's not a problem now *because* he's dead, it's a problem now because you and his daughter and Cal fucking Franks are digging around like dogs after a bone, stirring up all kinds of shit. *That*'s the fucking problem.'

'Right . . .' I said slowly, tapping ash from my cigarette. I stared in silence at the ashtray for a while, reminding myself that it was a waste of time picking holes in his story, because that's all it was, a story. And even if it was based on elements of the truth – and for all I knew Leon *had* been part of this shadowy ghost squad – the fact remained that the real reason Bishop was here was to cover his own dirty tracks. And that in itself was enough to convince me beyond doubt that he was responsible, directly or other-wise, for the murders of Leon and Claudia, and that the reason he'd killed Leon was to stop him revealing the truth about my father's death.

I looked at Bishop now – sitting across the desk from me, no more than a few feet away . . . staring at me with his soulless eyes. He knew that I knew, I was fairly sure of that. And I wondered again why he was bothering with this pointless charade. Did he enjoy it? Was his life so empty that this was all he had? Or was it just that he'd been doing it for so long – cheating, lying, twisting the truth – that he wasn't even aware he was doing it any more?

You're wasting your time again, I thought, stubbing out my cigarette and reaching for another. The packet was empty. I took a fresh pack from my pocket and opened it up. *Don't get involved with him*, I told myself, *don't try to beat him at his own game, just play along with it for now.*

I lit a cigarette, took a long drink of whisky, and looked at Bishop again. I knew I should have listened to myself, but it's not easy to play along with the man who shot your father in the head. I wanted to kill the fucker, not play along with him.

I closed my eyes for a moment, feeling the soak of whisky whirling in my head, then I took a deep breath, opened my eyes, and took a long drag on my cigarette.

'So that's it, is it?' I said to Bishop. 'That's your story?'

'You can call it what you like,' he said. 'But that's the way it is.'

'So you're just acting as a messenger really, is that it? You're simply trying to protect the reputations of these "people with influence". They want you to make sure that whatever Leon had on them stays buried, and that's why you're asking me to leave things alone.'

'I'm not asking you,' Bishop said calmly. 'I'm telling you.'

I smiled at him. 'You haven't really thought this through, have you?'

'Listen—' he started to say.

'I mean, apart from the more obvious holes in your story, and all the possibilities you've overlooked, you seem to have forgotten about Imogen in all this. She's Leon's daughter, remember? She's got every right to know how her parents died. And if she wants the truth, and she's willing to do whatever it takes to get it, do you honestly think she's going to take any notice of anything you have to say?'

'I doubt it,' he said, 'but I'm sure she'll listen to you.'

'Oh, right . . . so I tell Imogen what you've just told me, I tell her to leave things alone, and she says, "OK, John. Sounds fair enough to me."' I looked at Bishop. 'And that's it, end of story?'

'Pretty much.'

I nodded, still looking at him. 'And if, for any reason, it doesn't work out like that?'

'You make sure it does.'

'Or you'll arrest me, I suppose?' I said, unable to resist mocking him. 'Suspicion of murder, GBH, possession of a controlled drug . . . I mean, you can do whatever you fucking like, can't you? You could have me arrested on suspicion of terrorism and get me locked up for a month if you wanted to.'

'I could put you away for ever if I wanted to,' he said confidently. 'And that's always an option. But I get the feeling that you wouldn't last very long inside. You'd probably put a rope round your neck within the first year, or somebody else would do it for you.' He angled his head slightly, studying me. 'And you don't really care that much about your life anyway, do you?'

I didn't say anything, but I didn't have to. He knew he was right.

'You're a lot like me in that sense, John,' he went on. 'And we both know the benefits of having a detached view of life, don't we? If you can take it or leave it, there's not a lot anyone can do to you, is there?' He looked down, smiling sadly, and just for a moment his artifice left him and I could see the face beneath the mask . . . and there was nothing there. Nothing at all. Just a void of flesh and bone. Then he cocked his jaw, blinked hard, and when he raised his head and looked at me, the mask was back in place. 'How's Bridget, by the way?' he asked casually. 'Has she forgiven you yet?'

The sudden change of subject caught me by surprise, and it took me a moment or two to realise what he was saying. 'Oh, right,' I said, trying to sound unconcerned, 'so that's how you spend your evenings, is it? Creeping around in the dark, peeping through women's windows, taking naughty pictures . . .' I smiled at him, probably not very convincingly. 'I always wondered how you got your kicks. Do you just like looking at the pictures, or is it the thrill of emailing them to people that gets you off?'

It was a pretty pathetic attempt to hide my true feelings from him – especially as we both knew that he didn't personally take the photos of Imogen and me – and he was so unmoved by my juvenile comments that he didn't even bother responding to them. He just paused for a second, looking at me with mild disdain, then carried on as if I hadn't said anything at all.

'You see, John,' he said, 'the big difference between me

and you is that while you don't care for your own life, you do care for the lives of others. You have friends, loved ones, family, people that mean something to you . . . and that's a terrible weakness.'

'You think so?'

'I've never cared for anyone in my life.'

'What about your brother?'

'I killed him.'

'But you cared for him before that. You looked after him, protected him—'

'I did what I had to do. He never meant anything to me.' I shook my head. 'I don't believe you.'

'How's your sister?' he said.

'What?'

'Or should I say half-sister?' He looked at me, feigning curiosity. 'Does it make any difference to you, John? I mean, do you think you'd feel any closer to Robyn if you shared the same mother?'

I stared at him, unable to speak for a moment as my mind flashed back to Hale Island again and I saw a gaunt young woman sitting on a dirty bed in a grubby old caravan . . . her knees scrunched up to her chest, her arms wrapped tightly around them . . . her skin deathly pale, her eyes wide open . . . she's shaking, sweating, suffering . . . and then the image fades and I see her again, strung out and frightened, squatting down beside me in the hold of a fishing boat . . . *Hey, bruv*, she says, *how's it going?* And a wonderful sense of warmth surges through me, a rush of tenderness the like of which I haven't felt for a very long time . . .

And I could still feel it now, spreading into my head and tingling at the backs of my eyes . . .

I'd met Robyn Mayo for the first time just over two years ago, and until then neither of us had known of each other's existence. I knew my father had been seeing someone shortly before he died, and I knew her name was Serina Mayo and that she was only eighteen years old, but I didn't know that she'd borne his child. And until I'd met Robyn, and we'd lived through a nightmare together, I'd never realised just how primal the bond between brother and sister can be. But once I'd found out that she was my sister, even before we'd met, that was it. She was part of me, my blood, and whatever else she was, whatever she chose to do, no matter what, she'd always be my sister.

'She lives in Hey now, doesn't she?' Bishop said. 'In one of those squats at the far end of Dean Street?'

I was still staring at him, still unable to say anything.

'You know she was busted again last month, don't you?'

'She wasn't charged.'

'It's only a matter of time.'

'What do you mean?'

'Well, you know how it goes, John. She'll get away with it once or twice, but we know she's dealing now, and it's only a matter of time before—'

'She's not *dealing*, for Christ sake. She's spent the last couple of years trying to quit the fucking stuff.'

'Maybe she shouldn't live in a squat full of junkies then?'

'Maybe not . . . but she's never been a dealer.'

'It wouldn't take much to make her look like one though, would it? She's a known user, she's been done for possession before, she associates with other addicts . . . if she was arrested with a couple of grand's worth of smack on her, which could easily be arranged, I doubt if she'd even get bail. And if it turned out that the gear she was selling was laced with rat poison, and that some poor little kid who'd recently bought a £10 bag from her had just been declared brain dead . . . well, I don't have to tell you the rest, do I?'

I looked into his eyes. 'You'd fucking do it, wouldn't you?'

'I'll do anything if I have to, John. You should know that by now. And that's why you're going to do what I want you to do. Because if you don't, I won't just ruin your sister's life, I'll fuck up everyone you care about. Cal Franks, Bridget, Imogen . . . even that fat old bitch who works for you. I'll rip their fucking lives apart.' He gazed calmly at me. 'Is that clear?'

I nodded.

'Good,' he said, brushing a fleck of dust from his sleeve. 'And you do understand that if anyone else carries on looking into Leon's death, in any way at all, I'm still going to take it out on you?'

'Yeah, I understand.'

'So there won't be any second post-mortems, will there?'

'I don't see how I can do anything about that.'

'Well, it's up to you,' Bishop said dismissively. 'But if you don't do anything about it, you're going to spend the rest of your life wishing you had.'

'I don't have much choice then, do I?'

He smiled. 'There's always a choice.'

As I picked up my glass and drank deeply, I felt

something familiar stirring inside me, a whispered voice in my heart. It was very faint, like the trickle of a faraway stream, and although it was growing stronger and louder all the time, it was still too distant to be heard. I knew it was coming though, and there was something in its promise that made me realise that Bishop was right: I *did* have a choice.

My hand was at my side now, my fingers resting on the cold steel of the Beretta under my thigh.

It was my gun . . .

My history.

My justice.

My choice.

I could take it. I could kill him right now. Raise the gun, pull the trigger, shoot him in the head . . . I could do it. I could *see* myself doing it. The sudden movement as my hand whipped up, the momentary look of surprise in his eyes, the crack of the gun, the simultaneous flat whack of bullet on bone, the jolt in my arm, the hot stink of gunpowder, the slump and judder as the dead weight of his body hit the floor . . .

How would it feel?

It wouldn't feel like anything.

I knew I could do it.

I'd done it before . . .

The night is dark, no stars, no moon. It's three o'clock in the morning. I point the gun at Viner's head and walk him across to the edge of the car park.

'Stop,' I tell him.

He stops.

I look around at the empty night – no traffic, no people, no nothing. There's nothing here, just me and the man who killed my wife and baby. And both of us are less than nothing.

I put the gun to Viner's head and pull the trigger.

. . . I could do it again.

Not now, John, the whisper in my heart said. *Just wait. There'll be another time, another place.*

'Hey Stace,' I muttered, closing my eyes. 'I've missed you.'

'What are you *doing*?'

I opened my eyes and looked at Bishop. He was staring at me with a mixture of alarm and disgust in his eyes.

'Who were you talking to?' he said.

'When?'

'Just then . . . were you talking to your *wife*?'

'Stacy's dead.'

'I know she's fucking dead.' He shook his head. 'Jesus *Christ* . . . what's the matter with you?'

'Nothing,' I said, closing my grip on the pistol. 'I'm fine. There's nothing the matter with me at all.'

He held my gaze for a moment, then I saw his eyes flick down to my right. My fingers tightened on the Beretta, but I kept my arm perfectly still.

'You've still got it then?' Bishop said coolly. 'Your father's gun.'

'It's not my father's,' I said, taking the Beretta from under my thigh. 'It never was, was it?'

Bishop watched as I brought up the pistol and rested it

gently on the desk in front of me. 'The safety's off,' he said, casually studying the gun. He looked up and smiled at me. 'Are you thinking of using it, John?'

'It's an option.'

He shook his head. 'Killing me won't change anything.'

'Letting you live won't change anything either. So what have I got to lose?'

He paused for a moment, smiling thoughtfully, then looked at his watch and said, 'How far's the market square car park from here? Five minutes? Maybe less?'

'What?'

'If I'm not back at the car park in exactly twelve minutes' time, a very capable man in an unregistered Volvo will check his watch, get out of the car, and start making his way up here. And even if you shoot me right this second, you won't have enough time to get rid of my body before he gets here. He'll restrain you, make a phone call, and within twenty minutes you'll be face down on the floor with your hands cuffed behind your back and a dozen angry coppers kicking the shit out of you. And then you'll be arrested, taken down the station, and charged with the murder of a senior police officer.' He brushed at his sleeve again, then went on. 'And in the meantime, while you're locked up in a shitty little cell, my very capable colleague will be following the instructions I left him. He's not quite as refined as me, I'm afraid, and I expect he'll take to the task of destroying your family and friends with a lot more vulgarity than is strictly necessary, but that's just his way. He likes hurting people. And he's very good at it too.' Bishop looked at his watch again, then turned

280

back to me. 'So what about it, John? You still think killing me is an option?'

'I don't see why not,' I said. 'I just shoot you, wait for Mr Capable to show up, and kill him as well.'

Bishop smiled. 'He won't just stroll up here and walk through the door, you know. Renny might be a little crude in his ways, but he's not stupid. And unlike you, he knows how to use a gun. So, yes, I suppose you could try killing him, but even without a gun he's always going to get the better of you. Like I said, he's very good at what he does. And let's face it, you're not exactly Jason Bourne, are you? I mean, look at you . . .' He shook his head. 'I doubt if you can see straight enough to shoot me anyway.'

'There are ten rounds in here,' I said, picking up the Beretta. 'I'd get you with one of them.'

'Well, now's the time if you're going to do it,' he said, buttoning his blazer and getting to his feet.

I raised my arm and levelled the pistol at his head.

No, John, I heard Stacy say. *Not now.*

As Bishop stood there staring at me, and I looked back at him, steadying the pistol sight between his eyes, it was hard not to admire his composure. There was no trace of fear in his eyes, no anxiety, no doubt. And I couldn't help wondering if he genuinely believed that I wouldn't pull the trigger, or if he genuinely didn't care if I did.

'Right then,' he said, putting his hands in his pockets and casually gazing around. 'I'd better get going.' And without so much as a cursory glance at me, he just turned round and sauntered away.

I watched him go, keeping the Beretta aimed at the back

of his head, and I didn't take my finger off the trigger until he'd opened the main office door, walked along the corridor, and started down the stairs. I listened to the sound of his footsteps as they gradually faded away – *tump, tump, tump, tump* . . . passing the second floor now . . . *tump, tump, tump, tump* . . . all the way down to the ground floor – and then, as I heard the muffled slam of the front door closing, I finally lowered the pistol.

My arm ached.

My hand was shaking.

I lit a cigarette and poured myself a drink.

'Another time,' I muttered, raising my glass in promise. 'Another place . . .'

A gust of snow rattled a loose pane in the window. I rubbed my arm, drank my whisky, then filled the glass and drank some more.

19

I don't know how long I sat there after Bishop had gone, just thinking and drinking in the silence, and as far as I know I wasn't consciously aware of any direction or reasoning to my thoughts – I was too far inside myself for that – but when I finally got to my feet, steadying myself for a moment as a rush of blood swirled into my head, I knew in my heart, if not my mind, what I was going to do. I had no idea if it made any sense or not, and only the vaguest notion of what it actually entailed, but that's how I spend most of my life anyway – not really knowing what I'm doing – and while it's not always the best way to be, it's not necessarily the worst either. And besides, if it's the only way you've got, there's not much you can do about it anyway. So you might as well embrace it.

And with that in mind, I took the wrap of sulphate from my pocket, snorted a hefty pinch, and chased it down with a mouthful of whisky. As the speed kicked in, I sniffed hard, wiped snot from my nose, then reached for the phone and called Imogen.

She answered almost immediately. 'Hey, John. Did you get it?'

'Get what?'

'I sent you a text with the name of the pathologist—'

'Oh, yeah . . . yeah, I got it. Gerald McKee.'

'Do you know who he is?'

'I've heard of him, yeah.'

'And?'

'Sorry, Imogen, but I really can't talk about it now. I'll tell you everything later, OK?'

'You'd fucking better,' she said. 'I'm relying on you, John. You know that, don't you?'

'I'll come round as soon as I can,' I told her, glancing at my watch. 'I need to sort out a couple of things first. I'm not sure how long it's going to take, but as soon as I'm finished I'll let you know—'

'Just come over whenever you can, John, all right? It doesn't matter what time it is. I'm not going anywhere.'

'Have you got someone with you?'

'Yeah, Jack Farren's here. He's worked for us for years. I think you know him, don't you?'

'Yeah, I remember Jack. He knows what he's doing.'

'He's just checking round the garden again at the moment.'

'Good. Is he staying all night?'

'He's arranged for someone else to come over at twelve to relieve him.'

'OK,' I said, lighting a cigarette. 'Listen, Imogen, I have to go now, but the reason I called . . . did you tell the Coroner's office you want a second post-mortem on your parents?'

'Yeah, but they said they can't do anything until Monday because they need a written request and instructions from my solicitor. I called the company solicitor just now and he's going to see what he can do about speeding things up so we don't have to wait—'

'You need to call him back,' I said. 'Tell him to leave it for now.'

'But I thought you said—'

'Please, Imogen . . . just trust me, OK? It's important. Call him right now and tell him not to do anything just yet. I'll explain later.'

'Well, all right, if you say so. But—'

'And leave Lisbie alone too.'

'What do you mean?'

'The fire investigator . . . you've been checking him out, haven't you?'

'Who told you that?'

'Is it true?'

'Well, yeah, but—'

'Have you got anything on him yet?'

'Nothing definite . . . but he's had a lot of disciplinary problems in the past which we're still looking into, and his personal life is a complete disaster.' She hesitated. 'I really think he's worth looking into, John.'

'You're probably right,' I said. 'But just leave it for now, OK? Don't do anything else about *any* of this until you've seen me. Don't talk to anyone, don't go anywhere . . . just sit tight and wait. Have you got that?'

She sighed. 'You're asking a lot without telling me much, John.'

'I know.'

'I hope you know what you're doing.'

I hesitated for a second, then said, 'I've got to go, Imogen. I'll see you later, all right?'

'John?'

'Yeah?'

'It's nothing really,' she said sadly, 'I was just . . .' She sighed again. 'It's nothing. I'll talk to you later.'

And before I could say anything else she'd gone. I hung up the phone and just stood there for a while, gazing out through the window at the snow-laden night, then I took a deep breath, let it out slowly, and ran my fingers through my hair. I was drunk to the core now, numbed and painless from the base of my neck to the pit of my groin, but it was a functional numbness, a deadened pillar shot through with an electric rush of amphetamine that made me feel invincible. I knew it was all an illusion, of course, a self-induced deception that I'd pay a steep price for later. But later can always be postponed. And, besides, however illusory a feeling might be, it's still how you feel.

I drained the last few inches of whisky from the bottle, put the Beretta in my pocket, and got going.

It was just gone eight-thirty when I emerged from the gloom of a backstreet alley into the brightly lit babble of the High Street. It was Saturday night and the town centre was coming alive. The pubs were packed, the pavements streaming with groups of young men and women, most of them pre-drunk and barely dressed despite the thickening snow. The sounds of the night echoed flatly around the empty shops and office buildings that lined the street – music thumping from cars and pubs, clacking heels, drunken shouts, shrieks of laughter – and as I made my way up towards the taxi rank, the cocktail of noise seemed to swirl all around me like a living storm, and every time a car passed by, wet tyres hissing through the mush of snow, I heard the sound of a giant sword slicing through the sky.

The taxi rank is halfway up the High Street, directly opposite a club called Liberty's. There were no cabs on the rank when I got there, but a handful of people were queueing up, and none of them seemed too impatient, so I guessed I wouldn't have to wait very long.

I lit a cigarette, took out my mobile, and called Cal.

When I told him the same thing I'd told Imogen – don't do anything else that's got *any*thing to do with Leon – he didn't press me for an explanation, he just asked me to clarify a couple of things.

'You want me to stop everything, yeah?'

'Don't even Google his name.'

'What about automated searches?'

'Close them down.'

'Even if they're not directly related to Leon's death?'

'Just shut it all down, Cal. Everything.'

'What about the other stuff you asked me to look into?' he said. 'Jamaal Tan, Kassim Mukhtar, the drug gangs . . .? Do you want me to keep working on that?'

'No,' I told him. 'Leave it all for now.'

'OK.' He paused. 'Is there anything else I need to know?'

I thought about what Bishop had said . . . *someone's been sniffing around after Leon's computer and email records, and it's not hard to guess who that might be . . .*

I'll fuck up everyone you care about . . . Cal Franks, Bridget, Imogen . . . I'll rip their fucking lives apart . . .

'Mick Bishop paid me a visit,' I told Cal. 'He knows you've been looking into Leon's email account.'

'*What?*'

'Well, he doesn't *know* it's you, but he knows someone's been poking around, and he mentioned your name.'

'Shit,' Cal said. 'That's not good . . . that's not good at all.'

'He's only guessing it's you—'

'That's not the point, John. What worries me is how he knows anything at all. There shouldn't be any way of tracking anything I've done . . . it shouldn't be possible.' He sighed heavily. 'Fuck it. I need to think about this . . .'

A car horn beeped, and when I looked up I realised that I was at the front of the queue and a taxi was waiting for me.

'I've got to go, Cal,' I said, 'I'll ring you later.'

'Yeah . . .'

'Be careful, OK?'

'Right . . .'

I could tell by the distraction in his voice that he wasn't really listening to me any more, and I wanted to make him listen, to warn him about Bishop's threats, but at the same time I didn't want to worry him too much. A couple of years ago he'd taken a really bad beating from two of Bishop's men, and although he'd recovered well from his physical injuries – broken arm, broken leg, fractured skull – I knew the memory of the attack still haunted him. So I didn't want to alarm him unless I really had to, and since I was reasonably sure that Bishop wouldn't bother him as long as he left things alone, it was probably best for Cal if he didn't know about Bishop's threats. On the other hand, though . . .

'Hey!' the taxi driver called out to me. 'You want to go somewhere or not?'

I looked at him – a whey-faced man with a bad moustache – and was tempted to tell him to fuck off. But the snow was really coming down now, thick white sheets whipping around in an icy wind, and a numbing coldness was eating into my bones.

'Cal?' I said into the phone. 'Cal?'

He'd hung up.

I put my phone in my pocket and got into the back of the taxi.

'Cowley Lane,' I told the driver.

He glanced at me in the rear-view mirror, checking me out with his cab-driver's eyes, then he started the meter, put the car into gear, and we headed off down the High Street.

I didn't give any thought to the possibility that Hassan Tan might not be at home. There was no point. I didn't know enough about him to guess if he went out on the town or not, or if he spent all his evenings training or working at Juno's, and if I'd called ahead to find out where he was, I'd have tipped him off that I was coming and lost the element of surprise. So there wasn't much I could do about it anyway. If he was in, all well and good. And if he wasn't . . .? Well, I'd think about that in due course. Right now, as the taxi pulled in at the far end of Cowley Lane, and I paid the driver and got out, I wasn't thinking about anything. My head was as empty as my heart was cold.

It was how I had to be.

I lit a cigarette and waited for the taxi to drive off, then after looking around for a few moments to get my bearings, I crossed the street and started making my way along the pavement towards Hassan's house. Cowley Lane is one of the major trunk routes into town, and even at this time of night the traffic is usually chaotic – cars and lorries racing up and down, horns blaring, the air choked with exhaust fumes – but now, with the heavy snow and the rapidly deteriorating driving conditions, the road was oddly hushed. Traffic was lighter than normal, no one was driving too fast . . . everything was slow and muted.

I couldn't work out if I liked it or not.

It didn't matter.

I'd reached the house now.

A young woman in a cheap duffle coat was standing at the top of the steps struggling to find her front-door key. Her arms were weighed down with Tesco carrier bags full of shopping and she was trying to get the key from her pocket without putting the bags down.

'Are you all right there?' I asked amiably, sauntering confidently up the steps.

She gave me a wary look.

'I'll get the door,' I said, stepping past her and reaching into my pocket. 'You look as if you've got your hands full.'

She nodded, cautiously grateful.

I rummaged around in my pockets, pretending to look for my keys. 'They're here somewhere,' I said, starting to pat my pockets. 'Sorry about this . . . I'm sure I picked

290

them up.' I gave her a slightly embarrassed smile, then frowned to myself and carried on searching.

'It's all right, I'll get it,' she said, shifting a heavy carrier bag from one hand to the other and trying to reach her pocket. 'I just need to—'

'Do you want me to hold that for you?' I asked, offering to take the bag.

'Thank you,' she said, passing me the shopping.

She found her key, opened the front door, and we both went inside.

'Thanks,' I told her, brushing snow from my coat. 'It's a good job you were here. I must have left my keys in my room.'

She nodded again.

'Are you going upstairs?' I asked.

She shook her head. 'Ground floor.'

'I'm on the third,' I said, passing back her shopping bag. 'Just moved in actually . . .'

'OK,' she said, clearly not interested. She nodded once more, gave me a tight little smile, and shuffled off down the hallway with her shopping.

I gave it a moment, then turned round and headed up the stairs.

The smell of marijuana drifting down the stairs was stronger than the last time I'd been here, and the muffled thump of booming music was a lot louder than before, but apart from that, everything was much the same. Scuffed walls, cheap smells, lightless air. The stairs were reasonably well lit, with ceiling lamps at the top of each flight, but there was something about the air itself that seemed to soak up and nullify the light. There was no brightness anywhere, no real colour to anything. It was all just a murk of brown and grey.

Despite the cold, I was drenched in sweat by the time I reached the third floor. My heart was pounding, my hands were shaking, and for a moment or two I couldn't seem to get any air into my lungs. I stopped on the landing and leaned against the wall, waiting for my heart to slow down. *It's nothing to worry about*, I told myself. *It's the speed, that's all. Too much speed. You're not used to it these days.*

I breathed steadily.

The sweat on my back ran cold, making me shiver.

After a minute or two, I felt OK again. I wiped my face, ran my fingers through my hair, and headed down the corridor. The booming music was even louder now, a hypnotic throb of bass and drums thumping down from the floor above, and as I approached Hassan Tan's flat, I wondered how anyone could put up with it. Not that I really cared. It was just something to think about, something to take my mind off what I was about to do.

I stopped at the door to Flat 8. I couldn't hear anything beyond the door, and there was no keyhole or letter box to peer through, but a faint strip of light was showing through a gap at the foot of the door, and although that didn't necessarily mean Hassan was in, I knew that he was. I didn't know how I knew, but something inside me was telling me he was there, and that was good enough for me.

I took the Beretta from my pocket, held it down at my side, and knocked on the door.

After a moment, I heard him call out, 'Yeah, who is it?'

'Me,' I called back.

'Who's *me*?' he said irritably.

'I've got something for you.'

'*What*?'

'Do you want it or not?'

'Fuck's *sake*,' he muttered, and I heard him approaching the door. 'Who are you? What do you want?'

'It's me,' I said again.

'I don't know who the fuck you are,' he said angrily, unlocking the door, 'but you'd better not be wasting my time.'

As a bolt slid back and the door swung open, it only took a moment for Hassan to recognise me, but before he could do anything with the knife he was holding, I stepped forward, put the Beretta to his head, and forced him back into the flat.

'What the *fuck*—?'

'Lose the knife,' I told him, stabbing the barrel into his cheek. '*Now!*'

'All right, all right,' he said quickly, dropping the knife to the floor and showing me his empty hand. 'It's gone, OK? There's no need to—'

'Shut up,' I said, moving back a step but still keeping the gun levelled at his head. 'Put your hands on your head.'

He did as he was told.

'Turn round,' I said.

'What are you going to—?'

'*Turn round!*'

He hesitated for a moment, blinking nervously, then slowly turned round. Without taking my eyes off him, I stepped back and kicked the door shut. The sudden sharp *slam* was louder than I'd imagined, and as Hassan flinched violently at the noise, I realised that he'd mistaken the sound for a gun shot. For a second or two he was too shocked to move, and as he stood there rooted to the spot – his eyes squeezed shut, his head bowed down, his shoulders hunched . . . cowering like a helpless child – it was almost too much to bear, and for a moment or two I wondered if I had the guts to go through with this. But as Hassan quickly realised that he hadn't been shot, and he straightened up slowly and looked round at me, my doubts disappeared. His fighter's instinct had kicked in, I could see it in his eyes – the resolve, the courage, the aggression. *I can take it*, he was letting me know. *Whatever you've got, I can take it.*

'Sit down over there,' I told him, indicating an unmade bed in the corner of the room.

He didn't move, just stood there staring me out.

I levelled the Beretta at his head.

He grinned at me, holding out his hands, daring me to shoot.

I lowered the pistol, aimed it just to the right of his left leg, and pulled the trigger. As the gun jerked in my hand, and the shot rang out, Hassan suddenly gasped, his face screwed up in pain.

'*Fuck!*' he hissed through gritted teeth, doubling over and clutching his leg. 'Fucking *hell*!'

I thought he was just acting at first, trying to make me think that I'd shot him, but when he let go of his leg for a moment and glared at the blood on his hand, I realised that he wasn't pretending. There was a ragged tear in the left leg of his trackpants, about six inches below his knee, and through the torn material I could see a strip of bloodied flesh where the bullet had grazed his skin. I wondered if it was my aim that was off or the pistol's.

'You shot me, you cunt,' Hassan said with stunned disbelief. 'You fucking *shot* me.'

'It's just a scratch,' I said dismissively. 'But the next one won't be.' I raised the gun again. 'The next time you don't do what I tell you, I'll put one in your elbow. And that *will* hurt. And if you carry on pissing me off, I'll do your other elbow, and maybe one of your kneecaps too, or both of them.' I stepped towards him, staring into his eyes, letting him see the truth in mine. 'I don't want to hurt you, Hassan, but I will if I have to. Do you understand? No one's going to hear anything, not with that fucking racket going on upstairs, so I can do whatever I want.' I moved even closer to him. 'It's up to you how it's going to go. You can either tell me what I want to know, and never see me again, or you can keep your mouth shut and spend the next six months in hospital, and when you get out, you'll never fight again.' I paused, still looking deep into his eyes. 'So, what's it going to be?'

He didn't answer immediately, and as I saw his eyes searching mine, looking for any sign of weakness, I thought for a moment that he was going to call my bluff. I almost made the mistake of wondering what I was going to do if he did stand up to me, but I managed to force the possibility from my mind. He had to believe I was capable of hurting him, and the only way I could truly convince him was by believing it myself. I emptied my head of conscious thought, unlocked my darkest memories, and let him see through my eyes what I'd done in the past and what I knew I was going to do again.

An age seemed to pass before he eventually blinked – although in reality it was probably only a couple of seconds – and then he sighed softly, his shoulders dropped, and I knew all the fight had gone out of him.

'All right,' he said wearily. 'What do you want to know?'

I waited while Hassan limped over to the bed and sat down, then I picked up the knife he'd dropped, put it in my pocket, and made my way over to a springless settee on the other side of the room. I sat down, lit a cigarette, and looked around for something to use as an ashtray.

'Do you have to do that?' Hassan said, eyeing the cigarette.

'Yeah, I do.'

I flicked ash into an empty cup. Hassan shook his head, then turned his attention to his injured leg. I watched as he gingerly rolled up the leg of his trackpants and leaned over to study the wound. From what I could see – a raw pink gash in the fleshy part of his lower leg – it didn't look too bad. It undoubtedly hurt like hell, and it could probably do with a few stitches, but it wasn't too deep, and it wasn't even bleeding that much. As he tore a strip from the bed sheet and began wrapping it round his leg, I drew on my cigarette and gazed round the room. There wasn't much to it. Apart from the bed and the settee, there were a few shelves, a table by the window, a small TV, and a couple of rackety old cupboards. There was a punchbag and a set of weights in one corner, and a cramped little kitchen area in another. Cooker, microwave, fridge . . . packets of rice and stuff on a shelf. A door on the left led through into what I guessed was the bathroom, and that was about it.

The music upstairs was still booming away – *d-doomp-doomp, doomp-doomp . . . d-doomp-doomp, doomp-doomp* – and my head was aching.

I glanced over at Hassan. He was tying off the bandage on his leg. 'Have you got anything to drink?' I asked him.

'Uh?' he said, without looking up.

'Have you got anything to drink?'

He shrugged. 'There might be some Red Bull in the fridge.'

'Nothing else?'

'Plenty of water.'

'Any whisky or anything?'

The way he looked at me, you'd think I'd just asked him for unicorn's milk. He went back to examining his leg, and I just sat there studying him for a while. He seemed a lot younger than the Hassan I remembered from Juno's. He still looked every inch the boxer – dressed in a sweat-stained tracksuit and a Lonsdale T-shirt, his left cheek still swollen from the beating he'd taken at Juno's, a butterfly-stitched cut over his right eye – but there was just something different about him now, and I couldn't quite pin it down. Maybe it was the surroundings, the situation, or just the fact that he was only a few feet away from me . . . or perhaps it was just me. But whatever it was, he definitely seemed more adolescent now, much more of a boy than a man. He was eighteen, if I remembered correctly, but he could easily pass for fifteen or sixteen. He was just a kid really. And that didn't make what I was doing any easier.

You're not doing this because you want to do it, I reminded myself, *you're doing it because you have to.*

I knew I was right. But it didn't make me feel any better. I still felt like a cunt.

Hassan had finished bandaging his leg now and was sitting on the edge of the bed cautiously flexing his left foot, checking for any damage.

'How is it?' I asked him.

'What do you fucking care?' he said, not looking at me.

I dropped my cigarette-end in the empty cup and lit another. Hassan glanced up at the sound of the cigarette lighter, shook his head, then looked down again and began rubbing his leg.

'Tell me what happened to Jamaal,' I said to him.

He paused for a moment, staring at nothing, then carried on examining his leg. 'What makes you think I know anything?'

'Because you're scared.'

'Am I?'

I nodded. 'You're scared of talking about Jamaal.'

'Maybe I just don't want to talk about him,' he said. 'I mean, maybe I don't want to talk to you about my brother because it's none of your fucking business.'

'It became my business when your aunt hired me.'

'No, it didn't,' he said.

The mention of his aunt had a curious effect on Hassan – quietening him somehow, shrinking him – and as he sat there on the bed with his head bowed down and his eyes lowered, like a troubled child, I couldn't help wondering what lay behind it. I remembered then what Bishop had told me about Ayanna. *The poor cow doesn't even know she's making things up most of the time*, he'd said. *She lives in the fucking clouds.*

I looked over at Hassan again, wondering what kind of life he'd had . . .

I couldn't afford to think about it.

'What happened to him, Hassan?' I said quietly. 'Who killed your brother?'

He slowly looked up at me. 'Do you know what's going to happen to me if I talk to you?'

'I know what's going to happen if you don't,' I replied, holding up the pistol to remind him.

He sighed and shook his head, a look of resigned contempt in his eyes. 'You're no different than the rest of them, are you? You think you are, but you're not. You're just another bastard *copper*.' He sucked air through his teeth, as if cleaning a bad taste from his mouth. 'You're all the fucking same, every single one of you.'

'Are you saying the police have threatened you?'

'Of course they fucking *threatened* me. That's what they do. And the only difference between the way they do it and the way you do it is—'

'Who threatened you? Was it Lilley?'

'*Lilley?*' Hassan said with a snort of derision. 'Lilley's got fuck all to do with anything. He's just . . .'

'Just what?'

Hassan hesitated, suddenly realising that he'd said more than he'd meant to say, and I knew that if I didn't do something to keep him talking, and do it right now, I'd have to resort to acting like a cunt again, and I really didn't think I could do that any more.

'It's Mick Bishop, isn't it?' I said, watching Hassan carefully. 'It's Bishop who's behind all this.'

At the sound of Bishop's name, Hassan took a sharp breath and went very still for a moment, and when he looked up at me, I could see the tension in his face, the fear and loathing in his eyes.

'You know Bishop?' he asked warily.

'Yeah, I know him,' I said, holding Hassan's gaze. 'I know what he does, what he's done, what he can do . . . I know all about Mick Bishop.'

'Really?'

I nodded.

Hassan stared thoughtfully at me for a while, mulling over what I'd just said, and I just sat there in silence, letting him draw his own conclusions. I didn't feel too good now. The effects of the whisky and speed were starting to wear off, and I could feel the beginnings of a desperate ache for more. My chest was tight, my mouth was dry, my head was clouding with a stale grey emptiness . . .

I needed a drink.

I *needed* it.

Shit, I thought, lighting a cigarette.

Why do you do it?

'It wasn't a drug thing,' Hassan said quietly.

I looked at him.

'That's the only reason I called the *Gazette*,' he went on. 'Because no one else was fucking listening to me. I didn't think there was a cover-up or anything, I just thought the cops didn't know what they were doing, and it really pissed me off.' He shrugged. 'That's all it was.'

'Right . . .' I said, confused, but trying not to show it. 'When did you call the *Gazette*?'

'A few days after Jamaal was killed. Lilley had given us all this shit about the gear they'd found in his pockets, and it was obvious they were trying to put it down as just another gang thing, you know, another drug-related murder, and I know for a fucking *fact* that as long as no one else is involved the cops don't give a shit about gang-killings. All they do is make all the right noises for a couple of weeks or so, then quietly forget the whole fucking thing. And I wasn't having that with Jamaal.' Hassan looked at me. 'Especially as it wasn't a gang-killing anyway.'

'How do you know it wasn't?' I asked.

'He was my kid brother . . . we grew up in Mogadishu. I looked out for him from the minute he was fucking born.' Hassan swallowed hard. 'He was my kid brother, OK? I knew him better then he knew himself.'

'So he wasn't mixed up with gangs?'

Hassan sighed. 'He hung around with them sometimes, down at Redhills mostly. He didn't know what he was doing . . . poor bastard never really did. He just . . . I don't know. He just didn't think sometimes, you know? Didn't think things through.' Hassan shook his head, a heavy sadness in his eyes. 'He did the odd bit of running for the gang kids now and then, but that was about it. He was never really *in* with them. He didn't have what it takes. He definitely never sold for them.'

'But he used drugs himself, didn't he?'

Hassan nodded. 'Jamaal was always pretty fucked up. I mean, we both went through a lot of shit when we were kids, and I was just as bad as Jamaal for a while . . . you know, doing everything I could get hold of – coke, weed, Ecstasy . . . whatever. But it was never really a big deal for me, I could always take it or leave it, and when I started getting into boxing I just didn't need it any more. I didn't want to keep fucking myself up, so I packed it all in. But Jamaal didn't have anything else, you know? All he ever wanted to do was get wasted.'

'What did he take?' I asked.

Hassan shrugged. 'Anything . . . everything. Whatever he could get his hands on. As long as it did *some*thing to him, he didn't care what it was.'

'So the stuff they found in his pockets, the crack and the heroin, that *could* have been his?'

Hassan shook his head. 'He'd *take* any crack or junk he could get, and if he'd had enough money to buy the amount they found on him – which is highly unlikely – or if the chance came along for him to nick that much . . . well, I can see him doing that. But there's no way he would have gone down the subways at that time of night, on his own, with half a grand's worth of shit in his pockets. Jamaal might have been stupid, but he wasn't fucking suicidal.' Hassan sighed again, absentmindedly scratching at the stitches over his eye. 'And even if I'm wrong,' he went on, 'and Jamaal did go down there with a load of gear on him, the idea that it was some kind of gang-killing still doesn't make any sense.'

'Because whoever killed him would have emptied his pockets,' I said.

Hassan looked at me. 'Exactly. And they wouldn't have stabbed him so many times either. They would have just killed him, robbed him, and fucked off.'

'And is that what you told the reporter from the *Gazette*?'

He nodded. 'Not that it did any good.'

'Why not?'

'I don't know . . . I mean, he sounded really interested on the phone, asking me all kinds of questions and stuff, and he told me he'd look into it and get back to me . . . but he never did. And nothing ever got printed.'

'What was his name?'

'Jason Morgan.'

'Did you try getting in touch with him again?'

'I was going to,' he said quietly, 'but the day after I'd called him, Bishop came round.'

'Bishop came round here?'

Hassan nodded, staring at the floor. 'The bastard . . . comes in here with his fake fucking sympathy, telling me how *sorry* he is for my loss, then asks me if I wouldn't mind coming down the station with him to answer a few questions . . .' Hassan paused for a moment, then looked up at me. 'I told him to fuck off. And that's when he pulled the bag of coke from his pocket and told me to think again. He said I could either come down to the station with him of my own accord, or he'd arrest me for possession and have me taken down in cuffs. So I didn't really have much choice, did I?'

'What happened when you got there?'

'The fucker did me for the coke anyway.' He shook his head. 'He had it all planned out . . . I was put in a cell on my own at first, but about five minutes after I'd seen the duty solicitor I was taken out and moved to a cell at the end of the corridor. There were two of them in there, big nasty fuckers covered in swastika tattoos . . . like fucking psycho-Nazis or something.' Hassan shrugged. 'I held them off for a while, but they were always going to get me eventually. Bastards whacked the fuck out of me. I couldn't piss for two days afterwards.'

'How long were you in there for?'

'I don't know . . . I passed out during the night, and when I woke up, the two of them were gone. I kind of lost track of the time then, but it was light outside when they finally opened the door and took me up to Bishop's office. He didn't waste much time on me. He said that I wasn't being charged on this occasion, but if I ever spoke to anyone about Jamaal's murder again, anyone at all, he'd put me away for good. And that was it really. All I had to do, he told me, was go home and keep my mouth shut, and everything would be OK.' Hassan looked at me. 'So that's what I did . . . and everything *was* OK.'

'And then I showed up.'

'Yeah, and now you're going to do me if I *don't* talk about Jamaal. So basically I'm fucked if I talk to you and fucked if I don't.'

'Not necessarily.'

He looked at me.

'Bishop's not here, is he?' I said.

'So?'

'So how's he going to know that you talked to me?'

'What do you think Dempsey's going to do when he finds out I've been shot in the leg?'

'Why does he *have* to find out?'

'He's my fucking manager, remember? I'm supposed to be training for another fight. How am I supposed to hide a bullet wound from my manager?'

I shrugged. 'Tell him it was an accident, you got mixed up in a gang shooting or something—'

'He's still going to check it out with Bishop, isn't he? And then Bishop's going to start asking me questions . . .' Hassan shook his head. 'He'll find out it was you.'

'How?'

'He just will. He always finds out.' Hassan looked at me. 'I mean, how do I know that *you* won't tell him I've talked to you?'

'I'm not going to tell him anything. Why would I tell Bishop anything?'

'How do I fucking know?' he said. 'You're a liar, a drunk, you shot me in the fucking leg . . . you really expect me to trust you?'

'All right,' I admitted, 'I suppose you've got a point. But at least if you talk to me you'll be buying yourself some time with Bishop, won't you? I mean, I'm *here*, I'm going to fuck you up right now if you don't talk to me, and even if Bishop does find out, he's not going to find out immediately, is he?'

'So what am I supposed to do?' Hassan said. 'Jump on a plane to fucking Mexico or somewhere?' He shook his head. 'Knowing that bastard, he'd still probably find me.'

'Yeah, well,' I sighed, wearily raising the pistol, 'it's up to you, Hassan. I can't decide for you. But if I was in your shoes, and I knew I was fucked whatever I did, I'd at least try to make sure that something came out of it.'

He stared at me. 'Like what?'

'The truth,' I said. 'And who knows, if you tell me what really happened to Jamaal, I might even bring his killer to justice.'

'And what good's that going to do?' Hassan said. 'Jamaal's still going to be dead, isn't he? Even if you do get the fucker who did it, and even if he does get charged and brought to trial, which I very much doubt—'

'Who said anything about bringing him to trial?'

Hassan stared at me, and as I looked back at him, making sure he understood what I meant, I got the feeling that one or two doors were beginning to creak open in his mind. They weren't opening very much, just a few cautious inches, but they weren't being slammed shut either. And eventually, after we'd sat there together in the thumping silence for perhaps a minute or so, I saw something change in Hassan, an indefinable yet unmistakeable shift in his demeanour, and I knew then that he'd made up his mind.

'I warned Jamaal he was going to get himself killed,' he sighed, shaking his head. 'I fucking *told* him, but he just wouldn't listen . . .'

I lit a cigarette, sat back, and listened to Hassan's story.

306

20

Before signing up with Curt Dempsey, Hassan had heard lots of whispers and rumours about Juno's, but it wasn't until he'd been training there for some months, working out at the club every day, that he began to realise that not only were most of the rumours true, but that they barely even scratched the surface of what really went on at Juno's.

'And that's partly because Dempsey puts a lot of effort into the legitimate side of the business,' Hassan told me. 'It really is a good fitness club. The facilities are excellent – swimming pool, sauna, state-of-the-art gym – and it's very well managed, which is a lot more than you can say about most gyms. I mean, Juno's might be a front, but it's not *just* a front, if you know what I mean.'

'What's it a front for?' I asked him.

'Pretty much everything you can think of – drugs, prostitution, protection, porn, extortion . . .' He shrugged. 'I mean, if you think about it, it's kind of obvious really.'

'What do you mean?'

'Well, it's a fitness club . . . it's all there, isn't it? Half-naked bodies all over the place, girls *and* boys, muscle-bound thugs, guaranteed privacy . . . and as for drugs, they're fucking everywhere. Whatever you want. Your personal trainer can get you anything – steroids, uppers, downers, grass, roofies, Viagra, dolls, K, candy, smack . . . a lot of them use smack these days. You want a girl, a boy, both . . . you want a business rival beaten up . . . whatever you want, you just have to ask. There's private rooms, *very* private rooms. There's a bar, a restaurant . . . it's all very respectable. A lot of members hold their "business meetings" at Juno's.'

'And how does it work? I mean, if I'm a member, and I want something, what do I have to do?'

'What do you want?'

'I don't know . . . say I want a girl.'

'No problem. You just have a quiet word with one of the managers. He'll show you to a room, give you a menu, a price list, hourly rates, then he'll take your order and leave you to it. The cost shows up on your quarterly bill as something else, training services or something.'

'What's on the menu?'

'Everything – girls, boys, girl-boys . . . all colours, all ages . . .'

'What about drugs?'

'Pretty much the same thing. You have a meal, a quiet drink, then have a quiet word with your waiter and he'll sort it all out for you.'

'Protection . . . ?'

'Well, say you're a businessman, you own a string of shops . . . sports shops, say. Someone comes along and opens up a new shop down the road selling cheaper gear. You start losing business. So you go to Juno's and talk to Dempsey. A couple of days later, the owner of the new sports shop is lying in hospital with a ruptured spleen.'

'How does Dempsey keep all this quiet?'

'It's membership only, for a start. Very exclusive, *very* expensive. And all applications for membership are vetted really thoroughly.' Hassan looked at me. 'That's one of the things that Bishop deals with.'

'The vetting?'

'Yeah . . . Jamaal told me that Bishop runs background checks on everyone who applies, and no one's accepted as a member *unless* they've got something to hide. And since they're all either very powerful or very rich, they've all got a few secrets hidden away. So if any of the members start shooting their mouth off about anything, Dempsey's always got something on them.'

'So Bishop's in with Dempsey?'

Hassan nodded. 'They've known each other for years. Bishop protects Dempsey, keeps the cops off his back, and in return Dempsey gives him a cut of everything. It's like a two-way thing, you know? They're both so deep in each other's pockets that they *have* to look out for each other.' He looked at me. 'Did you hear about Tony Gameiro?'

I had to think for a second before it came to me. 'The guy who got killed in a hit-and-run outside his house, the dealer . . .?'

'Yeah, that's him. He used to work at Juno's, but he got greedy and started dealing outside the club. I don't really know what happened when he got busted, whether Dempsey set him up or not, or if he just got word that Tony was thinking of doing a deal and ratting out Dempsey in return for a lighter sentence . . . but when the news came out that he'd been run over and killed, everyone at Juno's knew it wasn't an accident.'

'You're saying Dempsey did it?'

Hassan shrugged. 'No one was ever caught, the car was never found . . . I mean, the cops made a show of looking into it for a week or two, but they needn't have bothered really. No one gave a fuck about Tony Gameiro. Why should they? He was just another small-time dealer, a worthless piece of shit . . . he had it coming, didn't he?'

'So Dempsey had him killed and Bishop covered it up.'

Hassan just looked at me.

'And that's what happened to Jamaal?' I said, staring back at him.

After a moment's pause, Hassan nodded.

Jamaal was only twelve years old when he first went with a man for money, and when Hassan had found out about it, and asked him why the hell he'd done it, his brother had just shrugged and said, 'Why not?'

'He said he was hungry,' Hassan told me. 'Said he really wanted some KFC. So he tossed off this old fucker in the toilets at Tesco's for the price of a bucket of fried fucking chicken.'

He never really *worked* as a rent boy, but if he needed money – for whatever reason – he didn't think twice about selling himself.

'He was always a good-looking kid,' Hassan said, 'and once he'd found out how piss-easy it was – you know, twenty quid for sucking a guy's dick for a few minutes . . .' Hassan shook his head. 'Shit, I mean . . .

310

I don't know . . . it just didn't seem to bother him what he fucking did . . .' Hassan's voice trailed off and he sat there in silence for a while, picking at his fingernails, staring at the bed.

I lit a cigarette and waited for him to go on.

'I don't suppose he ever had much of a chance,' I heard Hassan mutter. 'I mean, if your mother's a whore, and she fucks off and leaves you with her sister who's just as fucking bad—'

'You mean Ayanna?' I said, surprised.

Hassan looked up at me. 'She gave you the story, did she?'

'What story?'

'She looked after us, she did her best, she tried to shield us from our mother's wicked ways . . .?' He smiled bitterly. 'She's told it like that so many times that I think she actually believes it. But it's all bollocks. She was just as much a whore as our mother . . . still is, for all I know.'

I didn't want to believe him, for Ayanna's sake if nothing else, but I couldn't think why he would lie about her. And everything about him – his voice, his bearing, the look in his eyes . . . all seemed perfectly genuine. But Ayanna had seemed perfectly genuine to me too . . .

So what the fuck did I know?

I needed a drink.

That's what I knew.

'Jamaal didn't have a part-time job at Juno's, did he?' I said to Hassan.

He shook his head. 'He wasn't interested in boxing, didn't really give a shit about what I was doing, but when

Dempsey took me on, Jamaal started coming along to Juno's with me, just for something to do, you know? He'd hang around the gym for a bit, then wander off on his own . . . it didn't take him long to realise what was going on there. And once he found out that the whole place was swimming in drugs . . . well, you couldn't keep him away. He was like a kid in a sweet shop.' Hassan sighed. 'I should have known what would happen . . . I should have done something. But I was too wrapped up in myself . . . you know, training, boxing, trying to do something with my life. I just kind of forgot about looking after Jamaal. Next thing I know, he's on the fucking menu, being pimped out to any old fucker who wants him . . . and no one gives a *shit*, you know? No one cares. He's just a piece of dark meat, a new fucking toy to play around with . . . and there was nothing I could do about it, fucking *nothing*. If I'd told the cops, Bishop would have found out, and Dempsey would have had me whacked, and they'd probably have taken out Jamaal too, just to be on the safe side. And Jamaal couldn't do anything either. He was part of it all now, and once you're part of it, you can't stop being part of it . . . so he just kept doing it.' Hassan shook his head again. 'Do you know what he told me once? He said that compared to all the shit we'd been through, it wasn't such a bad life really. He was making a bit of money, getting free drugs . . .' Hassan closed his eyes for a moment, reliving the bitter memory, then he took a deep breath, blew out his cheeks, and went on. 'Anyway, one Sunday night, Jamaal came round here before going off to Juno's. He was already fucked out of his head on something, jabbering away like a madman, and he started telling me about this big idea he's got. We're going to be rich, he says, we're getting out of this shithole and fucking off to the Caribbean or some-where . . .' Hassan smiled sadly. 'He really believed it, you know? He really thought he had it all worked out.'

'What was his big idea?' I asked.

Hassan sighed. 'You know who Meredith Chase is?'

'The MP for Hey West?'

Hassan nodded. 'I think he's something in the government now, a minister or something . . .'

I shook my head. 'He's never been a minister. He used to be the *shadow* defence minister, but he resigned from the shadow cabinet in 2006.'

Hassan looked at me. 'How come you know so much about him?'

'I've had dealings with him before.'

'So you probably know what he likes then.'

I nodded. 'He likes young boys.'

'Yeah, and that's why he goes to Juno's whenever he can.'

'Chase is a member?'

'He's a *privileged* member, which basically means you don't have to pay for anything . . . well, not directly anyway. They all pay in the end, of course, one way or the other. But yeah, Chase is a member. It was around June last year when he first picked Jamaal from the menu. Jamaal didn't have a clue who he was then – he could have been the fucking Prime Minister for all Jamaal knew – but Chase really took a liking to Jamaal, and pretty soon he was asking for him every time he went to Juno's. Jamaal didn't like the guy, he didn't *like* any of them, but he told me that Chase was different to the others, that he didn't just want to fuck him, he wanted to talk to him as well. And that's how Jamaal found out who he was, because the stupid old bastard told him. Told him who he was, what he was, what he did, where he worked . . . like he was trying to impress Jamaal, you know? As if he fucking cared.' Hassan paused for a moment and started to get up off the bed. But then, remembering the gun in my hand, he stopped halfway and looked across at me. 'Just getting a drink, yeah?'

'OK.'

'Don't shoot me, all right?'

I smiled quietly, watching him as he carried on over to the fridge, took out a can of Red Bull, popped it open, took a long drink, then went back and sat down on the bed again.

'So that Sunday night,' he continued, 'Jamaal started telling me how he'd been with Chase the night before, and Chase had been drinking on and off all day, so he didn't know what the fuck he was doing, and he started mouthing off to Jamaal about Dempsey, telling all these stories about him, like they're best fucking buddies or something, you know? And that's when he told Jamaal about this big favour he's doing for Dempsey, something to do with a contract that one of Dempsey's companies is bidding for.' Hassan took another drink, finishing off the Red Bull and crushing the can. 'Chase told Jamaal that he's working with Dempsey to make sure his company gets the job . . . says he knows a guy at the Ministry of Defence who's got a say in who gets the contract. Jamaal reckoned Chase had something on this guy, some kind of hold over him . . .'

'Did he mention his name?'

Hassan shook his head. 'Chase was still drinking, and by this time he was so pissed he could hardly speak. I mean, he was totally fucking wrecked, apparently, just lying there on the bed, barely conscious, half-naked, mumbling away about God-knows-what . . . and that's when Jamaal gets his big idea. He sees him lying there, this sad old bastard, and it suddenly hits him that he's not just a sad old bastard, he's an MP . . . he's *somebody*, you know? And he's bent, he fucks young boys, he does "favours" for people like Dempsey . . .' Another sad smile came to Hassan's face. 'Jamaal told me that when he was standing there looking down at Chase, all he could see was a big sack of cash. He said it reminded him of that Bugs Bunny cartoon when Bugs is stranded on a desert island with two starving castaways, and they're so hungry they start hallucinating, seeing each other as burgers and hot dogs and stuff . . . he said it was just like that, only instead of seeing Chase as a giant burger lying on the bed, he saw him as this big sack of cash, with like pound signs on the side, you know?' Hassan sighed. 'He loved all those old-fashioned cartoons, you know, Bugs Bunny, Tom and Jerry, Roadrunner, shit like that. He'd watch them for hours . . .'

Hassan stared silently at the bed for a while, lost in his thoughts and memories, and I just sat there, smoking another cigarette, letting him have as much time as he needed. I'd already worked out what had happened to Jamaal now, so apart from my aching desire to get out of this room and get myself something to drink, I was in no great hurry to hear the rest of Hassan's story. So as we sat there together in the still-booming silence, I took the opportunity to start searching through my own dimmed memory, trying to remember the details of the article in the *Gazette* that I'd seen on Cal's laptop, the piece about Dempsey and Morden Hall. I was fairly sure the article had mentioned something about the Ministry of Defence, and that one of Dempsey's companies was bidding for a multimillion-pound contract to develop Morden Hall, but no matter how hard I tried, I just couldn't come up with anything else. I could see the article in my mind – the shape of it, the form of it – and I could even see the memory I'd had when I'd read it – the remembered image of the old brick ruins across the misted vale – but my head was just too clouded to see any facts or details.

'He took photographs,' Hassan said.

I looked up. 'Photographs of Chase?'

Hassan nodded. 'He used the camera on his mobile. Chase was too drunk to know what Jamaal was doing. He took some of Chase on his own, lying half-naked on the bed, then he undressed him and took some more, and then he stripped off and took a whole series of shots that clearly showed the two of them doing all kinds of stuff together, you know . . . and he got a couple of videos too. He was going to take more videos but the battery ran out on his mobile.'

'Did he show you the pictures?'

'I saw some of them, yeah . . . the ones of Chase on his own. I couldn't look at the others.'

'Right . . . and he told you he was going to use the pictures to blackmail Chase?'

Hassan nodded again. 'Said he was going to hit him for fifty grand. I *told* him . . . I mean, I went fucking *crazy* at him, you know? Screaming and yelling, trying to get him to see how fucking stupid it was, how all he was going to do was get himself killed, but he wouldn't listen. He just kept telling me not to worry, he had it all worked out . . .' Hassan shook his head. 'I gave up trying to reason with him then, I just went for him, trying to get hold of his phone so I could delete all the pictures . . . and I nearly got it. I was so close, you know . . . I had hold of him, I *had* him, and I was just getting the phone out of his pocket, and then . . . I don't know . . . I don't know how he did it. He just kind of twisted round and slipped out of my arms, and before I knew it he was gone. The last time I saw him he was legging it out of my flat, grinning like a little kid, slamming the door shut in my face.' Hassan looked at me. 'He was killed the following night.'

'When do you think he threatened Chase with the pictures?'

'Sunday night, probably. He either saw him at Juno's or found out where he lives and went round to his house. He probably showed Chase the photos and told him how much he wanted for them, and then Chase probably told him he needed time to get the money together or something . . . and then as soon as Jamaal had gone, Chase would have got in touch with Dempsey and told him everything.' Hassan shrugged. 'Dempsey tells him not to worry, he'll sort it out . . . and that's what he does. He sorts it out.

And the next night my brother's lying dead in a subway – beaten up, raped, stabbed to death . . .'

'I don't suppose he made copies of the photographs, did he?'

Hassan shook his head. 'Not that I know of. By the time I was allowed into his flat, the police had already been through everything, so even if he did make copies, Bishop would have got hold of them.'

'What about the original photos on his mobile?'

'According to the police report, no phone was found with the body. I thought about calling his mobile the day after they found him, just in case he'd just left it somewhere or something, but then I realised that Dempsey or Bishop might be monitoring his number, you know, just in case someone else knew about the pictures . . . and if they found out I was calling Jamaal, they'd probably come after me . . .'

I nodded. 'Would Dempsey have killed Jamaal himself?'

'No, he doesn't do his own dirty work.'

'Any idea who did do it?'

'Not really . . . I mean, Dempsey knows a lot of people, he has a lot of people working for him. Any of them could have done it.'

'No, they couldn't,' I said quietly. 'Jamaal wasn't just killed, he was beaten and raped, stabbed twenty-two times . . . it takes a certain kind of man to do that.'

Hassan hesitated for a moment. 'There's a guy at Juno's called Renny Surnam . . . I mean, I don't *know* if he did it or not, it's only a feeling . . . but Surnam's a serious fucking headcase, and I've heard some really sick stuff about him. Things he's done to people – men and women, kids – fucking awful things . . . the kind of stuff that real fucking psychos like doing, you know?'

It took me a few moments to remember where I'd heard the name Renny before, but suddenly it came to me. It was when Bishop had been telling me about his 'very capable colleague', the one who 'likes hurting people'. *Renny might be a little crude in his ways*, Bishop had said, *but he's not stupid*.

'Everyone's shit-scared of him,' Hassan went on, 'even the people he works with. They all keep away from Surnam. I saw him break a kid's arm once. Dempsey found out that one of his fighters was trying to make a deal with another promoter, so he asked Surnam to teach him a lesson. He was a big strong guy, this kid, a light-heavyweight – and a fucking good boxer – but Surnam took him by surprise, got him down on the floor, twisted his arm up behind his back, and just snapped it like a twig . . .' Hassan looked at me. 'And while this kid was still lying there, screaming his head off, Surnam leaned down and whispered something in his ear, then punched him so hard in the balls that the guy ended up having one of them amputated.'

'What does Surnam look like?' I asked.

Hassan frowned. 'He doesn't actually *look* that scary . . . well, he does, but not in an obvious way, if you know what I mean. It's kind of hard to describe . . .'

'Is he big?'

'Six foot, maybe, pretty solid. But he's not massive, you know?'

'Mid-thirties?'

'Yeah . . .'

'Old-fashioned haircut, dirty-blond hair?'

'You know him?'

'I think so,' I said, picturing the guy at Juno's who'd grabbed me by the balls. 'What does he actually do for Dempsey?'

Hassan shrugged. 'Whatever he's told.'

'Does he work for Bishop too?'

'Probably . . . how do you know Surnam?'

I thought back to the moment I'd first seen Mick Bishop at Juno's that night – standing with Dempsey and another man outside a closed door at the far end of the corridor. I'd barely even glanced at the third man then, dismissing him as just another security guard, but I was fairly sure now that he was Renny Surnam, and that Surnam was Bishop's 'very capable colleague'.

I put out my cigarette, stood up and stretched, then walked stiffly over to the window and pulled back the curtain. The window was misted. I wiped my hand across the glass and peered out into the night. The snow had stopped. The street-lit pavements were still mostly white, tracked here and there with scuffed black footprints, but the road itself was already turning to slush.

'Is that it?' I heard Hassan say. 'Are we done now?'

I turned round and looked at him. 'You haven't told anyone else about this, have you?'

'I wouldn't be here if I had. I'd be lying in the fucking mortuary—'

'Have Bishop or Dempsey said anything to you? I mean, do you think they suspect you of knowing anything?'

He shook his head. 'I'm sure it occurred to them, but apart from that night I spent in the cells, and Bishop's warning to keep my mouth shut, neither of them have said or done anything that makes me think they're particularly worried about me. And like I said, if they suspected I knew anything, and they thought I might talk, they'd have killed me already.'

'No one's going to kill you.'

He laughed.

I shrugged and put the gun in my pocket. 'If it's any consolation,' I said, 'I wouldn't have hurt you. I just needed you to tell me what happened.'

'You *did* fucking hurt me. You shot me in the leg—'

'Yeah, sorry,' I said, half-smiling. 'That was a mistake.'

'You think it's funny?'

'No—'

'I suppose you think everything's all right now, do you?' he said, his voice full of loathing. 'I mean, Christ, what kind of a cunt *are* you? You come in here and shoot me in the fucking leg, you scare the shit out of me, and then you tell me you didn't *mean* it, you weren't *really* going to hurt me . . . and you think that's going to make me feel better?'

'I didn't mean it like that. I was just—'

'Ah, fuck off,' he said quietly. 'Go on, just go.'

I looked at him for a moment, but I couldn't think of anything to say, so I just turned round and crossed over to the door. The music upstairs stopped for a second, and the unfamiliar silence was deafening, but as I paused at the door, checking to make sure I had my cigarettes, the thumping bass beats started up again – *d-doomp-doomp, doomp-doomp, d-doomp-doomp, doomp-doomp, d-doomp-doomp, doomp-doomp* . . .

I turned back to Hassan. 'Just one more question, OK? And then I'll go, I promise.'

'What?' he sighed.

'Why did you throw the fight?'

'What fight?'

'At Juno's . . . your fight against Rooney.'

'Who said I threw it?'

'I was there, I saw what happened. You were totally in control, you were just playing with Rooney. You could have put him down whenever you wanted. But you let him knock you out.'

Hassan glared at me for a second, trying to look insulted, but I could tell his heart wasn't in it. 'It's just a game,' he said wearily. 'All of it . . . boxing, living, dying . . . everything. It's all just a fucking game.'

I waited for him to go on, but that was it. He'd said all he was going to say. He wanted me gone now, out of his room, out of his life . . . and the way I saw it, after all I'd put him through, the least I could do now was oblige him. I opened the door, went downstairs, and headed off in search of a drink.

21

The first pub I came to was a ratty little place in a residential side street just off Cowley Lane. It didn't look very appealing – a shabby grey pub in a shabby grey backstreet – and it was so lifeless and dim that at first I didn't think it was open. But it was. And no matter how shabby it was, it was a pub. And the faded sign on the wall promised *REAL ALE, SPIRITS, HOT FOOD, SHELTERED SMOKING AREA*, and that was more than enough for me.

It was busier inside than I'd thought, and noisier too, and from the looks I got when I went up to the bar, I guessed that most of the customers were regulars, and that most of them probably lived nearby. The atmosphere wasn't exactly *un*welcoming, and I was even greeted with a few wary nods from some of the older drinkers, but it definitely wasn't the kind of place that welcomes strangers with open arms and a hearty smile. Not that I cared. It was a pub, it served alcohol . . . I didn't give a shit whether I was welcome or not. All I wanted was a drink.

I found a space at the far end of the bar, waited patiently to get served, and when the barman finally made his way over to me – raising his eyebrows to ask what I wanted – I ordered a large Teacher's and a pint of Stella. He nodded, fetched the whisky, and I drank it down while he was pouring the Stella.

'Anything else?' he said, eyeing the empty whisky glass as he placed the pint on the bar.

I gave him a twenty, asked for another large Teacher's, and took a long swallow of beer.

By the time the barman came back with my change and a fresh glass of whisky, I could already feel the sedative heat of the alcohol sinking down into my belly and spreading its comfort into my soul.

'Where's the smoking area?' I asked, tipping the whisky into the Stella.

'Through there,' the barman said, indicating a back door with a jerk of his head.

'Toilets?'

'On your way out, on the right.' He looked at my empty glass again. 'You want another one in there?'

'Yeah,' I said, passing him the glass. 'Why not?'

After finishing off the last of Cal's sulphate in the toilets, I went out to the smoking area – a brick-walled yard – and sat down at a wooden picnic table sheltered by a heated parasol. The heat was barely noticeable, and the parasol gave no shelter at all from the bitter wind whipping around the yard, but I didn't mind. I could smoke and drink out here, that was the main thing, and because it was so cold I virtually had the place to myself. And I needed some privacy now. I could feel Stacy's presence in my heart again, and it's not easy talking to your dead wife when other people are around. I glanced over at a twenty-something couple who were standing together by the door – a thickset squaddie in a short-sleeved T-shirt, and an overweight woman in a micro skirt and heels – both of them hunched over and shivering, taking short hard drags on their cigarettes, desperate to get out of the cold as quickly as possible.

They won't be long, Stace, I said silently.

Why aren't they wearing coats or jumpers? she asked. *I mean, look at that poor girl, she's freezing to death.*

If she was wearing a jumper no one could see her tattoos, I explained.

Oh, right . . .

The hunched couple had had enough now, and as they dropped their cigarettes to the ground and scuttled back inside, I lit one myself and drank some beer.

Can you talk now? Stacy asked.

'Yeah . . .'

Good. I like hearing your voice.

'I like hearing yours.'

Well, don't get too used to it.

'Why not?'

You've been fine without me, John. You've almost got yourself back together again. I don't want you throwing it all away.

'I need you, Stacy.'

No, you don't.

'I need you to tell me what I'm doing.'

What are you doing?

'I don't know,' I said, smiling. 'I mean, right now, I'm just getting drunk, staying drunk, talking to you, feeling sorry for myself—'

What about all that stuff with Hassan . . . what was that about?

'It was the only way I could get him to tell me what happened.'

Yeah, I know that. But why do you want to know what happened anyway? I thought you weren't interested in Jamaal any more?

'I'm not . . . well, I am . . . I mean, it's not that I don't care what happened to him, but that wasn't the point . . . and it still isn't really . . .'

You're not making any sense.

'Sorry . . . it's all a bit mixed up in my head at the moment. I'm still trying to make sense of it myself.'

You're going after Bishop, aren't you?

'He killed Leon and Claudia, Stace. He killed my father . . . and all these years he's let me think that Dad took his own life. And my mother went to her grave believing he'd killed himself. That's not right.'

I know.

'The trouble is, I don't think I can prove anything. And even if I could, even if there was a way of proving Bishop's guilt, I'm never going to get to it without him knowing. And Bishop doesn't make empty threats. If he thinks I'm still looking into Leon's death, or anything to do with Leon or my father, he *will* go after everyone I care about. He'll do what he promised – he'll rip their fucking lives apart.'

But aren't you risking that anyway by talking to Hassan?

'I don't think Bishop's that worried about Jamaal. I mean, he won't like it if he finds out I'm still working on the case, especially after I told him I was done with it, and I'm sure he'll make me pay for it somehow, but I don't think he'll want to take things too far.'

Why not?

'It'd be counter-productive. No one can prove what really happened to Jamaal, there's no evidence, no witnesses, Hassan's never going to talk . . . it's all wrapped up. Bishop knows that. He doesn't *want* me nosing around, asking questions, but he knows there's nothing I can do anyway, no matter how much I find out. So he'll warn me off, he'll get a bit tough with me, but he won't take it any further because he doesn't want to risk stirring things up. He wants to keep everything contained.'

But you think you can get to him through Jamaal?

'That's what I seem to be thinking, yeah.'

How are you going to do it?

'No idea.'

And what about this Renny Surnam, the one who's going to destroy your family and friends if you kill Bishop? What are you going to do about him?

'I've only just realised what I'm doing, Stace. I haven't had time to think any of it through.' I lit another cigarette and drained the last few drops of whisky from my glass. 'I'm tired, Stacy. I'm really tired.'

Go home, she said. *Get some sleep*.

'Yeah . . .'

And don't give up on Bridget, OK? Just call her, talk to her, tell her what happened. She'll understand.

'Would you?'

Before Stacy could answer, a young woman with a drink-flushed face came out of the pub into the smoking area.

She stopped by the doorway to light a cigarette, but just as she was taking one out, she looked up, saw me, and froze. I tried giving her a friendly smile, but she'd already seen me as I was – a drunken wreck with drug-crazed eyes, mumbling madly to himself in the cold – and I could tell she was having second thoughts about having that cigarette after all. Just as she was about to put it away though, the door swung open and another young woman came out, clearly a friend of hers, and as they both lit up and began talking excitedly about something, she soon forgot about me. I watched them for a second or two, wondering idly why women often stand with their arms crossed tightly beneath their breasts when they're talking to each other, then I lowered my eyes and looked away.

Do you know why they do that, Stace? I asked silently. *I mean, even when they take a drag on their cigarettes, they still leave the other arm where it is . . . Stacy?*

She'd gone.

I sat there for a minute or two, waiting to see if she came back, and when she didn't, I sat there for another minute or two, trying to get my head straight. And when that didn't happen either, I gave up and went inside to get another drink.

I don't know what time it was when I left the pub – maybe ten-thirty, eleven, something like that – and I don't really know if I was aware of where I was going or if it was just something that occurred to me on the spur of the moment as I passed by the Redhills estate on the way back to town. All I know for sure is that twenty minutes or so after leaving the pub I was sitting on the low brick wall opposite the dingy little café in the square off Redhills Lane, watching the comings and goings while I ate fried chicken from a box. The lights were off in the main part of the café, and a sign on the door said *CLOSED*, but by the time I'd finished two pieces of chicken I'd seen at least six or seven people enter the café and come out again. Some of them were just kids from the estate – Somalis, white kids, Asians, most of them in hoods and tracksuits – but it was clear that others had driven out here to get what they wanted. I also spotted one of the Somali kids I'd seen the last time I'd been here with Cal, the one with the gold tooth. I saw him come out of the café and go into the fried chicken place next door, and then five minutes later I saw him come out, clutching something under his jacket, and go back into the café. He didn't let on that he'd seen me, let alone recognised me, and it's quite possible that he didn't, but just as I was finishing my third piece of chicken, I saw him come out of the café again, and this time he headed straight over to me.

I wiped chicken grease from my hands, dropped the box of bones into a bin, and lit a cigarette.

'You want something?' Gold Tooth said, stopping in front of me.

I looked up at him. It was hard to tell how old he was – he had the figure of a thirteen-year-old kid, but his eyes were ageless. His hands were deep in his pockets, his arms straight and rigid, and he was looking to one side as he spoke to me. I didn't say anything, just stared at him.

He sniffed and spat. 'What do you want?'

'What have you got?' I said.

He turned his head, looking to the other side, then he sucked his teeth, spat again, and finally looked right at me. 'I'd go somewhere else, if I was you.'

'Yeah? Why's that?'

He sneered at me. 'You never know, do you?'

'You can say that again,' I said, smiling at him.

'You what?'

'Do you remember me from the other day?' I said, taking a drag on my cigarette. 'I was in a car with a friend of mine, we were parked just over there . . . in a Lexus.'

He frowned. 'I don't know what the fuck you're talking about.'

'You came out of the café with a bunch of other kids and an older guy who I'm guessing is your boss. The tall, scary-looking guy.'

Gold Tooth shook his head. 'What fucking "boss"? I ain't got a fucking—'

'Is he in the café now?'

'I just told you—'

'I want to see him,' I said. 'And when he knows what it's about, he'll want to see me. So unless you want to piss him off, I suggest you go back in there right now and tell him who I am and what I want to talk to him about. Do you understand?'

Gold Tooth just stared at me for a second or two, not sure what to do. It was a tricky decision to make – carry on stonewalling me and hope I was lying, or do as I asked and hope I was telling the truth? Either choice was potentially risky for him. But he wasn't stupid, and it didn't take him long to figure out that the second option was slightly less risky than the first.

'You going to tell me who you are then or what?' he said, glancing casually over his shoulder.

I took a business card from my pocket and offered it to him. He stared scornfully at it for a moment, then took it from my hand and shoved it in his pocket without looking at it.

'Tell your boss I'm investigating the murder of Jamaal Tan,' I said to him. 'And tell him I know that Kassim Mukhtar had nothing to do with it. Have you got that?'

Gold Tooth spat again, narrowly missing my foot, then turned round and sauntered back to the café.

I finished my cigarette, lit another, and waited.

After a few minutes, I saw him coming out again, this time with two older Somali kids. They were both in their late teens, both tall and rangy, and if I hadn't been so drunk, and I hadn't got a 9mm pistol in my pocket, they both would have scared the shit out of me. Not that I *wasn't* scared, because the fear was undoubtedly there – thumping away inside me like some kind of alien organ – but it wasn't all-consuming. I was afraid, but I wasn't afraid of the fear itself. It was just something I was feeling.

As the three of them approached, I stood up, keeping my hand on the gun in my pocket.

'That him?' one of the older kids asked Gold Tooth.

Gold Tooth nodded.

They stopped in front of me and the older kid looked me up and down. 'What's this about?' he said.

I looked at Gold Tooth. 'Did you tell your boss what I told you?'

'Well, yeah—'

'Is this guy your boss?'

Gold Tooth looked to the older kid for support. The older kid glared at him for a moment, then turned to me. 'You want to talk, talk to me.'

'I don't think so,' I said, turning to leave. 'I'm not standing out here in the fucking cold any more. You can tell your boss he had his chance, but he blew it.'

As I went to move off, the other kid stepped in front of me, blocking my way, and just for a moment I was tempted to pull the pistol from my pocket and crack it into his face, but even as my fingers were tightening on the grip, I heard him say, 'He'll give you five minutes, OK? Five minutes. And you'd better not be fucking around or you'll wish you never came here.'

They took me into the café and led me through the unlit seating area to the kitchens at the back, then up a flight of stairs and along a short corridor to a door marked *PRIVATE*. As one of them knocked and waited for a reply, I glanced up at the CCTV camera over the door and wondered idly who was watching me . . . and what did I look like to them? Did they see me as an Englishman? A white man? A European? Or perhaps, I thought – grinning to myself – perhaps they just saw me as a twat.

'Hey,' I heard someone say. 'You want to see him or not?'

I looked at the kid beside me and realised he was holding

the door open and waiting for me to go inside. I also realised he'd been watching me while I stood there grinning up at the camera like an idiot, and it was obvious from the look on his face that he *definitely* thought I was a twat.

I nodded at him, pulled myself together, and stepped through the doorway into a smoke-filled room.

22

There were four men in the room, all Somalis, all in their early twenties. Two of them were slumped on a brand-new leather settee, drinking beer and watching football on a widescreen TV with the sound turned off, and a third one was sitting cross-legged on the floor tapping away on a laptop. The two on the settee were smoking joints, the one on the floor was chewing on something and smoking a foul-smelling cigar. None of them were taking much notice of me. The fourth man, the tall Somali with the fearsomely gaunt face, was sitting at a desk across the room talking softly on a mobile phone. A half-smoked cigarette was burning in an ashtray in front of him, and as I entered the room he was pouring vodka into a tall glass of iced Coke. He glanced up at me and waved the neck of the vodka bottle, indicating a chair on the other side of the desk. I crossed the room, sat down, and lit a cigarette. As the tall guy carried on talking on the phone – in a language I guessed was Somali – I took a quick look around. The curtains were drawn, the room lit starkly by a bare light bulb hanging from the ceiling on a knotted flex. Apart from the settee and the desk, the only other furniture I could see was a long trestle table against the far wall and a small silver fridge to the right of the desk. The rest of the room was taken up with what I assumed to be stolen goods – boxed TVs and mobiles, brand-new laptops, games consoles, DVDs, boxes of trainers and piles of clothing in clear plastic wrapping ... there were even a couple of BMX bikes leaning against the wall, the price tags still tied to the handlebars. There was so much stuff piled up in there that the floor and the walls were virtually invisible.

'You want one?' I heard the tall Somali say.

I turned and looked at him – his raw-boned face, his burning black eyes – and I tried to smile, but my mouth was too dry. I licked my lips and swallowed.

'Sorry?' I said to him.

'BMX,' he said. 'You want one?'

His face and his voice were so empty of expression that it was impossible to tell if he was joking or not, which put me in the awkward position of not knowing how to respond, which was kind of unsettling. But I guessed that was his intention. He was a tough guy, and it was a classic tough guy's question – deliberately ambiguous, impossible to answer correctly. It didn't mean anything in itself, it was just his way of staring hard at me and saying 'Yeah? What are you looking at?' And, in my experience, the only way of answering a question like that is to not even try answering it. So I didn't. Instead, I just looked back at him for a moment, then glanced at the vodka bottle and said, 'That looks good.'

He blinked, hesitated for a second, then cracked the smallest of smiles. 'It's the best,' he said, taking another glass from a drawer. 'You want ice?'

'No, thanks.'

He picked up the bottle and half-filled the glass. 'Coke?'

I shook my head. 'It rots your teeth.'

He passed the glass over and watched as I took a long drink. As the vodka went down, and I breathed in the vaporous heat of alcohol, he opened a slim silver box and took out an untipped cigarette. He tapped it on the desk, studied one end, then put it in his mouth and lit it with a small gold lighter, sucking the smoke deep into his lungs. He breathed out, tapped ash from the cigarette, and glanced at the huge black watch on his wrist.

'You got about four minutes left,' he said, looking at me. 'Don't waste it.'

I took another swallow of vodka and put the glass on the desk. 'I'm looking into the murder of Jamaal Tan,' I said. 'You knew him, didn't you?'

The tall guy said nothing, just took a long drag on his cigarette and breathed out smoke through his nose.

'The police have got it down as a gang-killing,' I went on. 'Something to do with drugs. They're trying to make out that Jamaal was a dealer.'

Tall Guy let out a quiet snort.

I said, 'I know he wasn't a dealer, and I know it wasn't a gang-killing. I know what really happened to him.'

'Yeah?'

I nodded, lighting another cigarette. 'I also know that the police are going to pin the murder on Kassim Mukhtar.'

That got a reaction. I could tell from Tall Guy's studied indifference that I wasn't telling him anything about Jamaal that he didn't already know, and I got the feeling that he wasn't too bothered about it anyway, but when I mentioned

Kassim Mukhtar, the change in his attitude was immediate. Mukhtar clearly *did* mean something to him, and although he didn't show it in an obvious way, I knew he was surprised by what I'd just told him. The way he froze for just an instant, the quick glance over at the men on the settee, a sudden sense of urgency in his eyes . . . I'd stirred something in him. No question about it. I was getting somewhere. Where that might be, and why I wanted to get there, I didn't know. And as I picked up my glass and finished the vodka, it suddenly dawned on me that I had no idea at all what I was doing here. I was fairly sure that I'd *had* a reason, I could feel the place in my head where it had been, but there was nothing there now. All I had left was an empty space, a black hole in my mind . . . no purpose, no reason. No control. I felt like a blind man driving a car. And for a moment or two I was consumed by a sickening fear.

'You want another?' Tall Guy said, unscrewing the cap of the vodka bottle.

I looked at him, unable to speak.

'You all right?' he asked, refilling my glass. 'You look a bit—'

'Yeah,' I said weakly, reaching for the glass and quickly downing a mouthful of vodka, 'yeah, I'm fine.' I cleared my throat, took another drink, and lit a cigarette. The black hole was still there, still looming in my mind like a half-forgotten nightmare, but I wasn't a child, I told myself, I didn't have to be scared of nightmares. I could drink them away.

'Tell me about Kassim,' Tall Guy said.

I drank more vodka and told him about Kassim.

*

I don't have a problem with lying. It's not something that eats away at me in the small hours of the night – the shame of it, the guilt of deliberately deceiving someone . . . it's not even worth thinking about. We all lie, all the time – for good reasons, bad reasons, for no reason at all – it's what we do. We have to lie in order to survive. And if you don't believe it, try telling the truth all the time and see where it gets you. Or just ask yourself this: what is it about the truth that makes it so righteous anyway? It's just an option, isn't it? Just one way of seeing things. It has no inherent moral purity.

So naturally I didn't tell Tall Guy the whole truth about Kassim Mukhtar, I just told him what I wanted him to know . . . or at least what my instincts told me I wanted him to know. I was still struggling to understand what I was doing and what I was trying to achieve, but although I wasn't consciously aware of my purpose, there was something inside me that wasn't totally lost, and whatever it was, I had enough faith in it to follow its lead. And when it told me to tell Tall Guy that the police were going to charge Kassim Mukhtar with the murder of Jamaal Tan in addition to the murder he'd actually committed – the stabbing of Johnson Geele – I not only had to ignore the fact that it simply wasn't true, I also had to accept the fact that the only thing that linked Jamaal Tan with Kassim Mukhtar was me . . . but I was confused enough as it was, so I decided to ignore that too.

'I don't get it,' Tall Guy said when I'd finished lying to him. 'Why are they fitting up Kassim? It doesn't make sense. I mean, they've got him for the pub thing anyway, he's going down for that . . . so what's the fucking point in setting him up for Tan?'

'It's convenient,' I said. 'There are certain people, people with influence, who don't want an investigation into Tan's murder, they just want it to go away.'

'Why?'

'It's an irritant to them. A problem they could do without.'

Tall Guy sipped from his drink. 'Who are these people?'

'I don't know yet.'

He stared at me. 'Do you know who killed Tan?'

'Do you?'

He shrugged. 'Could have been anyone . . . Jamaal was a fuck-up, he was born to die. Know what I mean?'

'We're all born to die.'

'Yeah, but kids like Jamaal . . it's their fucking fate, man. They're born with low batteries, they're never going to make it past twenty. It's in their fucking DNA.'

I nodded. 'So what do you think happened to him?'

Another shrug. 'My guess would be he pissed off the wrong people.'

'What kind of wrong people?'

He almost smiled. 'You're the detective.'

I heard a quiet snort of laughter behind me, and when I looked round I saw the guy with the laptop grinning at me. He had bits of green leaves stuck in his teeth. I guessed it was khat, a stimulative plant that's popular in Africa but not so well known over here. As Laptop started chewing again, I turned back to Tall Guy.

339

'You don't think Kassim killed Jamaal?' I said.

'I know he didn't.'

'How can you be so sure?'

He just stared at me, as if the question was beneath him.

I said, 'Do you know Curt Dempsey?'

'I know *Cunt* Dempsey.'

I smiled. 'Mick Bishop?'

'Now you're talking.'

'How about Renny Surnam?' I said, my eyes fixed on his. 'Have you heard of him?'

'You know a lot of wrong people,' he said, nodding slowly. 'Maybe you're not so dumb as you look.'

'You think so?'

His eyes gave nothing away, but his silence said something. I sipped vodka and thought about it for a while, trying to work out what, if anything, he'd just told me, but I couldn't quite get hold of it. I was fairly sure it was there though, whatever it was. It had sunk in somewhere. I'd just have to wait for it to float back up again.

'Does it matter to you if Kassim is done for Jamaal's murder?' I asked him.

'Yeah,' he said. 'It matters.'

'Why? I mean, if he's going down for the pub killing anyway, another murder charge isn't going to make much difference to him, is it?'

'He didn't kill Jamaal. Jamaal was raped. Kassim didn't do that.'

'He stabbed someone to death for looking at him the wrong way.'

'So?'

'You think that's OK?'

'It's what he did.'

'But raping someone before you kill them . . . that's wrong, is it?'

Tall Guy's voice went cold. 'You ever see anyone getting raped?'

I shook my head.

'You ever seen a gang of men rape a woman, cut off her hands, then kill her fucking baby?'

'No . . .'

'So what the fuck do you know about right and wrong? You don't know *shit*.'

I almost left it there, and maybe I should have . . . maybe I shouldn't have said anything, but I couldn't help myself. 'Have you ever loved someone so much you'd die for them every day?' I asked him.

'What?'

'I was married once,' I said quietly, 'a long time ago. Her name was Stacy . . . we loved each more than anything. We were going to have a baby together. But then she was killed . . . murdered. A man broke into our house, raped her, stabbed her, ripped her apart . . . he killed her, killed our baby. I found her body.' I stared hard at Tall Guy. 'Hell doesn't know any boundaries,' I told him. 'It's fucking everywhere.'

He nodded thoughtfully. 'Did they find the guy who killed your wife?'

'I found him.'

'Yeah?'

'Found him, killed him.'

'Right . . .'

'Exactly,' I said, smiling.

He frowned at me for a second, not at all sure what I meant – which made two of us – then he took a breath, blew out his cheeks, and reached for my empty glass. 'So what are you going to do about Kassim and Jamaal then?' he said, pouring me a drink and passing it over.

'I don't know yet,' I admitted. 'I'm not sure I can do much about Jamaal's murder, not legally anyway. Even if I could prove who did it, and who was behind it, I doubt if anything would ever come of it. But I might just dig up enough to make the police think twice about pinning Jamaal's murder on Kassim.'

'Yeah?'

I nodded. 'I wouldn't have to prove he didn't do it, I'd just have to stir things up enough to make it too risky for them to bother charging him.'

'Yeah, well,' he said, 'that'd be good.' He hesitated for a moment, thinking something over, then looked at me and said, 'You need anything?'

I glanced round at the guy with the laptop. He was still just sitting there, chewing away, his cheap cigar lodged in his mouth, staring almost manically at the screen. I turned back to Tall Guy. 'Is that khat he's chewing?' I asked him.

He rolled his eyes. 'Fucker's old school . . . never stops.'

'Can I try some?'

'You don't want any of that shit,' he said, grinning. 'It rots your teeth. You need a pop?'

'What?'

'Try some of this,' he said, taking a small silver tube

342

from his pocket. He unscrewed the cap, leaned across the desk, and tapped out a thick line of white powder. 'Best coke in town,' he said, passing me a crisp £50 note.

I took the note from him and rolled it up, then paused for a second, asking myself what I was doing. Nothing came to me . . . I had no idea what I was doing. I put the rolled-up note to my nose, leaned over the desk, and hoovered up the coke.

23

Even now I can't remember much about the rest of that night. I have a vague recollection of sitting around in the smoke-filled room with Tall Guy and the other three – drinking vodka, snorting coke, smoking a few joints . . . and I'm pretty sure we hung around there for a while, just watching TV and talking about stuff, but I have no idea what we watched or talked about. All I can really recall is a general sense of feeling OK – numbed and high, comfortably drunk, quietly content with where I was and who I was with . . . I didn't feel out of place, I remember that. And leaving the café . . . I remember going down the stairs and passing through a room at the back where a bunch of young Somali kids were weighing out drugs and packing up wraps and vials . . . rap music playing . . . some of the kids singing along, shouting and laughing . . . and then I was following Tall Guy out through a fire door into an alleyway at the back of the café, and it was snowing again . . . and we got into a car, a sleek black thing with tinted windows . . .

And that's when it all starts to fade.

A club somewhere, some kind of basement building . . . hot and crowded . . . loud music . . . more drinks, more coke . . . and then nothing. The rest of the night is a formless blur. I can't remember anything at all.

It happens sometimes when I drink too much . . . my memory malfunctions. It's like looking down into the depths of a deep black pond. I can usually see a few scraps of things floating on the surface – bits of leaves, dead insects, sticks – and halfway down I can just make out the flickering trails of unknown living things, but beyond that – down in the depths – all I can see is a cold empty blackness.

It happens.

I can't remember.

It happens.

Sometimes, after a day or so, formless shapes wallow up to the surface and show me their truth, but mostly they don't. And even when they do, it's hard to tell if their truth is the same as mine. There's a distance to them, as if they belong to someone else. And, in a sense, they do.

When I woke up the next morning, to the urgent ringing of my mobile, I felt sicker than I'd felt in a long time. Gut sick, head sick, barely sentient. A frayed sponge was beating in place of my heart, a stone balloon filled my head, a jagged rock the size of a fist was lodged between my ribs.

My mobile was ringing . . .

I didn't know where it was.

I didn't know where *I* was.

My right arm was twisted up under my head, numb from the elbow down. I tried to sit up, fumbling in my pockets with my left hand, looking for my phone, and a surge of vomit rose up in my throat. I rolled over onto my side and swallowed it down, then cautiously tried sitting up again. A blunt pain stabbed dully in my chest, forcing a groan from my throat, but as I slowly straightened up, it didn't get any worse. I breathed steadily, looking down at the polished floorboards beneath my bare feet . . . there was something familiar about them. I belched, tasting vomit. I smelled bad, sour and sick. My mouth was bone-dry, my throat raw, my eyes stiff and swollen. I took a few more steadying breaths, then looked down to one side. I was sitting on a settee, shirt and trousers on, a sweat-soaked duvet scrunched up beside me. Like the floorboards, the settee seemed familiar. The light in the room was grey . . . veiled daylight. I raised my head, shielded my eyes, and tentatively looked around. I saw whiteness, space . . . a bright, modern room, floor-to-ceiling windows shaded by blinds . . .

Imogen's flat. I was in Imogen's flat.

I closed my eyes and put my hand to my head . . . trying to think, trying to remember. What was I doing in Imogen's flat? How the fuck did I get here? When did I get here? Where was Imogen? Did we—?

My mobile started ringing again.

I looked round, searching for the source of the sound. The duvet . . . it was coming from under the scrunched-up duvet. I reached over, pulled it to one side, and saw my mobile half-stuffed down the back of the settee. I picked it up, squinted at the screen . . . and my breath caught in my throat. It was Bridget. I quickly hit *ANSWER* and put the phone to my ear.

'Bridget? Is that you? Bridge—?'

'Hello, John,' she said quietly. 'Sorry if I woke you up.'

'God, Bridget,' I sighed. 'It's so good to hear—'

'Where are you? I tried you at home but you didn't answer.'

'Yeah, sorry,' I muttered. 'I was asleep . . .'

'You're at the house?'

'Uh . . . yeah,' I said, squeezing my eyes shut. 'Listen, Bridge, I'm really sorry about everything, OK? And I know what you must think—'

'I don't want to talk about it, John,' she said coolly. 'I'm just calling to let you know that I'm coming round to pick up a few things—'

'Nothing *happened*, Bridget. Please, you *have* to believe me . . . nothing happened. All it was—'

'I don't want to know.'

'But I wouldn't do that to you, Bridget . . . I wouldn't cheat on you, you *know* that.'

'You fucking lied to me, John.'

'I didn't *lie*—'

'You told me you were on a stake-out, in your car . . . you left me a voicemail message, remember?' I could hear the bitterness in her voice. 'You said you hadn't called me that night because you were on a stake-out and you fell asleep . . . but that was a lie, wasn't it?'

'Well, yeah, but it was a complicated situation . . . I didn't want to upset you.'

'A *complicated situation*?' She laughed coldly. 'Christ, John, is that the best you can do?'

'I was going to tell you everything, honestly—'

'You lied to me.'

'I know, and I'm sorry. I'm *really* sorry. But I just—'

'I thought you were different, John,' she said sadly.

347

I sighed, not knowing what to say.

'I'll be there in about half an hour,' she said. 'I just need to pick up some stuff from my flat, and then I'll be gone.'

'Please, Bridget . . . just give me a chance—'

I stopped at the sound of a door opening, and when I turned round I saw Imogen coming out of her bedroom and shuffling across the room towards me in her black silk dressing gown. Her hair was a mess and she was rubbing sleep from her eyes.

'What's going on, John?' she said.

I knew Bridget must have heard her, but I covered the mouthpiece anyway and put my finger to my lips, frantically shaking my head at Imogen, trying to tell her to keep quiet, but she was too sleepy to understand.

'What's the matter?' she said, stopping by the settee and frowning at me. 'Who are you talking to?'

'Bridget?' I said into the phone, waving Imogen away. 'Bridge? Are you still there?'

'That's her, isn't it?' she said, her voice cold and quiet.

'I can explain—'

'You bastard.'

Click.

'Bridget?' I said. '*Bridget . . .*'

She'd gone.

'Shit,' I hissed. '*Fuck* it.'

'I'm sorry, John,' Imogen said quietly. 'I didn't realise . . . I'm *so* sorry.'

I sighed heavily. 'It's not your fault . . .'

'God, what a mess. I suppose she thinks—'

'I need to borrow your car,' I said, looking around for my shoes and socks.

'You can't *drive*, John. Look at you, you're still drunk. You were so wrecked when you got here you could barely walk . . .' She glanced at a clock on the wall. 'You've only had about two hours' sleep—'

'I'm all right,' I told her, quickly putting my shoes on.

'No, you're not, for Christ's sake. I'll drive you.'

I shook my head. 'Bridget might see you. I can't risk that.' I got to my feet, grabbed my jacket off the back of the settee, and looked at Imogen. 'I don't have much time,' I told her. 'Bridget's coming round to the house in half an hour. If I'm not there when she turns up . . .' I shook my head. 'I have to be there.'

Imogen sighed.

I said, 'I *need* your car. Please?'

She looked at me for a moment, then shook her head and went over to a table by the door. As she picked up her keys and began separating the car key from the bunch, I put on my jacket and went over to her.

'I shouldn't be doing this,' she said, passing me the key.

'Thanks,' I said, taking it from her.

'Just be careful, for God's sake, all right?'

I nodded.

She leaned towards me and kissed me on the cheek. 'And good luck.'

It was almost eight o'clock when I drove off in Imogen's BMW. The Sunday-morning streets were quiet and the snow had cleared from the roads, so it was tempting to put my foot down and get home as quickly as possible, but Imogen was right – I was still drunk. Stale-drunk, hungover and sick, my head still buzzing with whatever drugs I'd taken . . . I shouldn't have been anywhere near a car. But I couldn't think about that. I didn't have time. And I had to concentrate on the road anyway – it kept splitting in two, one half floating above the other . . . so I had to compensate for that, and keep my speed steady, not too fast, not too slow, and if that wasn't enough, I was retching almost constantly now – my throat heaving painfully, nothing coming up, my eyes streaming with tears . . .

I couldn't *think* about anything.

I made it to Paxman Street in just over fifteen minutes. There was a parking space right opposite my house, and as I got out of the BMW and hurried across the street, I looked around for Bridget's van. There was no sign of it anywhere, and I hoped that meant she hadn't arrived yet. She could have already been and gone, I realised, and it was equally possible that she wouldn't show up at all, but there was nothing I could do about that. I just had to hope . . .

I fumbled my keys from my pocket and stepped up to the front door.

I knew something was wrong as soon as I went inside. There was a faint smell of earth in the air, damp earth . . . the scent of rotted leaves . . . and as I closed the front door, a seam of cold air drifted across my face and I heard the back door swing open and crash against the wall. I pulled the pistol from my pocket and stood still. The back door rattled in the wind, knocking loosely against the wall, then slammed shut. I didn't move. The house was deathly quiet.

'Bridget!' I called out. 'It's me . . . Bridget?'

There was no reply.

I looked down at the floor. The hallway carpet was littered with garden debris – dead leaves, bits of stick, clods of earth – and a trail of muddy bootprints led from the back garden to my door.

My door was unlocked, ajar.

I looked around . . .

Listened.

Too much silence.

Swallowing the rise of fear in my throat, I moved quietly along the hallway, stopped at my door, and nudged it open with the barrel of the pistol. I stepped back and listened again. Nothing. No sound, no movement. I waited a minute, two minutes, standing perfectly still, listening, staring at the muddy bootprints just inside my door . . . then I took a breath and went inside.

The curtains were closed, the light familiarly dim, and for a fraction of a second everything seemed just as I'd left it . . . but then I turned on the light, and that's when I saw it – lying on my bed, stiff and greyed, caked in mud, crawling with worms and insects . . .

Oh *God* . . .

It was a dead dog . . . long dead. Just a thing of bones and skin . . . a dried carcass. Tears clouded my sight as I stared at it – the poor muddied snout, the soil-clogged eye sockets, the dead grey fur still clinging to scraps of petrified skin . . .

'Walter,' I whispered. 'Jesus *Christ* . . .'

I sank down to the floor, numbed to the bone. Walter was Bridget's old greyhound, the love of her life. He'd died at the hands of Bishop's psychopathic brother just over two years ago, and at dawn the next day we'd wrapped him in his dusty old blanket and buried him in the back garden with his favourite toys – a rubber hammer, a chewed frisbee, a tennis ball in a sock . . .

And now someone had dug him up.

It wasn't hard to guess who was responsible.

I wiped my eyes and stared at the desecration on my bed. Teeth, cartilage, discoloured bone . . . the vague shape of a dog. Twisted feet, black and hard, tiny slivers of yellowed toes . . .

I couldn't look any more.

I just sat there and cried.

I was still sitting there when I heard Bridget's van pulling up outside. For a moment or two, I tried to convince myself that it wasn't her – it was just a neighbour, or maybe the Sunday papers being delivered – but there was no mistaking the sound of Bridget's old Escort van. The rattling exhaust, the creak of the handbrake, the rusty groan of the door opening . . . I'd know that sound anywhere.

It was Bridget.

Christ, I thought suddenly, staring at Walter's carcass. *If she comes in here . . .*

I couldn't let her see what they'd done to him. It would kill her. I had to stop her coming in. I jumped to my feet, ran out into the hallway and raced to the front door, and as I yanked it open and stepped outside, I almost ran into Bridget. She was right outside the door, digging in her pockets for her keys.

'John,' she said, looking up at me in surprise. The surprise turned to puzzlement as I closed the front door behind me. She frowned at me and said, 'What are you doing?'

I just looked at her, my mind blank.

'What's going on?' she said. 'I want to go inside . . . why are you—?'

'Sorry, Bridget,' I told her. 'But I can't let you in.'

'Why not?'

'I just can't, not now . . .'

'Don't be stupid, John,' she said dismissively, trying to get past me. 'I haven't got time for this . . .'

I blocked her way.

She stared at me, getting angry now. 'Get out of the way, John.'

I shook my head. 'Come back in an hour.'

'*What?*'

'Please? I'll explain everything then, I promise . . . just give me an hour, OK?'

'It's her, isn't it?' she said, glaring at me. 'It's fucking Imogen. She's in there, isn't she? You've got that bitch in our house—'

'No—'

'Jesus *Christ* . . .'

'No, listen—'

'Fuck you, John,' she said, starting to cry. '*Fuck* you.'

I instinctively reached out for her.

'Fuck *off*!' she spat, pushing me away. 'Don't you *dare* fucking touch me . . .'

I stepped back, meekly holding up my hands. 'I'm sorry . . . I didn't mean—'

'Just *fuck* off,' she spluttered, sobbing uncontrollably now. 'Fuck off.'

As I stood there staring helplessly at her, wishing I could put things right, I heard Stacy's voice whispering urgently in my heart. *Tell her, for God's sake, John. Tell her the truth.*

'I can't.'

'You can't *what*?' Bridget said nastily, angrily wiping tears from her face.

'I can't,' I said quietly, dying inside. 'I just can't . . .'

She stared at me for a second, broken with hatred and hurt, then she shook her head, turned round, and headed back to her van. As I stood there watching her go, I nearly called out to her to come back – half-opening my mouth, half-raising my hand, half-stepping after her . . . but as she got into the van, and I saw our dog Finn looking out at me through the back window, smiling his dog-smile, I remembered the mud-caked skull on my bed – the clogged eye sockets, the broken teeth, the pink worms crawling on yellowed bone . . . and I knew I had to let her go.

She could never see that.

She could never know.

It would be the death of her.

I watched as she started the van and pulled away, and I watched the van driving off . . . tyres crunching, exhaust rattling, Finn's heavy head motionless in the window . . .

and I watched it disappear round the corner at the top of the street . . . and then I just stood there for a minute or two watching the empty road . . .

It was snowing again.

I looked up at the falling whiteness, seeing my heart in the wintered black sky, then I wiped a tear from my cheek, opened the door, and went back inside.

I'd bolted the front door shut and was halfway along the hallway when the realisation suddenly hit me – why hadn't I just bolted the door in the first place? If I'd gone out into the hallway and bolted the door when I'd first heard Bridget's van, she wouldn't have been able to get in. And all I would have had to do was keep quiet, stay in my room, and wait until she went away. Why hadn't I thought of that? I wouldn't have had to tell her she couldn't come in, and she wouldn't have assumed that Imogen was here, and then maybe . . .

'You fucking idiot,' I muttered.

But there was no real feeling in my voice, no anger. I was too desolate for self-recrimination. I carried on down the hallway to the back door. One of the glass panels was smashed and the key was still in the lock. I shook my head. It hadn't been difficult to get in. I went out into the back garden. The snow was falling heavily now, grey-black clouds hanging low in the sky, and as I looked over at the tree-sheltered spot where we'd buried Walter's body, I could see the ruination of his grave – freshly dug earth scattered across the lawn, his blanket and toys thrown carelessly aside, a garden spade lying in the dirt. It would soon all be carpeted with snow, hidden from sight . . . just another buried sin.

I went back into the house and did what I had to do.

It was one of the hardest things I've ever done – cradling Walter's carcass in my arms, taking him out into the garden, laying him gently back in his grave . . . drenched in sweat, shaking and retching, a hollow sickness aching in my belly – and for a while I didn't think I was going to make it. But giving up wasn't an option. I had to do this, no matter what. If it took me all day, all week . . . if it took me the rest of the year, so be it. I'd do it whatever it took.

The tears came again as I wrapped Walter in his blanket and resettled him in his grave with his toys, and for the next twenty minutes or so I couldn't stop crying, the cold tears streaming in silence as I filled in the hole and patted down the earth, trying to put everything back as it was so that Bridget would never know . . .

It wasn't easy, but I did my best.

Then I put the spade away and went back inside and began cleaning up the hallway and my flat. I swept up the worst of the mud, the ruined duvet went in the bin, and the rest of it – the garden debris, the trodden-in soil – I hoovered up as much as possible. It was still a mess by the time I'd finished, but at least it wasn't quite so obvious what had happened. It was just a random mess. And if it was still there when Bridget came back – and I guessed she'd have to come back at some point to pick up all her stuff – she'd hopefully just ignore it.

It was ten-thirty by the time I'd finished cleaning up. I

slumped down on the settee beneath the front window and reached into my pocket for my cigarettes. I was exhausted, filthy, soaked in cold sweat, and I smelled like death. As I took out a cigarette and put it in my mouth, I realised that it was the first of the day. I'd been awake for almost three hours and I hadn't even *thought* of smoking . . . I couldn't quite believe it. I wondered for a moment if something had changed in me . . . if I'd lost something, or maybe found something, something that had taken away my need for nicotine, perhaps my need for *any*thing. And as I took the cigarette from my mouth and studied it for a second or two, I even went so far as to briefly consider throwing it away . . .

'Yeah, right,' I muttered, putting the cigarette back in my mouth.

As I reached into my pocket for my lighter, I felt something I wasn't expecting to feel – something soft and plasticky. I paused for a second, trying to work out what it could be – what did I have in my pocket that was soft and plasticky? – but nothing came to mind. I cautiously got hold of it and pulled it out. It was a small plastic bag, the sealable type, and it was half-filled with white crystalline powder. It looked like cocaine. I opened the bag, licked a finger and dipped it in, and touched the tip of my finger to my tongue. It *was* cocaine. Very good cocaine.

I lit my cigarette and tried to remember where I'd got the coke from. Had I bought it? When? And who from? Or had someone given it to me . . . Tall Guy maybe, or one of the other Somalis? I couldn't remember.

It didn't matter.

I put the bag of coke on the arm of the settee and glanced at the bottle of Teacher's on the corner table. The thought of whisky – the taste of it, the smell of it – made me feel nauseous, but that didn't mean anything. Nausea is irrelevant to a drunk, it's just another reason to drink. Just like everything else.

But I didn't want to drink anyway . . . not yet.

I put out my cigarette, got up, and went into the bathroom. I turned on the shower, setting it as hot as it gets, then I got undressed and sat down on the lavatory and began the process of emptying myself. As the steam from the shower built up, misting the mirror and opening my pores, the sweat started oozing out of me. I just sat there for a while, barely conscious of what I was doing, then I got up, flushed the lavatory, and pulled back the shower curtain. As I was getting in, a sudden pain ripped through my belly, stabbing up into my chest. My body convulsed and I jack-knifed to the floor, and for the next five minutes I just lay there, naked, my face pressed into the lino, writhing and groaning, retching, sweating, coughing up blood and bits of stuff . . . until eventually the coughing subsided and the pain inside me began to ease. I stayed where I was for a while, breathing slowly, letting things settle, then I got to my knees, gingerly got to my feet, and leaned against the sink. My head was throbbing, and my belly felt pretty fucked up, but apart from that I was OK.

I spat blood into the sink, ran the cold tap and rinsed out my mouth. The mirror above the sink was steamed up, so I was spared the indignity of looking at myself. When the worst of the sickness had passed, I turned down the heat of the shower, cautiously stepped in, then turned up the heat again. I stood there for a long time, washing away all the dirt and sweat, scouring the smell of death from my skin, and then I turned the shower to cold and stood in the stream of freezing water for as long as I could stand it, which wasn't long.

I got out and dried myself, cleaned up the bloody mess on the floor with toilet paper, then went into the bedroom and dressed in clean clothes. Finally, I went into the kitchen and had two raw eggs in a glass of milk, followed by four paracetamol tablets with a pint of cold water, then I went back to the settee, sat down, and lit a cigarette.

Now I was ready for a drink.

24

I didn't drink too much before I left the house – just enough to numb my body and make me feel relatively stable, and I didn't overdo it with the cocaine either, just a couple of lines to get me going and give me some kind of confidence in what I was about to do. I knew I was deluding myself again, relying on the false confidence of drugs and alcohol, but at least I was aware of the delusion. I knew what I was doing to myself. And I knew that if I didn't do it, I'd never leave this room again. I'd sit here for ever, unable to move, unable to think . . . incapable and insensible for the rest of time. And as tempting as that was, there were things that needed doing.

By midday, I was ready to start doing them.

I filled my pockets – gun, wallet, cigarettes, cocaine, keys – and placed my mobile on the bedside table, making sure it was still turned on. I put on my coat, emptied my whisky glass, lit a cigarette, and left the house without looking back.

The snow began to ease off a little as I drove into town, but driving conditions were still quite bad, and I almost came off the road a couple of times. But I wasn't the only one finding it difficult – there were shunted cars all over the place – so I wasn't too worried about getting stopped. I parked in my usual spot, the council car park in the old market square, and walked up the steep stone steps that link the car park to Wyre Street. The streets were busier than normal for a Sunday – families out together in the snow, kids throwing snowballs, shops selling sledges and furry hats – and there was an unfamiliar sense of innocence to the town, a communal playfulness that's usually only seen in old movies and TV adverts. I doubted it would last very long – by tonight the streets would be running with blood and beer again – but it was nice to know that innocent Sunday afternoons did still exist in the real world. The trouble with *nice* things though, is that unless you're part of them, or you have someone to share them with, they can really make you feel like shit.

It didn't take long to do what I needed to do in my office, and half an hour later I was back in my car, heading out of town towards the leafy suburb of Eastwoods, a well-to-do area on the outskirts of Hey. The address I had for Gerald McKee was 13 Orchard Close, a quiet cul-de-sac at the north end of Eastwoods. I'd looked it up on my office PC and printed out a map, so it wasn't too difficult to find, and by the time I pulled up outside McKee's house I'd only taken three wrong turnings, which wasn't bad for me.

It was a fairly large detached house – four or five bedrooms, I guessed – with a hedge-lined front garden, a wrought-iron gate, and a stepped pathway leading up to a canopied front door. I turned off the engine and sat in the car for a minute or two, smoking a cigarette and watching the house, but there was no sign of any movement, no indication that anyone was in. But I knew that didn't necessarily mean anything, and I wondered why I was even bothering to look. It was just habit, I suppose. When you spend half your life sitting in cars watching houses, it's easy to forget that you can get out of the car, walk up to the house, and knock on the front door.

Just as I was about to do that though, the door opened and an old man came out with a King Charles spaniel on a lead. The man had a small face and small features, wispy white hair, and the broken-veined complexion of a heavy drinker. I didn't have to check the printout of McKee's picture I'd taken from the Internet to know it was him, but I took it from my pocket and glanced at it anyway, just to make sure. It was definitely McKee. I watched him as he shuffled down the pathway and opened the wrought-iron gate, dragging the unenthusiastic spaniel behind him, and then as he turned left and began heading along the pavement, I got out of the car and went after him.

I caught up with him just as he was turning the corner at the end of the street.

'Dr McKee?' I said, moving alongside him.

'Hmm?' he said, looking at me without stopping, his mind clearly elsewhere.

'My name's John Craine,' I told him. 'I'd like to talk to you for a minute.'

'*Leave it*, Rolly,' he said irritably to the spaniel, pulling it away from a lump of fresh dog shit. '*Bloody* dog . . .' He turned back to me. 'I'm sorry? What do you want?'

'I'm John Craine,' I repeated, looking into his eyes. 'My father was Jim Craine. Do you remember him?'

McKee blinked, suddenly hesitant. 'I'm sorry, Mr Craine, but I really don't think—'

'Twenty years ago you performed the autopsy on my father's body,' I said. 'You falsified the post-mortem report.'

He stopped walking, glanced nervously around, then looked at me. 'If you don't leave immediately, Mr Craine,' he said, 'I'm afraid I'll have to call the police.'

'Go ahead,' I told him, taking my voice recorder from my pocket. 'Call Mick Bishop. And when he turns up, I'll play him the recording of the conversation you had with Leon Mercer in August 2010.'

McKee stared at the recorder in my hand.

'Sit down,' I told him, indicating a wooden bench on the pavement behind us.

He looked over his shoulder at the snow-covered bench. 'It's wet . . .' he muttered.

'Just fucking sit down.'

The bench was set back in a crescent-shaped seating area that backed onto a children's playground. The playground was empty, the swings and roundabouts resting quietly in the cold. McKee brushed snow from the bench and reluctantly sat down. I lit a cigarette and sat down next to him. Rolly the spaniel started shivering and whining, but McKee just ignored him.

'This doesn't have to be difficult, OK?' I said to him. 'All you've got to do is keep your mouth shut and listen to me, and tell me the truth when I ask for it. If you do that, it'll all be over in ten minutes. But if you fuck me about, I *will* make things very unpleasant for you. Do you understand?'

He went to say something, then saw the look in my eyes, and just nodded instead.

'Good,' I said, looking down at the voice recorder in my hand. I hadn't transferred the whole of Leon's audio file to the recorder, just enough to remind McKee of what he'd done. I hit the *PLAY* button, and as Leon's voice came out of the recorder, I held it up for McKee to hear.

. . . were there any significant injuries to DI Craine's body that you failed to include in your report?

I'm not sure I understand—

Yes or no, Doctor?

There was some bruising . . .

Where?

Around the neck, the upper arms.

Fresh bruising?

I believe so.

Did you form an opinion as to the cause of this bruising?

It's possible he may have been involved in a struggle of some kind.

It's possible?

Yes.

Did you mention this possibility in your report?

No.

Why not?

Silence.

Dr McKee? Do you understand the question?

Yes . . .

Then please answer it.

I think you know—

I didn't ask you what you thought, Doctor. I asked you why you failed to mention the bruising in your post-mortem report. You have two seconds to answer the question. One—

Bishop told me to ignore it.

DI Bishop?

Yes.

Detective Inspector Michael Bishop?

Yes.

He told you to ignore the bruising on the neck and upper arms of DI Craine's body?

Yes.

And that's why there's no mention of any bruising in your post-mortem report?

Yes.

Why did DI Bishop ask you to lie about your findings?

I didn't lie, I just—

Answer the question.

He said it was a very sensitive case, and it was in no one's interests to muddy the waters.

What did you take that to mean?

I honestly didn't know.

Did you ask him to explain?

No.

You just did as he asked.

Yes.

Why?

You know why.

Say it.

He threatened to reveal oversights from a previous post-mortem examination.

Ciara Reed's post-mortem?

Yes.

Which you carried out.

Yes.

And by oversights you mean the gross errors you made that led to a serious miscarriage of justice and the subsequent death of Darren Feeney?

More silence.

I'll take that as a yes.

You have no idea—

I turned off the recorder and looked at McKee. He was staring at the ground, his drink-ravaged face as pale as the falling snow.

'I've only got a couple of questions for you,' I said to him. 'But before I ask them, you need to know that I'm *not* Leon Mercer. Leon was a good man, he had principles, he was honourable, he cared about people. He could have ruined your life, but he didn't. But I'm not like that, do you understand? I'm not a good man, and I don't give a fuck about anyone, especially a bastard like you. So I'm not going to offer you anything, I'm not going to promise to leave you alone if you give me what I want. I might just fuck you up anyway. Or I might just decide to kill you instead. It all depends how I feel. But the one thing I can guarantee is that if you so much as hesitate when you answer my questions, if I detect even the slightest hint of a lie, you *will* go to bed one night and not wake up in the morning. Is that clear?'

'Yes,' he said very quietly.

'OK, first question. Do you think my father took his own life?'

'I strongly suspect that he didn't.'

'Suspect?'

'If it wasn't for the suicide note, I'd say there was a 99% certainty that your father was murdered.'

'Have you ever seen the note?'

McKee shook his head. 'But I've seen documentation from independent sources that confirm it was written in your father's hand.'

I nodded, putting out my cigarette and lighting another. 'You recently performed post-mortems on Leon and Claudia Mercer, is that correct?'

'Uh, yes.' He glanced anxiously at me, aware of his hesitation. 'Yes,' he added quickly, 'that's correct.'

'Did you falsify their post-mortem reports?'

'Yes.'

'Why?'

'DCI Bishop told me to.'

'So they didn't die from smoke inhalation?'

'No.'

'How did they die?'

'The cause of death in Mr Mercer's case was a massive blunt force injury to the head. His wife was most likely suffocated. She also had a significant quantity of temazepam in her system.'

'Any other injuries to either of them?'

'It was hard to tell given the condition of the bodies, but there were some indications that Mr Mercer had suffered a serious physical assault shortly before his death.'

'So Leon was beaten up then killed by a heavy blow to the head, is that right?'

'In all probability, yes.'

'And Claudia either took, or was forced to take, a significant quantity of sleeping pills, and then she was suffocated?'

McKee nodded. 'My guess would be that a pillow was held over her face.'

I looked at him. 'Why didn't you mention any of this in your reports?'

'DCI Bishop told me not to.'

'Did you ask him why?'

'No.'

'Did he threaten you?'

'Yes.'

'Have you ever thought of standing up to him?'

'No.'

'Did you carry out the post-mortem on the body of a young man called Jamaal Tan?'

'Yes, I did.'

'Did you falsify that report too?'

'Not in terms of the post-mortem itself, but the DNA testing was taken out of my hands.'

'By Bishop?'

'Yes. He personally took charge of all DNA samples

recovered from the victim – blood, saliva, semen . . . everything.'

'Is that unusual?'

'It's a serious breach of procedure.'

'Why do you think he did it?'

'He told me he wanted it fast-tracked.'

'Did you believe him?'

McKee looked at me. 'Do you know DCI Bishop, Mr Craine?'

I nodded.

'Then you'll know as well as I do that believing or disbelieving him is of no account whatsoever.' McKee gazed into the distance, slowly shaking his head. 'Bishop functions on a different level to the rest of us . . . his is a world without truth or lies. There's simply no point in questioning his actions.'

'And you think that justifies what you've done?' I said.

McKee shook his head. 'I gave up trying to justify my actions a long time ago, Mr Craine.'

I looked at him, trying to see him as he was – a self-serving and self-pitying fool – but all I could see was a feeble and frightened old man. His dog started whining again, tugging on its lead, desperate to get out of the cold.

'You should get him a coat,' I said.

McKee looked at me. 'I'm sorry?'

'Your dog,' I said, getting to my feet. 'He's cold. You should get him a coat.'

And with that I walked off and left them there, shivering in the snow.

25

I'd imagined Meredith Chase's house to be some kind of a stately affair, with ivy-clad walls and mullioned windows, perhaps a couple of statues in the front garden, but of course it wasn't anything like that. He was a backbench MP, not an investment banker. The hilly street where he lived was in a quiet district on the north side of Hey, an area favoured by dental surgeries, veterinarian practices, and herbal health specialists. Chase's house was the same as most of the others in the street – a grey-walled four-storey town house with a paved front garden and a stone porchway. The pavement was lined with sycamore trees.

As I pulled up outside the house, I noticed a snow-covered Range Rover in the driveway, but I had no idea if it was Chase's or not. It could belong to his wife. And even if it was Chase's, it didn't mean he was at home. He could be anywhere – in Westminster, in a restaurant, a pub, a hotel room, sitting in First Class on a train down to London . . .

I got out of the car, flipped my cigarette end into the gutter, and went straight up to the front door. *No waiting around this time*, I told myself, reaching up to ring the bell. *Just fucking do it.*

I heard the bell ringing inside the house. It sounded faint

and distant, a long way away. I turned my back to the door and watched the snow tumbling silently from the sky, and I found myself wondering *why* it was snow. Why wasn't it hail? *What's the difference?* I wondered. *What makes snow snow and hail hail?*

'Who cares?' I muttered to myself.

I heard bolts being unlocked then, and I turned round to see the front door opening and Meredith Chase peering out at me.

'Yes?' he said.

It sound like *Yaas?*

He was wearing a tatty blue cardigan with brown leather buttons and a tie-less Tattersall shirt. He was older than he looked on TV, nearer seventy than sixty, and up close his face was doughy and pale. His thinning grey hair was limp and dull, and he had the uneven teeth of a long-term pipe smoker. A pair of rimless reading glasses hung low on his nose.

'Can I help you?' he asked.

'My name's John Craine,' I said. 'I'm a private investigator.'

He blinked rapidly, several times. I didn't know if it was a nervous reaction to my name or just something he did. The smell of cooking drifted out of the house – the smell of other people's food – and I heard a woman call out, 'Who is it, dear?' As Chase glanced over his shoulder, I caught a glimpse of a fussy-looking woman in a floral print dress standing in a doorway at the far end of the hall. She had a wooden spoon in her hand and an apron tied round her waist. Chase's wife, I assumed. Just back from a 1950s-themed fancy dress ball.

'It's all right, Maddie,' Chase told her. 'It's nothing to worry about. I won't be a minute.'

Maddie glanced at me, frowned, then went back into the kitchen. Chase turned back to me, removed his glasses and began wiping the lenses with his fingers. 'I'm not sure what I can do for you, Mr Craine. Is this a constituency matter? If it is, I'm afraid you'll have to make an appointment with my secretary—'

'Jamaal Tan,' I said, looking at him.

'I beg your pardon?'

'I've been hired to look into the murder of Jamaal Tan. I know what happened to him, and why. We need to talk about it.'

'I'm sorry,' he said, putting his glasses in his cardigan pocket. 'I don't know anyone of that name. Now if you don't mind, I'm just about to have Sunday lunch with my wife.'

'We can talk about it inside,' I said to him. 'Or we can talk about it out here. If you want your neighbours to know you like to fuck teenage boys, that's fine with me.'

Chase glanced anxiously over his shoulder, half-closed the front door, then leaned forward and looked out into the street.

'I've got the photographs that Jamaal took,' I told him.

He blinked nervously again, his face stiff and tense, his jaw clamped tight. If I'd had any kindness in me, I would have felt sorry for him. But I didn't. He was just a sack of bones to me, a means to an end. I looked calmly at him, waiting for him to make up his mind. He glared back at me for a moment, trying to brazen it out, then all at once his entire frame seemed to deflate. He breathed out heavily, his shoulders sagged, and a look of resigned surrender came into his eyes.

'You'd better come in,' he sighed.

The house was bigger than it looked from the outside, with long corridors and high ceilings and broad oak doors leading through into spacious rooms intended for glittering social occasions . . . but there was no sense of joy or occasion in this house, just a palpable sense of loss, of what might have been. It was a sorrowful house, haunted with the aura of dried-up tears.

I waited in the hallway while Chase went into the kitchen and spoke briefly with his wife, then I followed him up a wide flight of creaking stairs to the second floor. The stair carpet was old and worn, as dull and colourless as the lifeless landscapes fixed unlovingly on the stairway walls. At the top of the stairs, a few pewter ornaments sat forlornly on the sill of an alcove window, and ruched white curtains hung rigidly from a brass rail. A blackened brass vase stood empty on the floor. Chase passed these things by as I imagined he'd passed them by for years, with barely a thought. He walked along the second-floor landing, opened a door halfway down, and motioned me into a small and stuffy study.

I went inside. He followed me in and shut the door. I looked around. It was an old man's room, an old politician's room – writing table, armchair, bookshelves and filing cabinets, 18th-century cartoons on the wall showing rotund fellows in powdered wigs, copies of Hansard, battered box files. I could picture Chase sitting at the table replying to constituents' letters, bored out of his mind, writing to bus companies and chambers of commerce and half-dead people with nothing better to do than moan about junk-food litter and skateboard ramps. Next to the armchair, a small corner table was cluttered with well-thumbed books, magazines, and half a dozen pipes in a pipe rack. There was an unassuming TV set on a low table, DVDs stacked in a plastic rack. Pearl light from a pewter lampstand reflected on a row of lead-crystal decanters on a narrow mantelpiece above the blackened grate of a small open fire. The fireplace was bare and the room was cold.

'Sit down, please,' Chase said, indicating a cushioned chair against the wall.

I sat down.

'Can I get you anything to drink?' he asked.

I looked up at the decanters. 'Whisky, if you've got it.'

He moved slowly, like a condemned man, pouring out a good measure of whisky into a plain glass tumbler. I took the glass from him and drank deeply. He watched me with a strained frown, as if I'd just farted, or he was about to. Then he sighed again and reached for one of the decanters.

'You'll be driving in a while,' I told him.

He looked at me. 'I'm sorry?'

'Driving . . .' I mimed the movement of a steering wheel. 'It doesn't bother me if you have a drink. I just thought I'd let you know.'

He gave me a puzzled look for a moment, then shrugged and picked up the decanter. With some care, he poured himself a very small drink – brandy, by the smell of it – and then carefully put the stopper back in the bottle. He took a ridiculously tiny sip from his glass, placed it deliberately on the mantelpiece, then looked down at me.

'What exactly do you want, Mr Craine?'

Despite the cold, my palms were moist with sweat. I took out a cigarette and took my time lighting it, keeping Chase waiting, playing the game. But it was hardly worth the bother. Chase wasn't a player, I already knew that. He was just a reasonably intelligent man who'd always known what he wanted and how to get it, a man who'd made himself good at one thing and used that skill to take himself to places he'd otherwise never have got to.

He was just an old man.

Just like McKee.

A sack of bones.

Just like me.

'Mr Craine?' he said.

'Just a second,' I told him, closing my eyes, trying to remember what I was doing. My mind had suddenly gone blank again, empty of purpose and reason, and just for a second I could feel the fear coming back to me, the fear of the black hole in my head . . . but then, as suddenly as I'd lost everything, it all came crashing back. I knew what I was doing, I'd always known. Of *course* I knew what I was doing.

I opened my eyes and looked at Chase. 'What did Curt Dempsey do when you told him that Jamaal was black-mailing you?'

Chase just stared at me for a few seconds, then he reached for his glass and lowered himself wearily into the armchair.

His face had died now. He looked old and pathetic, staring into his brandy as if he were staring at his own death. After a while, he sighed heavily and looked up at me.

'I thought this was finished,' he said.

'Maybe it is.'

He nodded slowly, then looked down into his drink again, angling the glass, gently swilling the brandy around. An old railway clock ticked loudly on the wall. I glanced up and watched the second hand sketching its slow, blind circle. A moment in time – gone. And another. And another. And another . . .

The seconds passed.

Outside, the snow was still falling.

The light in this room was old.

Chase raised his eyes and looked at me. 'Do you believe in sin, Mr Craine?'

'I don't believe in anything.'

'Retribution, perhaps?'

'I can take it or leave it.'

He nodded. 'I meant no harm to come to Jamaal. I was very fond of him.'

'Right, I said. 'So when you told Dempsey he was black-mailing you, what did you think he was going to do? Send him a stern letter? Remind him of his responsibilities?'

Chase shook his head. 'I don't know . . . I wasn't thinking. I was just—'

'You were just trying to look after yourself, protect your reputation.'

'I suppose so . . .'

I smoked my cigarette and studied him, looking for the

public face, the face I'd seen on the TV and in the newspapers, but it was hard to imagine him anywhere else but right here, in this stuffy little room – a sad old man sitting in an armchair with a small brandy in his hand and a look of repressed fear on his face.

'Look,' I said to him, 'I don't give a shit about your private life, OK? I couldn't care less what you do, or why you do it, or how you feel about it. It doesn't mean anything to me. Do you understand?'

He smiled sarcastically. 'You're not here to judge me?'

'You seem quite happy to do that yourself.'

'Someone has to.'

'You're not listening,' I said. 'This isn't about *you*. I don't give a fuck about you. If you do what I tell you to do, I'll get rid of the photographs and forget I ever saw them.'

'And if I don't?'

'I'll send them to the Sunday papers and tell them everything I know. I'll tell them about Juno's, about you and Jamaal and all the other boys, about Curt Dempsey and Mick Bishop, and what they did to Jamaal. And I'll tell them about the Morden Hall contract too. You'll be finished.' I paused and took a drink, looking at Chase to see how he was taking it so far. Not too well, it seemed. His eyes had sunk into his head and his cheeks were pale and gaunt. He looked half dead. 'You'll probably end up in jail,' I continued, 'but that won't be too hard. A year or two in an open prison . . . I'm sure you could cope with that. But by the time you get out, you'll be fucked. No job, no money, no pension, no wife probably, nowhere to live. Your reputation, such as it is, will be ruined. There'll be no more favours for you, no more VIP treats. You'll spend the last few years of your life in a dirty little bedsit somewhere, cutting coupons out of free newspapers.' I stubbed out my cigarette. 'Of course, it could be worse. Dempsey and Bishop might decide it's too risky to let you live . . .'

Chase sniffed. 'How do I know you won't contact the press regardless?'

'You don't.'

'I see.'

He got to his feet, took the empty glass from my hand, then made his way over to the fireplace. He refilled my glass, added another drop of brandy to his, passed me mine, then went over to a small lead-framed window and gazed out into the night. I studied the back of his head as he stood there, wondering where his devil dwelled and what shape it took. What was it in that decrepit old body that moved him to do what he did? Was it the same thing that moved me? The same thing that drives us all? And, if it was, what did it look like? I stared hard at the back of his skull, trying to see inside, but all I could imagine was the substance of things: blood, cells, snot, chemicals, fat, bone, meat . . .

He turned from the window. 'What do you want me to do?'

When I asked him to tell me more about the Morden Hall contract, he took his time answering, and as he moved slowly back to the armchair and sat down, I could see him thinking things through, wondering how much I really knew, and how much he could get away with. I let him sit down, let him have his moment's hope, then I took a drink of whisky, lit a cigarette, and brought him back down to earth.

'You sit on the Defence Select Committee,' I told him. 'You were the shadow secretary of state for defence between 2002 and 2006, and you still have a number of very close contacts in the Ministry of Defence. You've been leaning on one of those contacts to make sure that Town Developments gets the contract for the multimillion-pound operations centre the MoD is planning to build at the Morden Hall site in Stangate Rise. Town Developments is one of Curt Dempsey's companies.' I looked at Chase. 'Dempsey *owns* you, doesn't he? You sold your soul to him a long time ago, and now he's calling it in.'

Chase sighed. 'Actually, he's been calling it in for quite some time now, but this . . . well, this is a different matter altogether. I *told* Dempsey it was out of my league. I promised him I'd do my best, and I'd try to find out as much as I could, but that wasn't good enough. He told me, in no uncertain terms, that if I didn't cooperate, and if Town Developments lost the contract, then graphic evidence of a very personal nature would be made public.' Chase looked at me. 'Sounds familiar, doesn't it?'

'Has Dempsey got the contract yet?'

'Not officially. Nothing's actually been signed yet, but the deal's as good as done.'

'What's Bishop's involvement?'

'What do you mean?'

'Does he know about the deal? Did he play a part in it?'

'Of course he did,' Chase said, seemingly surprised by the question. 'He and Dempsey are partners, they've worked together for years. It's not a legal partnership, obviously – you won't find Bishop's name on anything – but to all intents and purposes he shares ownership in most of Dempsey's companies, if not all of them.' Chase took a small sip of brandy. 'The two of them have what I believe is called a symbiotic relationship – an association of dissimilar organisms to their mutual advantage.' He smiled ruefully. 'Dempsey's business interests used to be of a far more down-to-earth nature than they are today, but he thrived by cultivating the right contacts in the right places. Mick Bishop was always in the right place, and he realised a long time ago that an association with Curt Dempsey would be a profitable affair.'

'So the Morden Hall contract is as important to Bishop as it is to Dempsey?'

Chase nodded. 'Absolutely.'

I drank more whisky, sipping it slowly, and glanced up at the window. The snow-dimmed skies were darkening now, the winter light of the afternoon already beginning to fade, and I guessed it wouldn't be long before the night came down. I looked at my watch. It was three-fifteen.

'I want you to call Mick Bishop,' I said to Chase.

'*What?*'

'You asked me what I wanted you to do. That's what I want you to do.'

He shook his head. 'You can't be serious . . . surely.'

'Do I look like I'm joking?'

'But *why*, for God's sake? I mean, Mick Bishop . . .? What on earth do you want me to say to him?'

I told Chase what I wanted him to say.

He wasn't happy about it, to put it mildly.

'It's madness,' he said, shaking his head, 'utter madness. He won't believe me, he'll know there's something going on—'

'Make him believe you,' I said.

'I really don't think—'

'I'm not asking you to think, I'm telling you what to do.' I lit another cigarette. 'There's nothing for you to think about. You either do it or you don't. And if you don't . . . well, you already know what I'll do if you don't.'

'What if he says no?'

'He won't.'

'But what if he does?'

'Are you going to do it or not?' I said.

Chase let out a sigh. 'Shall I use the landline or my mobile?'

'Mobile.'

He nodded, taking a mobile from his pocket. 'Do you want me to put it on speaker?'

I thought about it for a moment, weighing up the pros and cons, then nodded. 'Put it on speaker, but ignore me when you're talking to him, OK? Don't even look at me.'

'What if there's a problem?'

'You're an MP, for fuck's sake. It's your job to deal with problems.'

He looked down at the phone in his hand and began

scrolling through his contacts. He found Bishop's number, stared at it for a second or two, then took a steadying breath, let it out, and drained the last drop of brandy from his glass.

He glanced at me. 'Ready?'

I nodded. 'Do it.'

He pressed the screen – once to dial the number, a second time to activate the speakerphone – then, as the ringing tone began, he leaned back in the chair, cleared his throat, and stared up at the ceiling.

After half a dozen rings, Bishop's voice barked out from the phone. 'Chase?'

'Is that you, Mick?' Chase said.

'Yeah, what do you want? I'm busy.'

'Sorry, but I really need to see you about something. It's rather urgent—'

'What is it?'

'There's a problem with the Morden Hall contract.'

'What problem? I thought it was all sorted out.'

'Well, it was, but something's come up.'

'Since when?'

'I've only just this minute found out—'

'Found out *what*, for fuck's sake?'

'I don't think it's safe to talk on the phone. That's why I need to see you.'

Bishop said nothing for a moment, and I could almost hear him mulling over what Chase had just said. 'What makes you think the phone's not safe?' he asked, instinctively lowering his voice. 'Have you heard something? Has someone said something to you?'

'It's probably best if I don't name names just now.'

'Right . . .' Bishop said hesitantly. It was hard to tell from his voice alone if he was hesitant because he was confused, or because he suspected something. 'This phone thing,' he said cautiously. 'Is it connected to the contract problem? Or are we talking about two separate things?'

'I'm not sure . . . I was hoping you might know.'

'All right. Where are you now?'

'I'm at home.'

'OK, I'll come over in a couple of hours—'

'No, I need to show you something.'

'So show me when I get there.'

'It's at Morden Hall.'

'What?'

'I need to show you something *at* Morden Hall.'

As the phone line went quiet again, I held my breath, waiting for Bishop to respond. This was it now, the moment of truth. He was either going to go for it, or see right through it. If he decided that it was a set-up – and there was no doubt in my mind that he'd seriously consider the possibility – all I could hope for was that he'd be so pissed off with Chase for trying to set him up that he'd agree to meet with him anyway just to show him what happens to people who fuck around with Mick Bishop.

'Let me get this straight,' he said warily. 'There's something at Morden Hall you need to show me, is that right?'

'Yes.'

'And it's got something to do with this contract problem.'

'Indirectly, yes.'

'But you can't tell me what it is over the phone.'

'No.'

'You wouldn't be fucking with me, would you, Meredith?'

'Of course not. Why would I—?'

'You don't want to fuck with me, old man.'

'I'm just trying to *help* you, Mick, that's all.'

'Why me? Why didn't you call Curt about this?'

'Because . . .'

'Because what?'

Chase sighed. 'Just let me talk to you first, Mick, OK? Just the two of us. I'll explain everything then, and you can decide what's best.'

'All right,' Bishop said, still far from convinced. 'I've got a few things to do this afternoon, but I should be free around six.'

'So six o'clock at Morden Hall?' Chase said.

'Yeah.'

'Thanks, Mick. And I'm sorry if . . . hello?'

Bishop had already hung up.

Chase looked at his phone, then thumbed the screen, wiped a sheen of sweat from his brow, and turned to me. 'How did I do?'

'You're a very convincing liar,' I told him.

He half-smiled. 'I'm a politician, it's my job.'

'You did very well.'

'Do you think he believed me?'

'I'm not sure, but I'd be surprised if he didn't show up.'

'You really think so?'

I nodded. 'He'll be very cautious, and he'll do everything he can to eliminate any possible risks.'

'Such as?'

'He'll probably get in touch with Dempsey, see if he can get anything out of him. If he's absolutely convinced he can trust him, he might bring him along to Morden Hall, but if he's got any doubts at all, he won't.' I looked at my watch. 'And if I was Bishop, I wouldn't go straight to Morden Hall, I'd come round here first to catch you off guard.'

Chase stared at me. 'You think he'll come here?'

'I would.'

'What am I going to do? I can't let him—'

'It's all right,' I said. 'You won't be here.'

He frowned. 'I don't understand.'

'Bishop's expecting to meet you at Morden Hall, isn't he?'

'Well, yes . . . he's expecting to meet me, but you're going to be there instead. That's the whole point of this charade, isn't it?'

I nodded. 'But he has to think you're there, and if he doesn't see your car when he gets to Morden Hall, he's going to start wondering. And if he sees my car, he's definitely going to start wondering. So the only logical solution is for you to drive me out there.'

'You want *me* to drive you to Morden Hall?'

'If we go right now, you won't be here if Bishop does turn up.'

'What about my wife?'

I shrugged. 'Make up an excuse to get her out of the house.'

'Like what?'

'I don't fucking know. You're the one who's cheated on

her for years, not me. I'm sure you can come up with something.'

'But what if—?'

'Just do it, OK?' I sighed.

'Now?'

'Yeah, now.'

He looked at me for a moment, then picked up his phone and got to his feet.

'I'll take that,' I said, holding out my hand for his phone.

'You don't trust me?'

'No.'

He shrugged and passed me the phone.

'I'll wait here for you,' I said, getting up and going over to his armchair. I leaned over and picked up his landline phone from the table. 'Just in case,' I told him, pressing the speakerphone button and placing the handset on the table.

'Haven't you forgotten something?' he asked, smiling wearily.

I shook my head. 'You're worried enough as it is about what to tell your wife – you're not going to risk asking her if you can use her mobile.'

He grinned at me. 'You're very good, Mr Craine.'

'No, I'm not. I'm just better than you.'

While Chase went downstairs to talk to his wife, I helped myself to another glass of whisky, then left his study and went looking for the bathroom. Along the landing there was a stunted aspidistra in a tall brass pot, more dull landscapes on the walls, and not much else. The bathroom was at the end of the hallway. I went in and relieved myself, flushed the toilet, then closed the lid, sat down, and took the bag of cocaine from my pocket. The bathroom was filled with prissy little things – crocheted rugs, covers, mats, ornaments, air fresheners – anything to disguise the fact that this was a place where you pissed and farted and emptied your bowels and scraped the grime from your teeth. I thumbed a pinch of coke up my nose, then got up and went to leave. As I reached for the door handle, the blunt ache in my belly suddenly tightened and a net of pain shot up into my chest. I let out a groan and sank to my haunches, holding my breath, but the pain disappeared almost as quickly as it had come, and when I breathed out again the tingling tightness had gone.

Chase was waiting for me in the hallway downstairs. He'd put on an old Barbour jacket and a dusty tweed hat, and he had a rolled-up golfing umbrella in his hand.

'All right?' I said to him.

He nodded. 'Maddie's gone to visit a friend.'

'OK, let's go.'

Once we were out of the house and in the car, Chase became very talkative. He didn't seem particularly nervous, in fact, if anything, he appeared quite relaxed. It was almost as if he'd been waiting a long time to unburden himself, and now that he'd started he just couldn't stop. I wasn't all that interested in what he had to say – I already had all the information I needed – but I couldn't be bothered to shut him up. I was tired, running on empty, and I didn't feel too good. The Range Rover was a comfortable car – plush seats, plenty of room, smooth and quiet and warm . . . it made me feel safe and secure, like a little kid in the back seat of the family car, driving home from the beach on a rainy Sunday afternoon. The hypnotic tock-tock of the windscreen wipers, the quiet swoosh of the tyres, the purring engine . . . a winter's lullaby.

As Chase started telling me how he'd first got to know Curt Dempsey, I lit a cigarette, leaned my head against the window, and watched the streets roll by.

'. . . Dempsey was always around in those days,' Chase said, 'always organising things – fund-raising events, charity dinners – inviting the rich to salve their guilt by giving money to good causes. Curt has a very persuasive manner. He can make people do things without them realising it. I told him once he'd make a good politician. He laughed at that. He said the only good politician is a dead politician . . .'

I touched a button on the door and the window slid down. Snowflakes drifted in, moistening the side of my face. I touched the button again and the window slid shut. I wiped the snow from my face and licked the moisture from my hand. I felt sleepy, but wide awake at the same time. I could feel the cocaine racing numbly in my head, taking me out of myself, and as I glanced in the side mirror I thought I saw something that could have been me – a speck of something, a shape in the glass . . . a stick man. He was moving, jiggling around, fluttering in the wind like a dead fly caught in a web, and I saw him as a model of disordered movements and misguided energies, a vortex of tightening spirals, always trying to get somewhere but never knowing where he was going . . .

I closed my eyes.

Chase was still talking.

'. . . when I stood for election in 2005. Dempsey had no political experience, of course, but the offer seemed quite genuine, and I wasn't really in a position to say no. Hey West was a marginal seat. I'd only just held it in 2001. Labour were still riding high and my opponent was a clean young thing with telegenic looks and a law degree. I needed all the help I could get. So when Dempsey made his offer, I couldn't afford to say no. He was very . . . resourceful, shall we say? Very resourceful, indeed. When it comes to persuasion, Curt Dempsey commits himself with extreme efficiency. In the end, as you probably know, I was elected with a fairly comfortable majority.'

'What did Dempsey want in return?' I asked.

'Very little, at first. Respectability through association, the odd snippet of information . . . prior notice of local development deals, that sort of thing. Nothing out of the ordinary.' Chase shrugged. 'I have no real power, you see. Even when I was a member of the shadow cabinet I had very little genuine influence.' He grinned at me. 'I spend most of my time discussing dog excrement and housing estates.'

'But you know a man who does have power.'

He frowned. 'I'm sorry, I'm not with you.'

'In the Ministry of Defence.'

'Oh, you mean Simon?' He laughed. 'A man of power? He'd like that. Yes, I must remember to tell him that. A man of power . . .' His laugh faded to a wounded sigh. 'Simon has a lot of things, Mr Craine, but power isn't one of them. He just happens to occupy a position that, under certain circumstances, is open to abuse . . .'

We were leaving town now, heading out past Lexden Vale towards Stangate Rise. It was dark, the streetlights on, the falling snow glazed with a faint orange glow. I remembered the domed lamp on the wall outside Imogen's flat . . . the eerie light . . . the green-tinted whiteness tinged with a violet-blue glimmer . . .

I didn't feel well.

'. . . but Curt has a remarkable capacity for finding things out,' Chase was saying. 'He knows who's who, he knows what people know, and he knows . . . well, let's just say he knows how to get what he wants . . .'

I was really suffering now. An insistent pain was throbbing hard at the base of my skull, my hands had gone numb, my skin felt tight . . . I was sweating, too hot, too cold . . . and the air was too thick . . .

'. . . Simon's relationship with a high-profile senior minister. Very few people know about it. Of course, there's no reason why they should. They're both single . . .'

. . . a wooden stave was lodged in my chest. My hands were shaking, my heart pounding . . . I couldn't breathe. Jesus . . . I couldn't *breathe*. My heart stopped for a second . . . two seconds . . . three . . . *oh, fuck! I don't want to die in a car. Please don't let me die in a fucking car . . . it's all right, just keep still, don't move . . . you'll be all right . . . this isn't anything extraordinary, it's just something, a body thing . . . it'll pass . . . think of something . . . think of something . . . I think I'm dying . . .*

But then all at once something inside me kicked in again

and I gulped in a lungful of air, and all the pain and fear drained out of me. I wiped my face and ran my fingers through my hair. I was drenched in sweat.

'. . . but even in these so-called enlightened times there are still lots of people who take a very dim view of – good Lord! Are you all right, Mr Craine? You look *terrible*.'

I coughed, cleared my throat, and looked out of the window. 'You missed the turning.'

'I'm sorry?'

'The turn-off to Morden Hall, you just missed it. You'll have to go on up to the roundabout and double back.'

Chase couldn't keep his eyes off me. 'You really don't look very well, Mr Craine. Perhaps I should pull in for a minute—'

'Stop at that petrol station over there,' I told him.

We carried on up to the roundabout, doubled back round it, then Chase slowed the car, indicated left, and pulled in at the filling station. He parked by the air pump, turned off the engine, and reached under the seat.

'Here,' he said, passing me a bottle of water. 'How are you feeling now? You look a little—'

'Wait here,' I told him, opening the door and getting out.

As I crossed the forecourt towards the shop, I wondered if Chase would take the opportunity to drive off and leave me. I didn't think he would, mainly because he didn't have anywhere else to go, but I didn't really care either way. If he waited for me, fine. And if he didn't, fuck it. I'd just have to do without him.

I entered the shop and went up to the counter. It was

an old-fashioned garage shop, the kind of place that stays open late, even on a Sunday, and sells just about everything – bread, milk, newspapers, pies, bags of coal, toilet rolls, DVDs . . . and alcohol. I asked the girl behind the till for two packets of Marlboro, and as she turned to get them off the rack, loudly chewing gum, I scanned the rows of spirit bottles in a glass cabinet on the wall. There were no full-sized bottles, just miniatures, quarter-bottles, and halves.

'£13.58,' the girl said, passing me the cigarettes.

'And a half-bottle of Bell's, please.'

She opened the cabinet and took out a quarter-bottle of Famous Grouse.

'Not that one,' I told her. 'Bell's . . . the big bottle.'

'This one?'

'No, the one next to it. The one that says *Bell's* on it.'

'Oh, yeah.'

The Range Rover was still there when I went outside, still parked by the air pump, and as I went over and got in, lighting a cigarette and sucking the smoke deep into my lungs, Chase just looked at me and said, 'I'm not sure you're allowed to smoke here. It's a fire risk.'

'We'd better get going then, hadn't we?' I said, opening the Bell's and taking a good long drink.

He glanced at me, shook his head, then started the car and got going. We headed off back the way we'd come, and this time Chase didn't miss the turning. He swung the car to the right and turned down a narrow rutted track lined with ragged hedges and wind-blown trees. In the powerful beam of the Range Rover's headlights, I could just make out a wasteground plateau at the far end of the track, half-hidden behind broken fencing and silhouetted Scots pines, and behind the fencing, blocked against the starless black sky, I could see the snow-blurred ruins of Morden Hall.

'Can I ask you a question, Mr Craine?' Chase said as we headed off down the track.

'Is it about politics?'

'No.'

'Ask away.'

'Why are you doing this?'

'I've already told you, I'm investigating Jamaal's murder.'

'And all this – threatening me, forcing me to lie, making me drive you out here against my will . . . this is all just part of your investigation, is it?'

'It's what I'm doing.'

He looked at me. 'I'm not sure I understand . . .'

'You don't have to.'

Chase was about to say something else when the Range Rover ran over a pothole and lurched to one side, tugging the steering wheel from his hands. He quickly got hold of it and regained control of the car, but it was enough of a reminder for him to keep quiet and concentrate on driving until we reached the end of the track.

As we approached the fenced-off courtyard surrounding the derelict building, I leaned forward in my seat and peered out into the snow. In the harsh white light of the headlights, the glassless black windows of Morden Hall stared back at me like the sockets of long-dead eyes.

'Where do you want me to park?' Chase asked, slowing to pass through a gateless gap in the fencing.

'Over there somewhere,' I said, gesturing towards the front of the building.

The wire-mesh fencing surrounding the courtyard was as derelict as the building itself – rusted and buckled, sagging from its posts – and whole sections of it had collapsed and been trampled into the ground. The courtyard was a waste-ground of weeds and rubble – piles of bricks, broken glass, shattered tiles, rotting timbers. This carpet of rubble spread outwards from the base of the building, and the further it was from its origin, the less definition it had, merging like gravel, then soil, then sand, then dust, into the clumps of scrub and wild grass sprouting from the courtyard waste.

Chase parked the car next to the remains of an old cement mixer, facing the ruined building. He turned off the engine but left the headlights on. I took a hit from the whisky bottle and looked around, seeing the remains of bonfires, desiccated rabbit carcasses, iron poles and rusted chains . . . and standing in the midst of all this dereliction, I saw the skeleton of Morden Hall glowering down at me like a crippled old man surveying the memory of his youth.

It was an H-shaped building, the old brick frame still mostly intact, but a lot of the roof was gone, the bare timbers jutting out like broken limbs, and anything worth salvaging had been ripped out a long time ago – window frames, sills, chimney pots, doors. It was just the shell of a place. A hundred years ago, I imagined, it would have been a serene and splendid building – a three-storey red-brick mansion house, with quartered windows set in pale granite, domed towers, turrets, arches, columns, tall chimney stacks, rhododendrons at the foot of the wall, marble statues and fountains . . . a place for garden parties, for pleasant conversation, for well-dressed gentlemen and pale-skinned ladies in pearls and feathered hats . . .

And now it was all but gone.

The house had lost its state of grace.

But even in its ruination, the building retained something of its prime. Like the dead body of a great beast, it still had a desolate dignity.

'Have you got a torch?' I asked Chase.

'A torch?' he said, turning to me. He was looking a bit drawn and haggard now, the skin of his face unhealthily grey. 'Why do you want a torch?'

'Why do you think?'

He glanced over at the building. 'We're not going in there, are we?'

'That's the plan.'

'Are you sure that's a good idea?'

'What's the matter?' I asked him. 'Scared there might be ghosts in there?'

'No, I'm scared of being crushed to death by a collapsing wall, or falling through some rotten floorboards, or step- ping on an infected needle—'

'Here,' I said, passing him the whisky bottle. 'Stop worrying and have a drink.'

He looked at me for a moment, then took the bottle, raised it to his mouth and drank awkwardly.

'There's nothing to worry about,' I said, taking the bottle back from him and having a drink myself.

'Nothing to *worry* about?' He shook his head. 'You're not only asking me to risk my life by walking into a deathtrap, but Mick Bishop's going to be here soon. Do you realise what he's going to do when he finds out I've set him up?'

'He's not going to do anything to you.'

'Who's going to stop him? You?'

'He's just a man. He's not fucking God.'

'He's an animal.'

I looked at him. 'We're all animals.'

He held my gaze. 'You might not like me, Mr Craine, and you're no doubt disgusted by my predilection for young men, but my behaviour in that regard isn't illegal. Nor is it immoral. I've never done anything with anyone against their will. I may be a sinner in some people's eyes, but I'm neither a criminal nor an animal.'

I was tempted to put him right, but it served no real purpose, and I didn't care what he thought about anything anyway. He could think what he liked about himself, about me, about the boys he paid to have sex with him . . . his thoughts were his business. I had no interest in changing them.

'Have you got a torch or not?' I said, removing my penlight from my pocket. 'If you don't, we'll have to use this.'

He sighed, blowing out his cheeks, then reached round the back of his seat and pulled out a foot-long torch with a rubberised handle. He turned it on, checking it worked, then clicked it off again and offered it to me. It was an impressive piece of equipment – well made, weighty, strong and solid – and it made my slim plastic penlight look so tiny and pathetic that I couldn't help grinning.

'I'm glad you find the situation amusing, Mr Craine,' Chase said.

I clipped the penlight back in my pocket and looked at my watch. It was ten past four. Time to get going.

26

I told Chase to stay close behind me and led the way up a short flight of moss-grown steps to a pillared porchway at the front of the building. There was no door, just a gutted doorway, and as I shone the torch inside I saw a dank corridor scattered with broken bricks and chunks of sodden plaster. The corridor walls were cracked and mouldy, dripping with pale-brown water, and some of the floorboards were missing, either ripped out or rotted away.

'Mind where you put your feet,' I warned Chase, stepping cautiously through the doorway.

I stopped and shone the torch upwards, studying the ceiling. It was riddled with jagged holes, revealing broken timbers and cables and sagging pipes, and through the holes I could see another floor with another holed ceiling, and through that I could just about make out a few dark patches of snow-filled night. But all in all there was more ceiling than hole.

It was probably safe enough.

I moved carefully along the corridor, sweeping the beam of the torch as I went. I saw shallow puddles filmed with oil, flattened cigarette ends, dried lumps of cement, a perished shoe, scraps of foil and clingfilm, a petrified apple core . . .

'All right?' I asked Chase.

'It stinks in here.'

He was right. The air was thick with a cloying mixture of waste and decay – the smell of dead animals, dampness, dried shit, piss. I lit a cigarette and paused beside the bones of a staircase, shining the torch up into the darkness. There was nothing to see, but I could hear the wind whistling through the ruins, and the quiet scratting sounds of small animals – *tacktacktacktack* – birds, maybe, or rats.

I took a quick drink from the whisky bottle and went on.

The first room we came to was plainly the first room that others had come to. The door was half-broken off, hanging from a single hinge, and it was completely covered in illegible graffiti. I pushed it back and stepped inside. There was a rusted filing cabinet in one corner, the drawers broken open and half-filled with filthy water, and lying on the floor was a stained and sodden mattress. It was surrounded by empty beer cans, bottles, used condoms, needles, dried faeces, and unidentifiable items of soiled clothing. One wall was pocked with hammer marks, another was smeared with shit. Every available surface was covered in more graffiti – tags, crude drawings, obscene or lunatic messages. I didn't bother trying to read any of them. Their authors were hopeless souls draped in rags, with ratted hair and facial tics and murderous addictions – there was nothing they could tell me that I didn't already know.

'Good God,' Chase whispered from the doorway behind me. 'How could anyone bear to be in here? It's *repulsive*.'

'It's better than nothing,' I told him, edging back out through the doorway.

There were a lot more empty rooms along the corridor, and some of them showed similar signs of vagrant occupation, but the addicted and the homeless have no interest in adventure for adventure's sake – once they've got what they need, that's generally enough – so the rooms furthest away from the entrance were mostly untouched, just bare walls and stripped floors, empty and abandoned.

'What are you looking for?' Chase asked me as we carried on down the corridor.

'I'm not sure,' I admitted. 'I'll know it when I find it.'

There were several staircases leading up to the second floor, but they were all either gutted – the stairs and fittings torn out – or too precarious to risk using, so my wandering was confined to the ground floor. As we approached the furthest end of the central corridor, we came to a vast room with huge double doors, one of them missing. The room stretched away to our left, taking up an entire section of the building, and as I shone the torch around I saw the rusted remains of industrial machinery, massive steel frames, enormous racks of shelves . . .

'It's the main research laboratory,' Chase said.

I looked at him.

'What's left of it anyway,' he added, gazing around.

I suddenly felt immensely tired, almost too weary to speak.

'I need to sit down,' I muttered.

Chase nodded.

I went over and sat down on a rust-streaked girder resting

against the wall, and after a few moments Chase came over and joined me.

'Are you all right?' he asked.

'Just tired.'

I wanted to close my eyes and lean my head back against the wall and drift away, just for a minute or two, but I knew I couldn't. If I closed my eyes now I'd never be able to open them again. I took the bag of cocaine from my pocket, tapped out a ragged line on the back of my hand, and snorted it up. The rush kicked in almost immediately, filling my head with an energising burst of white light, but within seconds it started to fade, straining and stuttering like the flame of a slightly damp match, and I knew my tank was empty now and I was pretty much running on fumes. But it was OK. There wasn't far to go now. The end was almost in sight, and one way or another I'd soon have time to rest.

I lit a cigarette and shone the torch around the vast derelict room. Snow was blowing in through a partially collapsed wall at the far end, and the three remaining walls were little more than crumbling ruins streaked with moss and swathes of brown algae. The stone floor was strewn with broken slate and smashed porcelain and rain-soaked timber, and beneath the heaps of debris I could just make out the rusted scars of huge steel bolts that had once held great banks of machinery and laboratory apparatus.

'What did they used to do in here?' I asked Chase.

'I'm not exactly sure,' he said. 'A company called Xylonex owned the building for years. They were an industrial plastics company, and as far as I know this was their main research and development facility.' He shrugged. 'They went out of business in '79. I assume this was where they developed and tested new products.'

I gazed out over the wreckage, imagining roaring furnaces and vats full of molten plastic, heavy steel worktops, aluminium shelving, test tubes and beakers . . . and I could see the laboratory men in their long white coats, boiling up their plastics by day and dreaming their plastic dreams by night . . .

And then I saw the door. There was nothing extraordinary about it, it was just a closed door in the wall, over to my left, much the same as all the other doors in the building – a decrepit old wooden thing, the frame warped, the paintwork faded and flaking away. But there was something about it, something that drew me towards it, and as I got to my feet and shuffled across the rubble-strewn floor, I had a feeling that I was about to find what I was looking for.

The door opened outwards, and when I shone the torch inside I saw a steep flight of wooden stairs leading down into the earthen darkness of a stone-walled basement. I called Chase over and told him to wait by the door while I went down and checked it out.

The stairs looked solid enough, and were guarded by wooden rails on either side, but I didn't take any chances, carefully studying each step in the beam of the torch before putting any weight on it. The air in the basement didn't feel quite as cold as the rest of the building, and it smelled different too – an underground smell, damp and organic, slightly musty . . . but not unpleasant. I stopped at the foot of the stairs and slowly swept the torch around, taking my time, taking everything in. It was a roughly square room, with bare brick walls, a dirt floor, and a flat stone ceiling. Odds and ends were scattered all over the floor – piles of sacking, coils of rope and wire, empty boxes, rags, wooden crates, metal piping. On the left-hand side of the basement, four rows of benches were built up in a semi-circular terrace that reached from the middle of the floor to halfway up the outside wall. The benches were made of heavy wood, greased and worn, like railway sleepers, but the terracing itself was solid concrete. There were no windows anywhere, just a small metal grille fixed high in the wall above the terracing. On the other side of the basement was a raised platform – also constructed of wood on concrete – and at the back of the platform, half a dozen rusty animal cages were strung along the wall on a length of wire.

'Is everything all right down there?' Chase called out from above.

'Yeah,' I called back. 'Just a minute.'

I went over to the terracing and clambered up the wooden benches. Standing on tiptoe, I could just see through the metal grille. I raised the torch and shone it through the grille, and the beam lit up the courtyard outside. I could see the parked Range Rover, the stone porchway, the entrance to the building. I could even see a little bit of the rutted track in the distance.

I climbed back down, sat on a bench, and lit a cigarette. I

looked over at the stairs. There was an empty space beneath them, a brick-lined alcove set back into the basement wall.

'Chase?' I called out.

'Yes?'

'You can come down now. Leave the door open.'

'I can't see anything.'

'Sorry,' I said, directing the torch beam at the top of the stairs. 'Is that better?'

I guided him down with the torch. He came down sideways, one step at a time, never letting go of the guard rail, and never taking his eyes off his feet. When he reached the bottom and finally raised his head, he was quite taken aback by what he saw.

'What on earth . . .?' he muttered, his eyes widening. 'What *is* this place?'

'I've no idea,' I said.

As he gazed around at the cages, the raised platform, the makeshift terracing, he shook his head in bewilderment. 'It almost looks like some kind of theatre, or perhaps a lecture room? But what are the cages for?'

'Laboratory animals?' I suggested.

'Maybe . . .' He looked at me. 'Did you know about this place?'

I shook my head, taking a drag on my cigarette.

Chase just stood there looking at me. 'I don't understand *any* of this . . . I mean, why are we here?'

I flicked the beam of the torch at the metal grille in the wall. 'You can see the courtyard from up there,' I explained. 'We'll see Bishop coming, but he won't see us. And it's relatively dry down here too.'

Chase sighed and shook his head again. 'And when he shows up . . . *if* he shows up, what then? What are you actually going to do?'

'You don't need to know,' I said.

'Excuse *me*, but I think I have the right—'

'None of us has a right to anything,' I said. 'That's what people like you don't understand. There *are* no rights. You either get what you're given or take what you want.' I looked at him. 'I'm not giving you what you want. It's up to you if you want to try taking it.'

Chase frowned. 'I was merely asking—'

'Well don't. I'm too fucking tired.' I pulled the half-bottle of Bell's from my pocket and took a drink. 'As long as you do as I say,' I told Chase, 'nothing's going to happen to you. All you've got to do is wait here with me until Bishop gets here, and then you can go.'

'Go where?'

'Wherever you fucking want.'

'I can just go?'

I nodded.

'And that's it?'

'That's it.'

'What about the photographs, the pictures that Jamaal took?'

'I haven't got them.'

'What do you mean you haven't got them? You said you'd get rid of them—'

'I haven't got the photographs. I never had them. I've never even seen them.'

'You *lied* to me?'

'Yep.'

He went quiet for a few moments, staring at the dirt floor, and I could hear him breathing heavily. I looked at my watch. It was ten to five.

Chase got to his feet. 'I think I'll go now.'

'Sit down,' I told him.

He shook his head. 'You have no hold over me, Mr Craine. Why shouldn't I just walk out of here right now?'

I took the pistol out of my pocket and levelled it at his belly. He took a step back, tottering slightly, and stared aghast at the gun. 'My *God*—'

'Just sit down, for Christ's sake,' I said wearily.

'What on *earth* do you think—?'

'*Sit down!*'

He shuffled over to the bench, his eyes never leaving the gun, and sat down about six feet away from me.

'Thank you,' I sighed, placing the pistol on the bench beside me.

For the next ten minutes or so, Chase said nothing, he just sat there like a sulky child – his head hanging down, his eyes fixed blankly on the floor. I was glad of the silence. I sipped whisky and smoked cigarettes and let my mind float away. I didn't want to think about anything. I listened to the wind in the courtyard, the muted drift of snow . . . I watched the movement of dusted air in the torchlight . . . I watched a shiny black ground beetle scuttling across the floor. It bumped into my shoe and stopped, its antennae twitching, and I wondered what it knew. Did it know it was snowing outside? Did it know where it was going? Did it possess a glimmer of reason? I watched as it turned round and moved away from my shoe, heading back the way it had come, and I hoped – for its sake – that it didn't know anything.

'Perhaps we'd better turn off the torch,' Chase said.

I looked at him.

'It's only just gone five o'clock,' he said. 'Bishop's not going to be here for another hour. We should save the batteries.'

'He'll be here long before six,' I said.

'What makes you think that?'

'Well, firstly,' I said, getting to my feet and listening hard, 'that's what I'd do if I was him. And secondly . . .' I looked over at the metal grille in the wall and saw a faint flicker of light in the darkness outside. 'He's already here.'

27

By the time I'd led Chase over to the alcove beneath the stairs and told him to get in there and stay out of sight, then clambered up the benches and positioned myself at the metal grille in the wall, the headlights of the approaching car were already sweeping around the courtyard, lighting up the weeds and debris in the billowing snow. I turned off the torch. The car was a dark-coloured saloon and it was moving slowly, its tyres crunching effortlessly through the snow-shrouded rubble. I couldn't see who was inside. It slowed even more as it approached the Range Rover and cautiously skirted round it, then it stopped for a moment or two in front of it, before finally reversing gently and rolling to a halt beside Chase's car.

Nothing happened for a while. The saloon just sat there, facing the building – its engine still running, exhaust fumes hazing in the snow, headlights blazing . . .

'*What's he doing?*' Chase whispered loudly.

'*Shut up*,' I hissed, without looking round.

The saloon's engine died, but the headlights stayed on. Steam rose gently from the bonnet of the car and the engine ticked to silence.

I waited, staring at the car.

My belly was starting to hurt again, the pain tightening

like a knotted rope in the pit of my guts, and for a second or two I thought I was going to throw up, but then the car door opened on the driver's side, and the sickness in my belly turned cold. As the interior light snapped on, I saw a heavyset man in a long waxed raincoat getting out of the car, and Mick Bishop sitting in the passenger seat, his face as cold and composed as ever. The man in the raincoat was Renny Surnam, the blond-haired security guard from Juno's who Hassan suspected of killing Jamaal, and who I suspected of being Bishop's 'very capable colleague'. He was also, of course, the man who'd calmly crushed my testicles and threatened to break my spine. I wasn't surprised to see him. It was almost inevitable that Bishop wouldn't come alone, he'd bring someone along to watch his back, and the most likely candidates were Dempsey and Surnam. The fact that Bishop had chosen Surnam suggested to me that he hadn't just come here to talk.

Surnam had crossed over to the Range Rover now and was shining a torch through the side window and peering inside. He moved to the rear of the car and did the same – raising the torch over his head and pressing his face to the glass – then he glanced over at Bishop and shook his head.

Bishop got out of the car, a torch in his hand, and went over to Surnam. They talked for a few moments, but I couldn't hear what they were saying, then they both turned towards the building and began scanning every inch of it with their torches – the doorway, the ruined windows, the collapsed roof, the courtyard. At one point, I saw the beam of Surnam's torch sweeping across the ground towards me, and I ducked down just as the light flashed through the grille, momentarily lighting up the basement.

'*What was that?*' Chase whispered.

I told him to shut up again, then cautiously raised my head and looked out through the grille. Bishop and Surnam hadn't moved, they were still just standing there, but they'd lowered their torches now and were talking again.

After a few moments, Bishop put his hand to his mouth and shouted out: '*CHASE! CAN YOU HEAR ME? ARE YOU IN THERE? CHASE!*' As he paused for a second or two, listening hard, waiting for a reply, I took the pistol from my pocket and looked over my shoulder.

'*Chase?*' I whispered.

'*What?*'

'*Stay exactly where you are and keep your mouth shut,*' I told him. '*If you so much as move, if you make any sound at all, I'll shoot you. Do you understand?*'

Before he could answer, Bishop shouted out again: '*DON'T MAKE ME COME IN THERE LOOKING FOR YOU, CHASE! I'M FUCKING WARNING YOU! IF YOU'RE IN THERE, YOU'D BETTER COME OUT RIGHT NOW!*'

'*Chase?*' I hissed. '*Did you hear me?*'

'*Yes, I heard you. And I can assure you that I have no intention of doing anything.*'

'*LAST CHANCE, OLD MAN!*'

I turned back to the grille. Bishop was still standing in front of the building but Surnam had moved over to the saloon and was opening the boot. He reached inside and took out a double-barrelled shotgun, leaned it against the car, then reached into the boot again and brought out a 20-litre petrol can. From the way he lifted it – his shoulders straining slightly – and the noise it made when he placed it on the ground – a heavy-sounding *dong* – I was fairly certain it was full.

'Shit,' I said.

'What is it?' Chase hissed.

'Nothing. Keep quiet.'

With the petrol can in one hand and the shotgun in the other, and the torch lodged under his arm, Surnam made his way back over to Bishop. Bishop said something to him. Surnam nodded, passed him the shotgun, and retrieved the torch from under his arm. They both took a last quick look around the courtyard, then Bishop patted Surnam on the shoulder, and Surnam moved off towards the doorway. Bishop gave it half a second before following on behind him. I watched them as they approached the doorway, moving very warily, and I watched Surnam go inside while Bishop waited in the porchway. After a short while, I heard Surnam calling out, presumably to let Bishop know it was safe, and then Bishop entered the building.

I waited a minute, making sure they didn't come out again, then I turned on the torch and began clambering back down the benches.

'What's he doing now?' Chase asked.

'They're in the building,' I said. 'Stay where you are.'

'They? It's not just Bishop?'

'He's with a man called Surnam.'

'Renny Surnam?'

'You know him?'

'I know who he is,' Chase said, his eyes white in the darkness. 'I've seen him at Juno's . . . he works for Dempsey.'

'Do you know what he does for him?'

Chase hesitated. 'Well, I've heard things, you know . . .'

'Like what?'

Chase just shook his head, either unable or unwilling to go any further.

I said, 'Did Surnam kill Jamaal?'

Chase lowered his eyes. 'I can't say for sure . . .'

'Might he have killed him?'

'Quite possibly.'

'Do you think he's capable of rape and murder?'

'Oh, yes,' Chase said quietly, looking up at me. 'Renny Surnam's capable of anything.'

'Yeah, well,' I said, going over to the raised platform. 'You don't have to worry about him. As long as you stay where you are and do exactly what I tell you, Surnam won't even know you're here.'

I hoisted myself up onto the raised platform and crossed over to the rusty animal cages strung along the back wall. Most of them were roughly rectangular, the kind of cage you'd keep a mouse or hamster in, but the one on the far end was a small domed birdcage. They were all empty – no exercise wheels or food bowls – just six bare cages strung at head-height along a length of wire. As I shone the torch over them, I wondered again what they were doing here – had they once served a purpose, or had someone just strung them up for the hell of it? I imagined the day the

412

laboratory closed down in 1979 . . . everyone busy packing up, getting ready to move out . . . and perhaps a bored young laboratory assistant (with long hair and glasses) stumbles across a cupboard full of cages, and with nothing better to do he strings them up along the wall, imagining – with a mischievous glint in his eye – the puzzled look on my face as I stand here thirty-three years later, trying to figure it all out . . .

Then Bishop's voice rang out in the distance – '*Chase! Where are you? CHASE!*' – and I shook the useless reverie from my head and got on with what I was doing. From the sound of Bishop's voice, they weren't that close yet, and even if they were moving quickly – which they wouldn't be – I guessed it would take them a good five minutes or so to get here. So there was no need to panic just yet. But I couldn't afford to waste any time either.

I positioned myself next to the birdcage, held the torch behind it, and looked across at the wooden stairs leading up to the open door. The beam from the torch easily reached the doorway, and there was no way the light couldn't be seen from the laboratory. I opened the cage door and began fixing the torch inside. It took a while to get it right, mainly because the torch was longer than the width of the cage, so I had to fiddle around with the door, bending it back on its hinges, and pull apart some of the bars at the back of the cage, but in the end I got it how I wanted it. I stepped back, lit a cigarette, and studied my work. The torch was fixed across the cage, jammed in at the front and back, and the beam was directed at the doorway. The cage was still swinging very slightly – the degree of the swing exaggerated by the beam of the torch – and I reached up with both hands and gently steadied it. When I let go, it started swinging again, but not as much as before.

It didn't matter. It would do.

I headed back across the platform, lowered myself down to the floor, and looked over at Chase. He'd moved out from beneath the stairs to watch what I was doing, but when he saw me looking his way, he edged back into the alcove again. I nodded to myself, satisfied that he couldn't be seen, and reached into my pocket for the bag of cocaine. *Just one more pinch*, I told myself, *before it's too late . . .*

I opened the bag and stuffed a pinch of coke up my nose. The hit barely registered. I felt a dull surge somewhere in the back of my head, and a strained quickening of my heart, but that was about it. I guessed there was nothing left to stimulate. As I dropped the bag back into my pocket and took another drink from the whisky bottle, the thoughts of a forgotten writer came back to me:

Sufficiency is enough for men of sense, he wrote, *but it's never enough for the drunk. We need to carry on pouring even when the vessel is full. That it overflows is fine; fullness isn't everything. It's the input that counts. And although we sometimes can't get any drunker, the need to carry on drinking is insatiable. We need to carry on drinking until we're dead.*

Across the basement, the birdcage had almost stopped swinging, but it still wasn't completely stationary. The resultant movement of the torch beam – scything to and fro through the basement darkness – had a weirdly mesmeric effect, and as I sat there watching it, my eyes transfixed, my head moving slowly from side to side, I found myself drifting away again . . .

I was back at the cemetery at St Leonard's church, sitting on a wooden bench in front of my parents' graves. A light rain was falling, the air was damp and earthy. It was early morning, the skies still dark, but the first faint flickers of a pale January sun were beginning to show on the horizon. As I gazed out over the low stone wall that borders the cemetery, I could just make out the soft grey outlines of the hills and fields beyond, and away to my right, on the other side of a misted vale, I could see the dark dereliction of Morden Hall glowering down from its hilltop plateau. I knew I was in there somewhere. I could see myself . . . my other self . . . sitting on a wooden bench in the torch-lit darkness . . . looking at the gravestones in front of me . . . reading the inscriptions in the granite . . . *James John Craine, 1945–1992 . . . Alice Craine, 1946–1997 . . .*

'Hey, Dad,' I muttered.

'Mr Craine?'

'Hey, Mum.'

'Mr *Craine*!'

I sat up straight, rubbed my eyes, and looked over at Chase. He was leaning round the corner of the alcove, staring anxiously at me.

'I think they're coming,' he said, his voice an urgent whisper. 'Listen . . .'

I held my breath and listened. I could hear the wind outside, a rustle of something skittering across the courtyard, the faint creak of the birdcage . . . but nothing else. I breathed out and carried on listening, and after another ten seconds or so, I heard it – the cautious tread of footsteps, not too far away. As I angled my head, trying to get a bearing, the footsteps stopped. I heard a door opening . . . muffled voices, then footsteps again. They were getting closer. Not quite at the laboratory yet, but not far off.

I got up off the bench and went over to the alcove beneath the stairs, waving Chase back inside as I went. When I got there, he was standing with his back to the wall, his eyes blinking rapidly and his face drained of colour.

'All right, listen,' I said to him, keeping my voice calm and low. 'They're going to be here any minute, OK? I don't know exactly what they're going to do when they see the light in the doorway, but eventually they're going to have to come down here. When they do, all you have to do is keep quiet and stay here, all right?' Chase nodded. 'Whatever happens,' I went on, 'whatever you hear, whatever anyone says, you stay here. Is that clear?' He nodded again. I paused for a moment, listening to the ever-closing sound of voices and footsteps, then I turned back to Chase. 'When it's safe to come out,' I whispered, 'I'll let you know.'

'But what if—?'

'Shh,' I hissed, glancing upwards at the sound of voices. 'They're here.'

They still weren't close enough for me to make out what they were saying, but I could hear the questions in their voices, the wariness and uncertainty, and I guessed they'd just entered the laboratory, seen the light in the doorway, and were standing there staring at it, trying to work out what it meant.

'*Move back a bit*,' I whispered to Chase, taking the Beretta from my pocket. He edged closer to the side wall, and I positioned myself directly beneath the stairs. I held up the pistol and quietly racked the slide, double-checking that there was still a round in the chamber, then I slid it back and held the pistol down at my side.

I heard careful footsteps moving towards the doorway.

Then Bishop's voice calling out: 'Chase? Is that you? Chase?'

Then silence.

More footsteps, a muttered voice: 'It's moving . . . what the fuck is it?'

No answer.

'*Chase!*'

Very close now, almost at the door.

'You think it's him?' Surnam's voice.

More silence . . . the scrape of a boot on concrete, a metallic *dong* – the sound of the petrol can being placed on the ground.

'It looks like a basement or something.' Surnam again.

'Can you see where the light's coming from?'

'Not from here. Give me the shotgun.'

'I want him alive, Renny.'

'I'm not going down there without the gun.'

'All right . . . but don't fuck it up this time.'

'Do *you* want to go down first?'

There was a slight pause, and I imagined Bishop looking at Surnam, thinking things through, then reluctantly passing him the shotgun.

'Just don't do anything stupid, OK?'

'Like what?'

'Like what you did to Tan.'

'It solved the problem, didn't it?'

Bishop sighed. 'We wouldn't even be here if you'd done what you were supposed to do.'

'So?'

'I'm just saying, that's all.'

'Right. So do you want me to go down there or not?'

A moment's silence, then a rustle of cloth . . .

'What are you doing?'

'I can't hold a torch *and* a shotgun, can I?'

'Do you need the torch?'

'No.'

'Give it to me.'

I heard Surnam edging closer to the doorway, his footsteps scuffing on the ground. I could feel my tattered heart beating hard, my lungs sucking in air . . . blood and oxygen pumping into my muscles, my cells, my nerves, heightening my senses . . .

I looked up as the top stair creaked and bowed . . . Surnam was coming down.

'Can you see anything?' Bishop asked him.

'Not yet.'

Another step . . . another . . . then another . . .

He paused.

'Fuck's that?' I heard him mutter under his breath.

'Renny?' Bishop said.

'Hold on.'

Another step.

'Shit . . .'

418

'What's down there?'

'I don't know,' Surnam said guardedly. 'There's some seats or something, benches . . . some kind of platform . . .'

'Some kind of *what*?'

Another step.

'It's a fucking *birdcage* . . .'

'What are you talking about?'

'The light . . . it's coming from a birdcage on the wall—'

'A *birdcage*?'

'There's a torch in the cage.'

'Shit, Renny, what the fuck are you talking about?'

'Come down and see for yourself.'

'Is there any sign of Chase?'

Another step, another pause . . . and I guessed Surnam was looking around the basement now, scanning every inch of it . . . I glanced at Chase. He was standing perfectly still, his hands down at his sides, his eyes closed.

'There's no one down here,' Surnam said.

'You sure?'

'It's safe, Mick. You can come down.'

As Surnam carried on down the stairs, still moving cautiously but no longer pausing at every step, I suddenly realised that I felt strangely perfect – emotionless, focused, unnaturally alert. I could see the slight bowing of every wooden board as Surnam came down the stairs. I could hear the sound of the dust beneath his feet as he stepped down onto the basement floor. I could see without seeing the calmly puzzled look in his eyes as he stared over at the torch in the birdcage.

'Are you there?' Bishop said from the top of the stairs.

'I thought you were coming down.'

'I am.'

As Bishop started down the stairs, I could hear the difference in his footsteps. They were lighter than Surnam's, not quite as sturdy-sounding. They were the steps of a man wearing shoes, not boots.

'What the fuck is that?' I heard him say.

'I told you . . . it's a torch in a birdcage.'

'What's it doing up there?'

'I don't know. Maybe someone lives down here, a tramp or something.'

'Why would a tramp put a torch in a birdcage?'

'Why would *anyone* put a torch in a birdcage?'

Bishop had reached the bottom of the stairs now, and I could hear him slapping dust from his clothes.

'*Some*one's been down here,' he said.

I heard them moving away from the stairs then, walking slowly across the basement towards the raised platform.

'Hold on,' I heard Bishop say.

The footsteps stopped.

I heard Bishop sniff.

'Cigarette smoke,' he said. 'Shit . . .'

When I stepped out from the alcove with the gun in my hand, everything registered instantly: Bishop to the right of Surnam, half-turned towards me, a look of sudden realisation in his eyes . . . Surnam with his back to me, gazing up at the birdcage, the shotgun held loosely at his side . . . the torch in Bishop's left hand, the torchlight from the birdcage slicing through the dusted air, the distorted shadows of cages on the wall, the white wind blowing in through the metal grille . . .

I saw it all in a timeless moment.

And then I raised the pistol, pulled the trigger, and shot Renny Surnam in the back.

28

Even as Surnam went down, hitting the ground with a heavy thump, Bishop was already moving. He was quick, lunging for the shotgun almost before Surnam had dropped it, but he wasn't quick enough. I aimed low and fired twice. The first shot clipped his ankle, knocking him off his feet, and the second shot ripped into his kneecap. As he fell back against the wall, screaming in pain and clutching his knee, I turned my attention back to Surnam. He was still alive, but only just, and as I moved towards him, holding the pistol at arm's length, he somehow managed to heave himself up onto his hands and knees and shuffle round to face me. I stopped in front of him. He looked like a huge wounded beast – crouched on all fours, his head hanging down, blood and spit drooling from his mouth. I watched curiously as he slowly lifted his head, stared into my eyes, and agonisingly straightened up. It took a massive effort, and as he sat there slumped on his haunches, smiling through bloodied teeth at me, I could see the life draining out of him. His face was white, his skin was clammy, his breath was bubbling in his throat. I glanced down at the shotgun. It was no more than a foot away from him.

I looked into his eyes. They were fading away.

I didn't have anything to say to him.

I just stood there, waiting.

Bishop had stopped screaming now. I glanced over at him. He'd propped himself up against the wall and was sitting there with his wounded leg stretched out in front of him, pressing a handkerchief to his shattered knee.

When I turned back to Surnam he was trying to reach for the shotgun. It was just to the left of him, but he couldn't move his left arm – it was just hanging there, dead and useless – so he was reaching across his body and trying to get to the shotgun with his right hand. But he had nothing left now. His head was lolling on his shoulders, his upper body wavering to and fro, his eyes dull and unfocused . . . he couldn't even see the shotgun, let alone get hold of it.

I picked up the shotgun, then stepped back, put the pistol to Surnam's head, and pulled the trigger.

The basement was heavy with smoke now, the smell of gunpowder thick in the air, and as I slipped the Beretta into my pocket and went over to Bishop, my ears were ringing from the sound of the gunshots. I felt high and floaty, weirdly detached from everything, yet at the same time totally engaged. I not only knew precisely what I was doing, but I felt as if I'd already done it all a thousand times before.

Bishop never took his eyes off me as I approached him. He tried not to show any emotion, but he couldn't help flinching slightly as I leaned down in front of him, and as I picked up his torch from the ground and turned away without looking at him, I wondered at the power of violence. It was all so straightforward, so elemental. The fear of pain: it's all you need.

I went over to the alcove and found Chase standing with his face to the wall, his hands over his ears, and his head tucked into his chest. He jumped when I touched his shoulder, jerking to one side and staring at me with stricken eyes. I stepped back to let him see that it was me, and after a few seconds he slowly took his hands from his ears.

'It's all right,' I told him. 'It's over now. You can go.'

He nodded, unable to speak.

'Here,' I said, passing him the torch. 'Can you remember how to get out?'

He nodded again.

'It's a bit of a mess out there,' I said, taking him by the arm, 'so it's probably best if you keep your head down and don't look at anything, OK?'

'Yes, I see . . . right . . .'

'Are you ready?'

'I think so . . .'

'Keep the torch on the ground,' I said, leading him out of the alcove to the stairs.

'Evening, Meredith,' Bishop said when he saw him, his voice already beginning to weaken and slur. 'Enjoying yourself?'

Chase ignored him and started up the stairs.

'How's Maddie?' Bishop said.

Chase paused.

'I was thinking of popping round to see her the next time you're away,' Bishop said. 'I know how lonely she gets.'

'Maddie has nothing to do with this,' Chase said sharply, turning round. 'You leave her—'

'He's not going to do anything to Maddie,' I told Chase. 'He's just fucking with you.'

Chase glared at Bishop for a moment, then looked at me.

'Go on,' I told him. 'Get out of here . . . go home.'

I thought Bishop was going to say something else as Chase turned round and trudged up the stairs – a parting shot, a final threat – but when I looked over at him, I could tell that he didn't have it in him. He was shocked white, dazed, breathing hard. The dirt floor beneath his leg was dark with blood, and the cloth of his trousers was saturated from the knee down. I leaned the shotgun against the wall – well out of his reach – then picked up an old wooden box and went over to him.

'Mind if I join you?' I said, upending the box.

He wearily waved his hand.

I sat down on the box and lit a much-needed cigarette. I smoked it in silence for a while, sucking the smoke deep into my lungs, then I took the bottle of Bell's from my pocket and took a long shuddering drink. I waited for the heat to soak down into my belly, breathing in the after-burn, then I had another quick mouthful, put the bottle back in my pocket, and took out the pistol.

The light from the birdcage was fading now, the torch batteries beginning to run out. In the growing gloom, I looked at Bishop. He was slumped against the wall, about four feet away from me, with his ruined leg stretched out awkwardly in front of him and the other leg propped up at an angle. The bullet wound in his ankle looked fairly bad – bloody and swollen, lots of torn flesh – but compared to his knee, it was nothing.

'Does it hurt?' I asked him.

'What do you think?'

I shrugged.

He went to say something else, but a sudden stab of pain made him grit his teeth and swallow his words. He squeezed his eyes shut and carefully adjusted his position, grimacing painfully as he straightened his back against the wall, trying to keep his leg still in the process. The effort tired him out, and for a moment or two he just sat there, breathing through his nose, waiting for the pain to subside.

I glanced at my watch. It was ten to six. I put out my cigarette and lit another. When I looked back at Bishop, he was gazing over at Surnam's body.

'You didn't give him much of a chance, did you?' he said.

'He raped and murdered a teenage boy,' I said simply. 'Beat the shit out of him, stabbed him to death. He didn't deserve a chance.'

'You shot him in the back.'

'What was I supposed to do? Challenge him to a duel?'

Bishop sighed. 'We didn't tell him to kill the boy. He was only supposed to rough him up a little, scare him off . . .' He shook his head. 'Renny had problems controlling himself—'

'Did you tell him to dig up my girlfriend's dog?'

'Is that what he did?'

I nodded.

Bishop shrugged. 'Well, I did warn you.'

I just stared at him.

He looked back at me. 'What do you want, John?'

'What do you think?'

'I don't think you're going to kill me.'

'No?'

He shook his head. 'You know I wouldn't come out here without making contingency plans.'

'Your only contingency plan is lying over there with his brains dripping out of his head. No one knows you're here.'

'I'm a senior police officer, John. Have you forgotten that? If you kill me, you'll have every cop in the country after you. And when they get you, which they will—'

'God, you're pathetic.'

He stopped and stared at me, genuinely quite shocked.

'Have some fucking dignity, for Christ's sake,' I said.

'*Dignity?*' he sneered. 'I'm sitting here bleeding to death—'

'You told me you didn't care much for your life, remember? You told me you could take it or leave it.'

'And you *believed* me?' he said, shaking his head in disbelief. 'Jesus Christ . . .' He looked disdainfully at me. 'You really don't get it, do you?'

I heard the Range Rover starting up then, and as I gazed over at the metal grille and saw the flicker of headlights in the darkness outside, I wondered if Bishop was right. I *had* come to think that he shared with me a detached view of life – and even now, as I remembered the depth of sorrow in his eyes as he'd uttered those words – *And we both know the benefits of having a detached view of life, don't we?* – I still found it hard to believe that there wasn't at least some truth to his sadness, if not his words. But maybe he was right – maybe I just didn't get it. Or it could be that he *was* telling the truth then, but lying about it now . . .

Does it matter? I asked myself, taking the whisky bottle from my pocket and having another drink.

Does anything matter?

The headlights had gone from the grille now, and I could hear the sound of the Range Rover fading into the distance. I pictured Chase in the driving seat, peering out through the windscreen at the falling snow, his eyes glazed with too many emotions – fear, relief, confusion, anxiety . . .

'I suppose you think he's a victim in all this, do you?' Bishop said.

The torchlight from the birdcage was very faint now, and I had to lean forward to get a good look at Bishop. His face was pale, drained of what little colour it had, and he was having trouble sitting up straight. He still sounded quite composed and relatively confident, but there was no strength left in his voice, and I could tell from his lack of movement that his body, if not his mind, had already begun shutting down.

'If you think Meredith Chase deserves any sympathy,' he said, 'you're even more naïve than I thought. Chase has been—'

'No more,' I said.

Bishop blinked. 'What?'

428

'You heard me.'

He hesitated, not sure what to say.

'I'm tired,' I said. 'I've had enough. I'm sick to death of playing games.' I looked at him. 'I know what you did . . . what you've done. I know you killed my father—'

'No—'

'And Leon and Claudia—'

'Your father took his own life.'

'You put this gun to his head,' I said, raising the Beretta. 'You forced him to write a suicide note, and then you shot him.'

'You're wrong, John,' Bishop said firmly, shaking his head. 'I don't know who you've been talking to, but whoever told you—'

'I've been talking to Gerald McKee.'

There was no mistaking the surprise in his eyes. He did his best to cover it up, composing himself almost immediately, but his reactions were dulling now, his mind slowing down, and I could see his mask beginning to slip. Telling the truth is easy, you don't have to think about anything when you tell the truth. But lying is hard work. And the more Bishop lied, the more energy he used, the heavier his mask would become.

'Listen to me, John,' he said, trying to keep his eyes steady, 'listen . . . McKee's a junky . . . a drunk . . . you can't trust him. He'll tell you whatever you want to hear—'

'You're wasting your breath,' I said.

'I did *not* kill your father,' he insisted. 'You have to believe me. I mean, think about it . . . if he knew I was

429

going to kill him anyway, how could I force him into writing a suicide note?'

'You did what you always do,' I said, wearily lowering the gun. 'You preyed on his weakness. You used his love for my mother to make him write the note. You told him you'd hurt her if he didn't write it.'

'No . . . that's not right—'

'He knew there was no guarantee that you'd leave her alone even if he did write the note, but what choice did he have? He'd already broken her heart. He couldn't bear the thought of her suffering any more. He had to write it.'

'I think you're forgetting something,' Bishop said. 'Your father accused me of corruption in his suicide note, he claimed that I'd planted the drugs and money in his locker.' Bishop looked at me. 'Why would *I* force him to write that?'

'So it would never occur to anyone that you *did* force him to write it.'

Bishop stared at me for a moment, his eyes unfocused, his face a veil of contrivance and pain, and then quite suddenly something changed in him, both physically and emotionally, and as he breathed in deeply and let out a long rasping sigh, I could almost see the strain of duplicity leaving him. He coughed weakly, turned his head to one side and spat, then wiped his mouth and looked back at me. 'Everybody dies, John,' he said simply. 'It's just a matter of how and when.' He smiled, seemingly at peace with himself. 'None of us are worth anything.'

We were there now, we'd come to another time and another place. There was nothing more to do. I shut my eyes for a second – closing my mind to all thoughts of reason – and when I opened them again, I knew we were both ready. I looked at Bishop, seeing nothing, and as he smiled back at me, his eyes glazed with calm acceptance, I raised the pistol and shot him in the head.

29

The torch in the birdcage was almost dead now, its beam fading to yellow, the shadows greying on the basement walls. I lit a cigarette and just sat there for a while, smoking quietly in the dying light. I felt nothing. I wanted for nothing. My head was blank and my heart was empty. I took the whisky bottle from my pocket, drained the last few inches, and stared vacantly at what I'd done. Bishop's body was lying crookedly against the wall, his arms at his sides, his head on his shoulder, his dead eyes gazing at nothing. A trickle of blood was seeping slowly from the bullet hole in his forehead, and a ragged arc of blood and matter was smeared on the wall behind him.

Matter . . . the substance of things.

There is no soul.

None of us are worth anything.

I finished my cigarette and wearily got to my feet. I'd never been so tired. I looked around at the odds and ends scattered all over the floor, then stepped over to my right and picked up an old piece of rag. After wiping the pistol with the rag, I moved back over to Bishop, crouched down beside him, and placed the gun in his hand. I fixed his fingers round the pistol grip and placed his hand in his lap.

I paused for a moment, vaguely aware that I was

forgetting something, but my head was too blank to think about it. It didn't matter. There was very little point to what I was doing anyway. I was just doing it – crossing over and picking up the shotgun, taking it over to where Surnam lay dead, aiming it at the wall above Bishop's body and firing both barrels, then wiping my prints from the gun and dropping it to the floor next to Surnam's body . . .

The torchlight flickered, almost gone.

I took a last quick look around the rapidly darkening basement, but nothing had changed. I'd seen all there was to see. As the torchlight finally faded into blackness, I took out my penlight, turned it on, and headed for the stairs.

There was no sense of past or future now, I was existing only in moments, and as I climbed the wooden stairs – one step, another step, another step – I had no conscious awareness of what I'd just done or what I was about to do. And although I acted without hesitation when I reached the top of the stairs and saw the 20-litre petrol can standing beside the basement door – leaning down and flipping open the lid – it wasn't a predetermined act of intent, it was just the act of that moment. The dull green can was heavy, and as I dragged it across to the top of the stairs, I could feel the weight of the petrol sloshing around inside. The can was almost full. I positioned it carefully, placing it on the floor about eighteen inches away from the top of the stairs with the spout facing the basement, and then I began to tip it forwards. The petrol spurted out wildly at first, spraying all over the place, but as I carried on tipping the can away from me, eventually lowering it to the floor, the flow of petrol settled itself and began gushing steadily down the stairs.

I stepped back and watched it . . .

Fire devours. It consumes, destroys, obliterates. It lays the world to waste.

I lit a cigarette.

Fire deforms. It craves disorder, its only purpose to burn and burn and light the skies until all that's left is dust.

I waited for the last drop of petrol to drip from the can, then I waited a little longer.

Fire has no limits. Everything burns: wood, plastic, stone, metal, flesh, bone, blood. And everything will burn in the end. Today, tomorrow, a thousand million years from now . . .

Long enough.

I drew hard on my cigarette, sucking heat into the glowing tip, then I took another step back and tossed the burning cigarette down the stairs. Half a second later, a massive *whoomp!* ripped through the air and the stairs erupted in a blaze of fire. The flames boiled and roared, the intense heat feeding upon itself, and as I turned away to shield my face from the fire, I could already hear the crackle and snap of burning wood from the basement. Thick black smoke billowed out into the laboratory as I crossed over to the double doorway, choking the air with the acrid stink of burning petrol, but I was close to sense-lessness now, barely aware of my surroundings, and as I made my way through the doorway and along the derelict corridor, the conflagration behind me was already fading away into the non-existent past.

My hands were dirty, my mouth was dry . . .

I was moving – one step, another step, another step –
going from one place to another . . . movement is time,
time is movement . . .

Motion, moment, time.

That's all there is.

30

I dream of leaving Morden Hall and walking home in the snow. Along the rutted track, stumbling through the darkness . . . the noise and glare of the night-lit road . . . traffic streaming past, headlights blazing . . . walking with my head bowed down, drunk eyes immersed in the world of the ground . . . sodden scraps of paper, dog shit, cellophane, wet cigarette ends, bits of rubber, sweet wrappers, a hubcap half-buried in the snow . . . then gazing up at the night, looking for the moon . . . my head whirling, falling over, cracking my knee on the kerb . . . it doesn't hurt . . . get up, keep going . . . along an endless road of dim verges and bare chestnut trees and blazing headlights beneath the winter sky, and then another road of railings and walls and trees and cars and hedges and snow . . . and then another . . . and another . . .

I dream of a dead dog at the side of the road, its skin torn apart, its black lips frozen in a rage of pain.

I dream of entering my midnight house and locking the door and guzzling whisky from the bottle, then doubling over and retching it all up on the floor in a wash of pink-flecked vomit. I wait for the sickness to subside, then drink again, squeezing my eyes shut to keep it down. Everything hurts. I don't know what's going to happen . . . I don't care. I get out of my dirty wet clothes and stand there looking down at the pale misery of my naked body, and I wonder why it doesn't just give up. Why is it so stubborn? What does it want from me? What is it trying to prove? That it's more resilient than me? No, it's nothing, just a mute thing of limbs and skin. A frame, a vehicle.

I can't stand my self.

I can't stand.

I waver, the room wavers. I want to smoke a cigarette but my fingers belong to someone else, and I can't keep my eyes open any more . . . and as I lower myself to the bed and lie down in the darkness, I wonder for a moment what it would be like to be something else . . .

It's only a dream, but it's all I have.

I don't know what day it is now. I don't know how long I've been here, lying in my bed, sucking on a whisky bottle. I don't know anything. The pale light of the moon is crawling in through the kitchen window, illuminating a half-empty whisky bottle on the bedside cabinet and an ashtray full of cigarette ends. My clothes are scattered on the floor and the room smells stale and sick. I pluck a half-smoked cigarette from the ashtray, straighten it, and light it. The stale smoke burns dry in my throat. When I turn my head to mute the cough in the pillow, a blunt saw cuts into my guts. Groaning like a sick old man, I sit up stiffly and reach for the whisky bottle. I can smell petrol. I can see dust and blood and cages and snow . . . I see it all as nothing. I drink from the bottle, wait for the nausea to pass, and lie down again. It's cold in here. I pull up the sweat-soaked duvet and curl up in bed like a middle-aged foetus, with a pillow clutched to my aching belly and my eyes fixed blindly to the neverness of the wall.

It's dark outside. Dark inside.

I'm never going to leave this house again. Never. I'm staying here for ever, wrapped in white in the darkness.

A Dance of Ghosts

Kevin Brooks

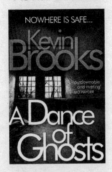

PI John Craine is struggling to cope with the weight of his past. Sixteen years ago his wife, Stacy, was brutally murdered. Craine found her body in their bed. And since then, to escape the pain and the unanswered questions, he has buried himself in work by day, and whisky by night.

But one phone call changes everything. The mother of missing young woman Anna Gerrish calls on his services, and Craine soon finds himself at the centre of a sinister web of corruption and lies that leads back into the murky waters of the past – and to the night that Craine has spent over a decade trying to forget. As he delves deeper and deeper into the case everything gets increasingly, terrifyingly, personal. And it's down to Craine to stop history from repeating itself.

arrow books

Until the Darkness Comes

Kevin Brooks

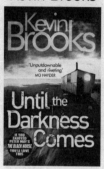

PI John Craine has come to Hale Island to get away from it all – the memories and the guilt, and a past that just won't let go.

But within hours he stumbles across the dead body of a young girl on the beach. When the police arrive the body has inexplicably disappeared. Or – in his already tormented state – did Craine imagine it in the first place?

Determined to get at the truth, Craine starts asking questions. But it seems no one on the island is talking. And all too soon he finds himself tangled up in a deadly network of fear and violence.

Someone has a dark secret to keep, and Craine is getting in the way.

arrow books

THE POWER OF READING

Visit the Random House website and get connected with information on all our books and authors

EXTRACTS from our recently published books and selected backlist titles

COMPETITIONS AND PRIZE DRAWS Win signed books, audiobooks and more

AUTHOR EVENTS Find out which of our authors are on tour and where you can meet them

LATEST NEWS on bestsellers, awards and new publications

MINISITES with exclusive special features dedicated to our authors and their titles

READING GROUPS Reading guides, special features and all the information you need for your reading group

LISTEN to extracts from the latest audiobook publications

WATCH video clips of interviews and readings with our authors

RANDOM HOUSE INFORMATION including advice for writers, job vacancies and all your general queries answered

Come home to Random House

www.randomhouse.co.uk